Excel As Your Database

Paul Cornell, Jr.

Apress®

Excel As Your Database

Copyright © 2007 by Paul Cornell, Jr.

ISBN-13 (pbk): 978-1-59059-751-4

ISBN-10 (pbk): 1-59059-751-6

Printed and bound in the United States of America 9 8 7 6 5 4 3 2 1

Lead Editor: Jim Sumser
Technical Reviewer: Judith M. Myerson
Editorial Board: Steve Anglin, Ewan Buckingham, Gary Cornell, Jason Gilmore, Jonathan Gennick, Jonathan Hassell, James Huddleston, Chris Mills, Matthew Moodie, Dominic Shakeshaft, Jim Sumser, Matt Wade
Project Manager: Sofia Marchant
Copy Edit Manager: Nicole Flores
Copy Editor: Jennifer Whipple
Assistant Production Director: Kari Brooks-Copony
Production Editor: Ellie Fountain
Compositor: Lynn L'Heureux
Proofreader: Patrick Vincent
Indexer: John Collin
Cover Designer: Kurt Krames
Manufacturing Director: Tom Debolski

Distributed to the book trade worldwide by Springer-Verlag New York, Inc., 233 Spring Street, 6th Floor, New York, NY 10013. Phone 1-800-SPRINGER, fax 201-348-4505, e-mail orders-ny@springer-sbm.com, or visit http://www.springeronline.com.

For information on translations, please contact Apress directly at 2560 Ninth Street, Suite 219, Berkeley, CA 94710. Phone 510-549-5930, fax 510-549-5939, e-mail info@apress.com, or visit http://www.apress.com.

The source code for this book is available to readers at http://www.apress.com in the Source Code/ Download section.

Contents at a Glance

Contents

About the Author

■**PAUL CORNELL, JR.** has been involved with helping folks get the most out of Microsoft Office Excel for more than seven years. Paul has written two previous books about Excel for Apress and one book about Excel for Microsoft Press. He has also helped Microsoft produce online documentation, written many technical articles, served as a web columnist, and blogged about the Visual Basic Language Reference for Office as well as Microsoft Visual Studio Tools for the Microsoft Office System. In his current role at Microsoft, Paul serves as a documentation manager on the Microsoft Visual Studio User Education team. He lives with his wife and two daughters among the mountains of the Pacific Northwestern United States.

About the Technical Reviewer

JUDITH M. MYERSON is a systems architect and engineer. Her areas of interest include middleware technologies, enterprise-wide systems, database technologies, application development, web development, software engineering, network management, servers, virtualized infrastucture, security management, information assurance, standards, RFID (radio frequency identification) technologies, and project management. Judith holds a Master of Science degree in engineering, and is a member of the Institute of Electrical and Electronics Engineers (IEEE) and ISA organizations. She has reviewed/edited a number of books including *Hardening Linux*; *Creating Client Extranets with SharePoint 2003*; *Microsoft SharePoint: Building Office 2003 Solutions*; and *Microsoft Operations Manager 2005 Field Guide.*

Acknowledgments

I first want to thank my beautiful wife and best friend, Shelley, for close to 20 years now of constant love. I could not have completed this book without her behind-the-scenes support, understanding, counsel, and encouragement. Shell, you are awesome.

A big thanks also to my two wonderful daughters, Zoe and Bailey, for their sacrifice of time so that Daddy could work on his books. Girls, you are the best kids that a dad could have.

I want to acknowledge my parents, Paul and Darlean, for their ongoing love and support.

I appreciate everyone at Apress who contributed to helping me produce this book, especially Gary Cornell, Jim Sumser, Sofia Marchant, Jennifer Whipple, Ellie Fountain, and Tina Nielsen. Also, many thanks to my technical reviewer, Judith Myerson.

I am grateful to you, the many readers who have shown such a great interest in my books over the past several years. Thank you for your continued support and feedback as I try to make each book better for you.

Finally, I give the ultimate thanks to God. He is the source of my skills, my talents, and my gifts. I'm also thankful for the gift of abundant and eternal life given to me by God through his son, Jesus Christ. I don't deserve what I've been given, but I'm immensely grateful for having received it, and I continually seek opportunities to share it with others.

Introduction

Naturally, Microsoft Office Excel is designed to work well with facts and figures. However, Excel can do much more than just crunch numbers. For certain types of data, Excel is an ideal database management system. Excel is very good for entering, storing, and analyzing small amounts of data. Excel is also, of course, a less expensive alternative to larger computing-intensive database management systems designed for business and academic institutions to store sizable amounts of data. For those who don't have the time or interest to study advanced data storage and data management techniques, Excel provides a much lower learning curve. Also, Excel provides data analysis features lacking in many more expensive database management systems.

If you have relatively small amounts of data, want to spend a minimum amount of time learning fairly powerful data analysis techniques, or have a limited computing budget or resources, you can use Excel as your database management system, and you can use this book to help you more quickly learn Excel database management and data analysis techniques that you can put to use right away.

Understanding how this book is organized and presented will help you find and learn these techniques faster.

Chapter Summaries

This book begins by introducing you to data basics and then moves on to help you define your data. You then learn how to enter, find, connect to, and analyze data. You also learn how to automate common data management and data tasks.

Chapter 1: Data Basics

Chapter 1 introduces you to the basic characteristics of various types of databases, including flat file databases, nonrelational databases, relational databases, and multidimensional databases. Being aware of these differences will help you better understand when you can use Excel as your database management system. You will learn how to normalize your data for easier data storage and retrieval. You will also be introduced briefly to other Microsoft database management systems such as Microsoft Office Access and Microsoft SQL Server. Knowing about these products can provide you with alternatives in case your database needs are greater than what Excel provides.

Chapter 2: Define Your Data

Chapter 2 provides you with strategies for determining the goals, results, or outcomes for your data. Understanding how to use these strategies will help you in turn to better determine your requirements for gathering, entering, storing, using, and analyzing your data. Once these requirements are understood, you can more efficiently design your data for best use with Excel.

Chapter 3: Enter Data

Chapter 3 instructs you in the basics of putting your data into Excel. This chapter covers data entry techniques such as the following:

- Copying and pasting data into worksheet cells.

- Filling repetitive or sequential data across worksheet rows or down worksheet columns.

- Entering data with a data form instead of directly into worksheet cells.

- Defining, creating, and applying named ranges to worksheet cells for easier, less error-prone data management.

- Formatting data and copying it across worksheet cells for more intuitive data visualization and analysis.

- Conditionally formatting data for even more intuitive, informative data analysis.

- Protecting data from intentional or inadvertent changes.

- Inserting functions and formulas into worksheet cells to summarize data from other cells.

- Validating data to help ensure that only the correct data is entered into worksheet cells.

- Importing data from other data sources to reduce data-entry errors.

Chapter 4: Find Data

Chapter 4 instructs you in techniques to locate your data. Techniques include using Excel's Find, Replace, Go To, offset, Lookup Wizard, HLOOKUP, VLOOKUP, and query functions.

Chapter 5: Connect to Other Databases

Chapter 5 shows you how to use Excel to work with data in other electronic files and database management systems without actually bringing the data into Excel itself. Files and database management systems include text files, other Excel files, Microsoft Office Access, Microsoft SQL Server, Microsoft SQL Server Analysis Services, and other assorted files and database management systems.

Chapter 6: Analyze Data

Chapter 6 provides techniques to help you gain insights and make more informed decisions based on your data. Covered data analysis techniques include the following:

- Sorting data.

- Filtering data.

- Subtotaling data.

- Creating and using data tables.

- Consolidating data.

- Grouping and outlining data.

- Creating and using lists.

- Creating and using scenarios.

- Using Goal Seek.

- Using Solver.

- Creating and using PivotTables and PivotCharts.

- Performing statistical data analysis.

Chapter 7: Automate Repetitive Database Tasks

Chapter 7 describes techniques for writing code that instructs Excel to repeat data entry, data analysis, and data interoperability tasks in order to improve your productivity. This chapter teaches you how to use the macro recorder to make Excel write code for you. You are also introduced to the Excel programming model and the Visual Basic code editor. Understanding this model helps you write more efficient code to make Excel do what you need. Automated tasks covered include the following:

- Sorting data for faster data analysis.

- Filtering data to show only the data you want displayed.

- Subtotaling data.

- Calculating worksheet functions such as data averages and highest and lowest data values.

- Using offsets and the HLOOKUP and VLOOKUP worksheet functions to locate related data in nearby worksheet cells.

- Creating PivotTables and PivotCharts for quicker, more robust data analysis.

- Changing PivotTable and PivotChart views for even more enhanced data analysis.

- Performing more advanced statistical data analysis.

- Connecting to data in other electronic files and database management systems.

Chapter Layout

With only a few minor exceptions, the sections in this book's chapters are organized similarly to help you more quickly find the specific information that you're looking for:

- The "Quick Start" portion of each section provides a summarized process, a set of keystrokes, or a set of mouse actions to more quickly perform the technique without additional information.

- The "How To" portion of each section expands on the information provided in the "Quick Start," providing additional details and notes.

- The "Try It" portion of each section gives you an opportunity to practice the technique, using sample data where applicable.

Reading Recommendations

This book was written with several groups of people in mind. Based on your specific needs, the following recommendations can help guide you to the chapters that you might be more interested in:

- If you are a database novice, you should focus on reading Chapters 1 and 2 first.

- If you feel that you are fairly proficient with database basics, you can safely skip Chapters 1 and 2.

- If you are a home user, you are probably very interested in getting directly into learning the most important data entry and data analysis techniques. You are probably less likely to worry about perfectly designing your data, writing computer programming code, or connecting to data in other database management systems. If these interests apply to you, you should focus on reading Chapters 3, 4, and 6.

- If you are a business professional, but you are neither an information technology (IT) professional nor a computer programmer, you are probably interested additionally in learning about designing your data to reflect your workgroup's data needs. You may also need to occasionally connect to data in other workgroups. As your data grows, you may need to consider working with your IT department to step up to a more expensive, more resource intensive database management system. If these situations apply to you, you should focus on reading Chapters 3 through 6.

- If you are an IT professional, you are most likely interested additionally in using Excel to interoperate with other more expensive, more powerful database management systems. If this is the case, you should focus on reading Chapter 5.

- If you are a computer solution developer, you are likely very interested in writing code to make it easier for your end users to perform repetitive tasks with Excel. If this interests you, you should focus on Chapter 7.

Text Conventions

Although in many cases it is faster and easier to work in Excel by using keyboard shortcuts or right-clicking shortcuts instead of clicking menus, this book's procedures are presented from the perspective of menus whenever possible. This is done to keep instructions brief, consistent, and predictable.

Tip In Excel 2007, you can display keyboard shortcut combinations by pressing the Alt key and then pressing keys corresponding to the key letters that appear next to the menus and commands. For example, to insert a blank worksheet, press Alt, H, I, S, as shown in Figure 1.

Figure 1. *Pressing the Alt key in Excel 2007 as a shortcut to invoke menu commands*

To keep instructions brief, in Microsoft Excel 2003, menu commands are designated with the *click* verb and are separated by the right arrow character (➤). For example, this book substitutes the phrase "on the File menu, click Open" with the phrase "click File ➤ Open," as shown in Figure 2.

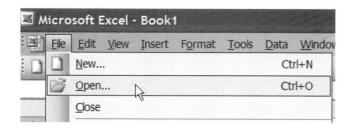

Figure 2. *Using the phrase "click File ➤ Open" for Excel 2003 as a substitute for the phrase "on the File menu, click Open"*

In contrast, when you click tabs (the equivalent of menus) in Microsoft Excel 2007, groups of commands appear in a "ribbon" instead of submenus. For example, when you click the Office Button (a circular button at the top-left corner of Excel with the Office System logo icon inside of it), a submenu still appears, as shown in Figure 3. So in this case, the phrase "click Office Button ➤ Open" is still used.

Figure 3. *Clicking the Office Button in Excel 2007 is equivalent to clicking the File menu in Excel 2003.*

However, clicking any tab in the row of tabs directly below and next to the Office Button displays a ribbon with several commands organized by groups. For example, clicking the Home tab in the row of tabs directly below and next to the Office Button displays a Clipboard group that contains a Paste command. When you click the Paste command in the Clipboard group, a submenu appears containing commands such as Paste Special. So this book substitutes the phrase "click Home, and in the Clipboard group click Paste, and then click Paste Special" with the phrase "click Home ➤ (Clipboard) Paste ➤ Paste Special." In this case, the word *Clipboard* is surrounded by parentheses as a visual indicator of where the Paste command is located, but you don't actually click the Clipboard group, as shown in Figure 4.

Figure 4. *Clicking the Home ➤ (Clipboard) Paste ➤ Paste Special command in Excel 2007*

Tip Many commands in Excel 2007 ribbon groups have an icon but no text. As you begin using Excel 2007, you may have to spend a few moments resting your mouse pointer on several of these icons to see their command names appear. For example, in the Home ribbon's Number group, the Format Cells: Number command is represented in the lower right corner by an icon with a down arrow. When you rest your mouse pointer on that icon, as shown in Figure 5, the Format Cells: Number command screen tip appears. When you click that screen tip, the Format Cells dialog box appears with its Number tab selected. As you continue using Excel 2007, you will find these commands much faster.

Figure 5. *Clicking the Home (Number) ➤ Format Cells: Number down arrow opens the Format Cells dialog box.*

System Requirements

This book was written based on the features and commands included with Microsoft Office Excel 2007 and Microsoft Office Excel 2003.

For Excel 2007 system requirements, see `http://office.microsoft.com/en-us/suites/HA101668651033.aspx`.

For Excel 2003 system requirements, see `http://www.microsoft.com/office/excel/prodinfo/sysreq.mspx`.

To practice some of the techniques in Chapters 1, 5, and 7, you will need access to a computer with Microsoft Office Access 2007 or Microsoft Office Access 2003 and Microsoft SQL Server 2005 Express Edition or greater installed. To practice techniques related to online analytical processing, you will need access to a computer with Microsoft SQL Server 2005 Standard Edition or greater installed. For system requirements, visit the following web pages:

- *For Access 2007*: `http://office.microsoft.com/en-us/suites/HA101668651033.aspx`

- *For Access 2003*: `http://www.microsoft.com/office/access/prodinfo/sysreq.mspx`

- *For SQL Server 2005*: `http://www.microsoft.com/sql/prodinfo/sysreqs/default.mspx`

Note Unless stated otherwise, the information in this book pertains to both the 2007 and 2003 versions of Excel and Access.

Sample Data

This book provides supplementary sample data to help you complete the "Try It" exercises provided throughout this book. Electronic files containing the sample data—and supporting files where needed—are available at the Apress web site's Source Code/Download page at http://www.apress.com/book/download.html. To help you locate the correct files for a specific "Try It" exercise within the download, the files generally follow the naming convention of ExcelDB_ChXX_YY, where *XX* is the chapter number, and *YY* is a single section number or a range of section numbers. For example, a sample file name corresponding to the first section in Chapter 6 (Section 6.1) would start with ExcelDB_Ch06_01. Likewise, a sample file name corresponding to the first three sections of Chapter 5 (Sections 5.1, 5.2, and 5.3) would start with ExcelDB_Ch05_01–03.

This book's sample Excel data is presented in Excel 97–Excel 2003 format with the file extension .xls. These files should be able to be opened in any version of Excel from Microsoft Excel 97 through Excel 2007. (These files should be able to be opened in earlier Excel versions as well, but this cannot be guaranteed.)

This book's sample Microsoft Access data is presented in Access 2003 format with the file extension .mdb. These files should be able to be opened in Access versions 2002, 2003, and 2007. These files are not guaranteed to open in earlier Access versions.

This book's sample Microsoft SQL Server data should only be able to be attached to Microsoft SQL Server 2005 instances. This data is not guaranteed to be able to be attached to earlier SQL Server versions.

■■■

CHAPTER 1

Data Basics

Data comes in many different forms. Whether the data is a personal contact history, a set of academic test scores, a catalog of products and prices, a group of scientific research facts, or a multinational corporation's general ledger entries for the past 20 years, data can be small or large, simple or complex, and summarized or detailed.

Understanding the differences between common database types—flat file databases, nonrelational databases, relational databases, and multidimensional databases—will help you decide whether to use Microsoft Office Excel, Microsoft Office Access, Microsoft SQL Server, or a similar database management system from another computer software manufacturer to enter, store, modify, and analyze your particular data.

1.1 Learn About Flat File Databases

A *flat file database* is a single electronic text file containing a list of data records with one record per line, usually with a newline character separating each data record. Each record contains one or more data fields with each field separated by a character, known as a *delimiter*, such as a comma or a tab character. For example, in a list of personal contacts, each data record contains an individual contact's information: the contact's name, address, and phone number are each a data field.

Flat file databases are ideal for storing simple data values, especially when those values are in data records with varying numbers of fields. However, flat file databases can be tough to enter data into; specifically, they are error-prone when entering multiple data field delimiters.

Flat file database data records and data fields usually are consistent in their definition, layout, and data format, such as the personal contact list described earlier, but this is not strictly required. For example, in a flat file database containing a list of students and their test scores, the first data record could contain a student's name and five numeric test score data fields, while the second data record could contain a student's identification number and seven alphabetic test score data fields.

Quick Start

A flat file database can most easily be represented as an electronic text file with each data record separated usually by a newline character. For each data record, each data field in that data record is separated by a common character such as a comma or a tab character.

How To

To quickly create a flat file database, use one of two ways. The first is the following:

1. Start Microsoft Notepad.

2. Type a series of data records with each data field value separated by a common character such as a comma or a tab character.

3. Press Enter after each data record.

4. Save the file.

The other way is the following:

1. Start Excel.

2. Type a series of data records with each data field in a subsequent worksheet cell.

3. Enter each data record on a subsequent worksheet row.

4. Save the file.

Tip

You should only use flat file databases for the simplest lists of data values. Flat file databases are prone to corruption, especially when two or more users or computer programs are trying to work with the same flat file database at the same time. Flat file databases are also prone to data entry errors. If you miss entering just one delimiter in a flat file database, you increase the probability of a database management system to not be able to correctly open, display, analyze, or store the data values.

Try It

In this exercise, you will open a flat file database in Notepad. Then you will open the same flat file database in Excel to see how Excel presents flat file data in rows and columns on a worksheet:

1. Start Microsoft Notepad.

2. Click File ➤ Open.

3. Browse to and select the ExcelDB_Ch01_01.txt file, and click Open. Notice that each data field is separated by a comma, and each data record is on a separate line.

4. Start Excel.

5. Click Office Button ➤ Open (for Excel 2007) or click File ➤ Open (for Excel 2003). In the Files of Type box, select All Files.

6. Browse to and select the ExcelDB_Ch01_01.txt file, and click Open. The Text Import Wizard appears.

7. Select the Delimited option, and then click Next.

8. Clear the Tab check box, select the Comma check box, and click Finish. Notice that each data field is in a separate worksheet cell, and each data record is on its own row.

9. Quit Excel, and quit Notepad.

1.2 Learn About Nonrelational Databases

The defining characteristics of a *nonrelational database* are that each data table (which is a collection of individual data records) in a nonrelational database is self-describing and self-contained. For example, in a nonrelational database containing a personal contact list, the contact list itself is a single data table; each contact is a data record; each contact's first name is a data field; and each contact's street address is another data field. Furthermore, the data field values are straightforward to understand, and the contact list does not depend on any other data tables to convey each contact's information.

Nonrelational databases are great for storing lists of data values with the following:

- The same number of data fields in each data record.

- Data values and data records that do not depend on other data tables to convey all of the information about each data record.

- Data values that are straightforward to understand.

- Data fields that are organized with similar data values grouped together.

There are two key differences between flat file databases and nonrelational databases. The first key difference is that a flat file database does not need to have the same number of data fields per data record. Nonrelational databases always have the same number of data fields per data record.

The second key difference between flat file databases and nonrelational databases is that flat file databases do not need to contain data field names. Nonrelational databases always contain data field names.

Quick Start

A nonrelational database is simply an electronic file containing the same number of data fields in each data record, and each data field has a name. Similar to a flat file database, you could represent a nonrelational database as a text file containing a set of data records, with each data record separated usually by a newline character. Each data field in a data record is separated by a common character such as a comma or a tab character. Each data record contains the same number of data fields.

How To

To quickly create a nonrelational database, use one of two ways. One way is the following:

1. Start Notepad.

2. Type a series of data field names, with each data field name separated by a common character such as a comma or a tab character, and press Enter.

3. Type a series of data records with each data field value separated by a common character such as a comma or a tab character. Make sure that each data record has the same number of data field values as data field names.

4. Press Enter after each data record.

5. Save the file.

The other way is the following:

1. Start Excel.

2. In the first row of a worksheet, type a series of data field names, with each data field name in a subsequent worksheet cell.

3. In the second and subsequent rows, type a series of data field values with a data field value or a null value for each data field name.

4. Enter each data record on a subsequent worksheet row.

5. Save the file.

Tip

A data field in a nonrelational database that contains no data value for a given data record is commonly known as a *null value* or a *null field*. Null values are commonly expressed as a blank value, the value Null, or the value N/A (for not applicable). Note that the value zero (0) is never used to convey a null value.

For most data entry, storage, and analysis tasks, Excel handles flat file databases and nonrelational databases the same.

Try It

In this exercise, you will open a nonrelational database in Notepad. Then you will open the same nonrelational database in Excel to see how Excel presents the data in rows and columns on a worksheet:

1. Start Notepad.

2. Click File ➤ Open.

3. Browse to and select the ExcelDB_Ch01_02.txt file, and click Open. Notice that the first line contains data field names; each data field is separated by a comma; each data record is on a separate line; and there are the same number of data field values for each data record.

4. Start Excel.

5. Click Office Button ➤ Open (for Excel 2007) or click File ➤ Open (for Excel 2003). In the Files of Type box, select All Files.

6. Browse to and select the ExcelDB_Ch01_02.txt file, and click Open. The Text Import Wizard appears.

7. Select the Delimited option, and click Next.

8. Clear the Tab check box, select the Comma check box, and click Finish. Notice that each data field is in a separate worksheet cell; each data record is on its own row; and there are the same number of data field values for each row.

▓Tip To see all of the data field names and data field values, click the Select All button (the blank button in the upper left corner of the worksheet), and click Home ➤ (Cells) Format ➤ AutoFit Column Width (for Excel 2007) or Format ➤ Column ➤ AutoFit Selection (for Excel 2003).

---

9. Quit Excel, and quit Notepad.

1.3 Learn About Relational Databases

Similar to nonrelational databases discussed in the previous section, *relational databases* store data records in two or more data tables. However, relational databases are different than nonrelational databases in one key aspect: the data tables rely on each other to capture all of the facts and figures in the database. For example, in a nonrelational database containing customer sales history, one data table contains all of the customers' names and addresses and all of the sales transactions for all of the customers. In contrast, in a relational database containing customer sales history, one data table would contain the customers' names and addresses, while another data table would contain all of the sales transactions for all of the customers.

You should consider using relational databases for all but the simplest of data lists. Very large flat file and nonrelational databases can be slow to open, tough to search in for specific data records, and prone to data-entry errors and data corruption.

There are two main benefits to using relational databases vs. nonrelational databases. The first benefit of using relational databases is the efficient use of database space. Using the example of the nonrelational database in the preceding section, there would be a lot of repeated customer names and addresses and therefore increased wasted space. The second benefit of using relational databases is the reduction of data-entry errors. Duplicating data can increase the probability of data-entry errors every time you retype the same customer names and addresses. Once you remove the repeated customer names and addresses to a separate data table in a relational database, you can update the customer names and addresses in just one table.

To declare relationships among data tables and cross-reference related data records in separate data tables to each other in a relational database, you use *primary keys* and *foreign keys*. A primary key is a data field containing a unique identifier—such as a sequential number, a part number, a customer ID, or a Social Security number—applied to each data record in the main table, also known as the *primary-key data table*. A foreign key then is a data field in the related table, also known as the *foreign-key data table*, containing the unique identifier from the related data record in the primary-key data table. For example, in the relational database example in the preceding section, you could assign each customer in the customer data table a unique ID number, and include the customer's unique ID number in each data record in the sales transactions data table for that customer.

Quick Start

To create a relational database, create two or more data tables, and then enter data records into each data table. Make sure that each data table contains a primary-key data field and that each data record in that data table contains a unique identifier in the primary-key data field. Also, for each related data table, create a foreign-key data field, and make sure that each data record in the related data table contains a primary-key data value from the related record in the primary-key data table.

How To

To create a relational database in Excel, do the following:

1. Start Excel.

2. Using one worksheet per data table, enter data records into each table.

3. Make sure that each worksheet contains a primary-key data field.

4. Make sure that for each worksheet, each data record in that worksheet has a primary-key data value in the primary-key data field that is unique to that worksheet.

5. Make sure that for each worksheet with data records related to the primary-key data table worksheet, the related worksheet contains a foreign-key field.

6. Make sure that each data record in the related worksheet contains a primary-key data value in the foreign-key data field, with that primary-key data value taken from the related record in the primary-key data table worksheet.

7. Save the file.

Tip

Foreign-key data tables should always also contain a primary-key data field. For example, a customer data table could have a related sales transactions data table, which in turn could have a related sales products data table. In this case, the sales transactions data table would need a foreign-key data field to cross-reference unique customers to sales transactions, and the sales transactions data table would also need a primary-key data field to relate unique sales transactions to unique sales products. (Of course, the customer data table would also need a primary-key data field to uniquely identify each customer, and the sales products data table would also need a primary-key data field to uniquely identify each sales product.)

Try It

In this exercise, you will examine a relational database in Excel. You will then use Access to import the relational data, examine the data in Access, define data table relationships, and examine related data:

1. Start Excel.

2. Click Office Button ➤ Open (for Excel 2007) or click File ➤ Open (for Excel 2003).

3. Browse to and select the ExcelDB_Ch01_03.xls file, and click Open. Notice that there are five worksheets in this workbook, one worksheet each for the Orders, Line Items, Suppliers, Products, and Salespeople data tables. In each worksheet, the primary key field ends in "PK," and any foreign key fields end in "FK."

4. Close the workbook.

Now, import the workbook data into Access.
For Access 2007, do the following:

1. Start Access.

2. Click Office Button ➤ New.

3. In the Blank Database pane, in the File Name box, type any name that's easy for you to remember for the database, click the Browse for a Location to Put Your Database icon and select a location for the database, and then click Create.

■**Note** You may need to scroll down the screen to find the Create button if the Create button is not visible under the File Name box.

---

4. Click External Data ➤ (Import) Excel.

5. Click Browse, browse to and select the ExcelDB_Ch01_03.xls file, click Open, and click OK.

6. Click the Show Worksheets option, select Orders in the list of available worksheets, and then click Next.

7. Select the First Row Contains Column Headings check box, and then click Next.

8. In the Indexed list, select Yes (No Duplicates), and then click Next.

9. Select the Choose My Own Primary Key option, select Order_ID_PK, and then click Next.

10. Click Finish, and then click Close. The Orders table is imported into the Access database.

11. Repeat steps 4 through 10 to import the Line Items, Suppliers, Products, and Salespeople worksheets into the Access database. Be sure to substitute in step 9 the values Line_ID_PK, Supplier_ID_PK, Product_ID_PK, and Salesperson_ID_PK for Order_ID_PK as appropriate. You can check your results against the imported worksheets in the finished ExcelDB_Ch01_03.mdb database file.

12. Open each of the tables in Access to ensure that the data in the Orders, Line Items, Suppliers, Products, and Salespeople data tables match the data in the Excel workbook. You can check your results against the imported worksheets in the finished ExcelDB_Ch01_03.mdb database file if needed.

For Access 2003, do the following:

1. Start Access.

2. Click File ➤ New.

3. In the New File task pane, click Blank Database, type any name that's easy for you to remember for the database in the File Name box, browse to a location to put your database, and then click Create.

4. Click File ➤ Get External Data ➤ Import.

5. In the Files of Type list, select Microsoft Excel.

6. Browse to and select the ExcelDB_Ch01_03.xls file, and click Import.

7. Select the Show Worksheets option, select Orders in the list of available worksheets, and then click Next.

8. With the First Row Contains Column Headings check box selected, click Next.

9. With the In a New Table option selected, click Next.

10. In the Indexed list, select Yes (No Duplicates), and click Next.

11. Select the Choose My Own Primary Key option, select Order_ID_PK, and click Next.

12. Click Finish, and click OK. The Orders table is imported into the Access database.

13. Repeat steps 4 through 12 to import the Line Items, Suppliers, Products, and Salespeople worksheets into the Access database. Be sure to substitute in step 11 the values Line_ID_PK, Supplier_ID_PK, Product_ID_PK, and Salesperson_ID_PK for Order_ID_PK as appropriate. You can check your results against the imported worksheets in the finished ExcelDB_Ch01_03.mdb database file.

14. Open each of the tables in Access to ensure that the data in the Orders, Line Items, Suppliers, Products, and Salespeople data tables match the data in the Excel workbook. You can check your results against the imported worksheets in the finished ExcelDB_Ch01_03.mdb database file if needed.

Next, create relationships among the data tables in Access:

1. For Access 2007, click Database Tools ➤ (Show/Hide) Relationships. For Access 2003, click Tools ➤ Relationships.

2. On the Show Table dialog box's Tables tab, with the Line Items data table selected, click Add. Repeat this step for the Orders, Products, Salespeople, and Suppliers data tables. Then click Close.

3. In the Orders data table, drag the Order_ID_PK data field to the Line Items data table's Order_ID_FK data field.

■**Note** Be sure to close all of the open data tables in Access before you complete the preceding step.

   4. In the Edit Relationships dialog box, select the Enforce Referential Integrity check box, and then click Create.

■**Note** Selecting the Enforce Referential Integrity check box ensures that Access will prevent you from deleting a data record in the primary data table when there are matching data records in a related data table. This prevents you from having "stranded" or "orphaned" data in related data tables.

   5. Repeat steps 3 and 4 for the following data fields:

   • In the Products data table, drag the Product_ID_PK data field to the Line Items data table's Product_ID_FK data field.

   • In the Salespeople data table, drag the Salesperson_ID_PK data field to the Orders data table's Salesperson_ID_FK data field.

   • In the Suppliers data table, drag the Supplier_ID_PK data field to the Products data table's Supplier_ID_FK data field.

   • You can check your results against the finished ExcelDB_Ch01_03.mdb database file.

   6. Click Office Button ➤ Save (for Excel 2007) or File ➤ Save (for Excel 2003).

   7. Close the Relationships window.

   Now that you have data table relationships defined, drill down into one of the supplier's sales order details in Access.

   1. Open the Suppliers data table.

   2. Click the plus sign symbol next to the Acme data row.

   3. Click the plus sign symbols next to the two products that are displayed to discover how many units were ordered on which orders.

   4. Quit Access, and quit Excel.

1.4 Normalize Data

Relational databases work best when data is normalized. When you normalize your data, you eliminate redundant data to help protect your data against data entry errors. You also ensure that the information in each data table is correctly linked so that you can properly cross-reference related data.

You normalize data when you have a lot of repetitive data in one or more data tables and you want to restructure the data to reduce data entry errors and possibly reduce data storage requirements.

To normalize data, you should follow a set of well-established rules called *normal forms*. There are three common normal forms. There are also several less common normal forms that are beyond the scope of this book.

The general strategies underlying the three common normal forms are the following:

- Eliminate repeating data in rows or data records.

- Eliminate repeating data in columns or data fields, moving the repeated data to other data tables.

- Use primary keys and foreign keys to cross-reference related data records among data tables.

For example, examine the following nonnormalized data in Table 1-1.

Table 1-1. *Nonnormalized Weather Data for Three United States Cities*

City, State	Date 1	High	Low	Air Quality	Date 2	High	Low	Air Quality
Portland, Oregon	15-Feb	47	30	Moderate	16-Feb	45	26	Moderate
Portland, Oregon	17-Feb	33	23	Good	18-Feb	39	27	Good
Salem, Oregon	15-Feb	47	27	Moderate	16-Feb	44	23	Moderate
Salem, Oregon	17-Feb	31	22	Good	18-Feb	39	23	Good
Spokane, Washington	15-Feb	35	18	Good	16-Feb	23	2	Good
Spokane, Washington	17-Feb	20	10	Good	18-Feb	32	14	Good

Notice the following facts in the preceding data table:

- The cities and states are contained in the same data field, with several duplicate cities and states listed.

- The date, high temperature, low temperature, and air quality data fields are presented in a peculiar manner: the weather for four dates is presented in more than four data records; and three city and state combinations are presented in more than three records.

- Many air quality data field values are repeated.

By moving repeating data to other data tables and linking the data tables together through primary keys and foreign keys, you could present the data in Tables 1-2 through 1-7.

Table 1-2. *Cities Data Table for Normalized Weather Data from Table 1-1*

City_ID_PK	City
1	Portland
2	Salem
3	Spokane

Table 1-3. *States Data Table for Normalized Weather Data from Table 1-1*

State_ID_PK	State
1	Oregon
2	Washington

Table 1-4. *Cities States Data Table for Normalized Weather Data from Table 1-1*

City_State_ID_PK	City_ID_FK	State_ID_FK
1	1	1
2	2	1
3	3	2

Table 1-5. *Dates Data Table for Normalized Weather Data from Table 1-1*

Date_ID_PK	Date
1	15-Feb
2	16-Feb
3	17-Feb
4	18-Feb

Table 1-6. *Air Qualities Data Table for Normalized Weather Data from Table 1-1*

Air_Quality_ID_PK	Air_Quality
1	Moderate
2	Good

Table 1-7. *Weather Data Data Table for Normalized Weather Data from Table 1-1*

Data_Record_ID_PK	Date_ID_FK	City_State_ID_FK	High	Low	Air_Quality_ID_FK
1	1	1	47	30	1
2	2	1	45	26	1
3	3	1	33	23	2
4	4	1	39	27	2
5	1	2	47	27	1
6	2	2	44	23	1
7	3	2	31	22	2
8	4	2	39	23	2
9	1	3	35	18	2
10	2	3	23	2	2
11	3	3	20	10	2
12	4	3	32	14	2

Normalizing this data results in the following benefits:

- The Cities, States, and Cities States data tables are extendable to allow a city with the same name to exist in multiple states.

- If a city or state changes its name, you only need to change a record in the Cities or States data table.

- If the representation of a date needs to change (for example, changing 15-Feb to 02/15 or 15/02), you only need to change data records in the Dates data table.

- If the air quality categories change, you only need to change data records in the Air Qualities data table.

As an added side benefit, sorting and averaging weather data is a bit more straightforward in the normalized Weather Data data table. In the nonnormalized data for example, averaging high temperatures for cities in Oregon for February 15 is more complicated: first you must filter for all rows where Oregon is somewhere in the City, State data field, then you must somehow collect all of the High data field values together where the corresponding Date 1 or Date 2 data field is 15-Feb (which is tough for many database management systems to do automatically), then you calculate the average high temperature. In the normalized Weather Data data table, you filter for all rows where the Date_ID_FK data value contains a matching data value in the Dates data table corresponding to 15-Feb and where the City_State_ID_FK data value contains a matching value in the Cities States and States data tables corresponding to Oregon; then you average the values in the High data field.

Quick Start

To normalize repetitive data, you eliminate the repeating data in data records and data fields, moving the repeating data to other data tables. You then use primary keys and foreign keys to cross-reference related data records among those data tables.

How To

To normalize data in one or more existing data tables, do the following:

1. Identify data fields with repeating data values or multipart data values (for example, contact name and address data values or product name and manufacturer data values contained in the same data field). Break these data values into multiple data fields (for example, separate data fields for name, address, product name, or manufacturer data values).

2. Group data fields with related data values into separate data tables (for example, a data table for contacts, a data table for products, or a data table for manufacturers).

3. Eliminate repeating data values in each data table (for example, a repeated address or a repeated product name).

4. Assign a primary key data field to each data table and a unique identifier for each data record in that data table (for example, a unique contact identification number or a unique product part number).

5. Add foreign key data fields as needed to cross-reference related data records contained in multiple data tables (for example, foreign key data fields describing the relationships between products and manufacturers, cross-referencing primary key data values in the separate product and manufacturer data tables).

6. Create additional data tables and use foreign keys as needed to store data records containing unique facts and figures (for example, a product sales transaction data table containing individual sales transaction details, cross-referencing primary key data values in the product/manufacturer data table).

Tip

A *one-to-many relationship* between two data tables is the most common type of relationship. A one-to-many relationship exists when a data record in data table A can have many matching data records in another data table B, but a data record in data table B has only one matching data record in data table A. For example, a sales order in one data table can have many matching sales line items in another data table, but each sales line item matches only one sales order.

A less frequent but still common type of relationship, a *many-to-many relationship*, exists between two data tables when a data record in table A can have many matching records in data table B, and a record in data table B can have many matching data records in data table A. A many-to-many relationship is made possible by creating a third table, called a *junction table*, that contains foreign keys from both data tables A and B. A many-to-many relationship is really two one-to-many relationships described by a third data table. For example, a sales order in one data table can have many matching product items in another data table, and each product item can appear in many different sales orders. A third data table is used to describe this complex relationship, matching sales orders to product items and product items to sales orders.

A very uncommon type of relationship, a *one-to-one relationship*, exists between two data tables when each data record in data table A can have only one matching data record in data table B, and each data record in data table B can have only one matching data record in data table A. This type of relationship is uncommon because this type of data is best described in a single data table. For example, a customer in one data table has a unique identification number in another data table, and each unique identification number belongs to only one customer. In this example, you may have needed to separate this information into two data tables for some type of security or privacy policy mandated by your organization.

Try It

In this exercise, you will practice using Excel and Access to normalize some nonnormalized data:

1. Start Excel.

2. Click Office Button ➤ Open (for Excel 2007) or click File ➤ Open (for Excel 2003).

3. Browse to and select the ExcelDB_Ch01_04.xls file, and click Open. Notice that there are six worksheets in this workbook, one worksheet with some nonnormalized data in it, and one worksheet each labeled Orders, Line Items, Suppliers, Products, and Salespeople.

You can use these worksheets to manually normalize the nonnormalized data, comparing your results to the ExcelDB_Ch01_04.mdb file. Or you can follow the remaining steps to import the nonnormalized data into Access, normalize the data, and use Excel to import the normalized data.

For Access 2007, do the following:

1. Start Access.

2. Click Office Button ➤ New.

3. In the Blank Database pane, click Create.

4. Click External Data ➤ (Import) Excel.

5. Click Browse, browse to and select the ExcelDB_Ch01_04.xls file, click Open, and click OK.

6. Select the Show Worksheets option, select Nonnormalized Data in the list of worksheets, and then click Next.

7. Select the First Row Contains Column Headings check box, and then click Next.

8. In the Indexed list, select Yes (Duplicates OK), and click Next.

9. With the Let Access Add Primary Key option selected, click Next.

10. Click Finish, and click Close. The Nonnormalized Data data table is imported into the Access database.

For Access 2003, do the following:

1. Start Access.

2. Click File ➤ New.

3. In the New File task pane, click Blank Database.

4. Click Create.

5. Click File ➤ Get External Data ➤ Import.

6. In the Files of Type list, select Microsoft Excel.

7. Browse to and select the ExcelDB_Ch01_04.xls file, and click Import.

8. Click the Show Worksheets option, select Non-Normalized Data in the list of worksheets, and then click Next.

9. Select the First Row Contains Column Headings check box, and click Next.

10. With the In a New Table option selected, click Next.

11. In the Indexed list, with the Yes (Duplicates OK) item selected, click Next.

12. With the Let Access Add Primary Key option selected, click Next.

13. Click Finish, and click OK. The Nonnormalized Data data table is imported into the Access database.

Next, use the Table Analyzer Wizard to help you normalize the data in the Nonnormalized Data data table:

1. With the Nonnormalized Data data table selected (but not opened), for Access 2007, click Database Tools ➤ (Analyze) Analyze Table. For Access 2003, click Tools ➤ Analyze ➤ Table.

2. Click Next three times.

3. Click the No, I Want to Decide option, and then click Next.

4. Drag the Order_ID data field from the Table2 data table (for Access 2007) or Table1 data table (for Access 2003) to a blank area of the workspace. Type **Orders**, and click OK.

5. Drag the Salesperson_Name data field from the Table2 data table (for Access 2007) or Table1 data table (for Access 2003) to a blank area of the workspace. Type **Salespeople**, and click OK.

6. Drag the Supplier_Name data field from the Table2 data table (for Access 2007) or Table1 data table (for Access 2003) to a blank area of the workspace. Type **Suppliers**, and click OK.

7. Drag the Product_Description data field from the Table2 data table (for Access 2007) or Table1 data table (for Access 2003) to a blank area of the workspace. Type **Products**, and click OK.

8. Drag the Unit_Description data field from the Table2 data table (for Access 2007) or Table1 data table (for Access 2003) to underneath the Product_Description data field in the Products data table.

9. Drag the Price_Per_Unit data field from the Table2 data table (for Access 2007) or Table1 data table (for Access 2003) to underneath the Unit_Description data field in the Products data table.

10. Click the title bar of the Table2 data table (for Access 2007) or Table1 data table (for Access 2003), click the Rename Table button, type **Line Items**, and click OK. Compare your results to Figure 1-1.

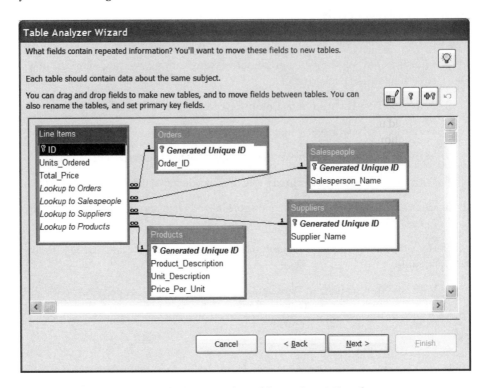

Figure 1-1. *The completed table design in the Table Analyzer Wizard*

11. Click Next five times.

■**Note** Each time you click Next, you will be asked if you really want to move on without changing anything. In each case click Yes.

---

12. On the final page of the Table Analyzer Wizard, with the Yes, Create the Query option selected, click Finish.

13. Click OK. (For Access 2003 only, a query simulating the contents of the original Non-normalized Data data table appears. Click File ➤ Close to return to the Database Objects window.)

14. Open and explore the contents of the normalized Line Items, Orders, Products, Salespeople, and Suppliers tables.

1.5 Learn About Multidimensional Databases

Microsoft Office Excel 2003 can display at most 65,536 data records or 256 data fields on a single worksheet. (Excel 2007 supports 1 million data records and 16,000 data fields on a single worksheet.) What happens if your data exceeds any of these limits? You have a few options, specifically the following:

- You could break up the data into a set of smaller data tables, although this approach could be very difficult to set up and maintain in Excel. Also, multiple data cross-reference operations could be a big drain on your computer's resources.

- You could use Microsoft Office Access 2007 or Access 2003 to store and manage your data, although with Access 2007 and 2003 you are still limited to 255 data fields in a single table. You are also limited to 4,000 characters in a data record for Access 2007 (2,000 characters for Access 2003), excluding a few special types of data fields.

- You could use other database management systems that are more robust for very large databases compared to Excel—for example, Microsoft SQL Server. But these systems are more expensive, are harder to learn and maintain, require greater computing resources, and lack most of Excel's great data analysis features.

There is, however, one more approach for representing in Excel large amounts of data that exceed Excel's limits, and that approach is to convert the data into a *multidimensional database*.

You should consider using a multidimensional database when you have a large amount of data that exceeds Excel's display limits, or when you have a large database for which you only want to work with summarized data and not necessarily the individual data values themselves.

A multidimensional database is a set of data records that summarize the most important facts and figures in a large database. The term *multidimensional* comes from the fact that the summarized facts and figures can be cross-referenced along several dimensions. Here are a few of the key terms you should know about when working with multidimensional data:

- *Dimensions* are categories or groupings of similar facts and figures such as time, geography, products and services, or organizations.

- Dimensions can be further broken down into *levels*. A time-oriented dimension could consist of years, seasons, months, and weeks. A geographical-oriented dimension could consist of continents, countries or regions, and states or provinces.

- Levels consist of *members*. A year level could contain the members 2004, 2005, 2006, and 2007. A country level could contain the members France, Germany, and Italy.

- *Measures* contain the summarized data values. Measures can be summarized by member, level, or dimension, depending on how much detail you are interested in working with.

- Dimensions, levels, members, and measures are stored in electronic files called *cube files*. Just as a physical cube has three dimensions, a multidimensional data cube file also contains dimensions.

■**Note** Cube files are not cubes in the strictly geometrical sense because they are not limited to three dimensions. However, the term *cube file* in this context is well understood and defined in the discipline of multidimensional data analysis.

Because a cube file contains various combinations of measures for members, levels, and dimensions summarized in advance, you can retrieve the summarized data very quickly. In fact, because cube files only contain summarized representations of the data records' key facts and figures, cube files are smaller in size than the data upon which they are based. Because of their smaller size, cube files can use fewer computing resources to work with.

You can use Excel to both create and work with cube files.

Quick Start

To create and save a cube file in Excel 2003, do the following:

■**Note** Excel 2007 does not support creating a cube file using MS Query. This feature has been removed from Excel 2007 due to technical issues. You can, however, create cube files based on cubes that exist in Microsoft SQL Server Analysis Services. You can also create cube files from relational databases using Microsoft SQL Server Analysis Services.

1. Start Excel.

2. Click Data ➤ Import External Data ➤ New Database Query.

3. With the Use the Query Wizard to Create/Edit Queries check box selected, on the Databases tab, click one of the items in the list to create a connection to an existing external data source (such as a dBASE file, an Excel workbook, or an Access database), and then click OK.

4. Follow the steps in the Query Wizard.

5. In the Query Wizard – Finish page, select the Create an OLAP Cube from this query option, and click Finish.

6. Complete the steps in the OLAP Cube Wizard to finish creating the cube file.

To open and work with a cube file in Excel 2007, do the following:

1. Click Data ➤ (Get External Data) From Other Sources ➤ From Microsoft Query.

2. With the Use the Query Wizard to Create/Edit Queries check box selected and the OLAP Cubes tab selected, select the name of a cube file in the list (or click <New Data Source>, click OK, follow the steps in the Create New Data Source dialog box, click OK, and then select the name of the new data source), and then click OK. The Import Data dialog box appears.

3. Click OK.

4. Create a PivotTable using the PivotTable Field List pane.

To open a cube file in Excel 2003, do the following:

1. Click File ➤ Open.

2. In the Files of Type list, select All Data Sources.

3. Browse to and select a file with the .cub file extension.

4. Click Open.

5. Create a PivotTable using the PivotTable Field List pane.

■**Note** For more information on creating and working with PivotTables, see Chapter 6.

How To

To create a cube file in Excel 2003, do the following:

1. Start Excel.

2. Click Data ➤ Import External Data ➤ New Database Query.

3. With the Use the Query Wizard to Create/Edit Queries check box selected and the Databases tab selected, click one of the items in the list to create a connection to an existing external data source (such as a dBASE file, an Excel workbook, or an Access database), and then click OK.

4. Follow the steps in the Query Wizard.

5. In the Query Wizard – Finish page, select the Create an OLAP Cube from This Query option, and click Finish. The Welcome to the OLAP Cube Wizard page or the OLAP Cube Wizard Step 1 of 3 page appears.

6. If the Welcome to the OLAP Cube Wizard page is displayed, click Next.

7. Complete the steps in the OLAP Cube Wizard to finish creating the cube file.

To open and work with a cube file in Excel 2007, do the following:

1. Click Data ➤ (Get External Data) from Other Sources ➤ From Microsoft Query.

2. With the Use the Query Wizard to Create/Edit Queries check box selected and the OLAP Cubes tab selected, select the name of a cube file in the list (or click <New Data Source>, click OK, follow the steps in the Create New Data Source dialog box, click OK, and then click the name of the new data source), and then click OK. The Import Data dialog box appears.

3. Click OK.

4. Create a PivotTable using the PivotTable Field List pane.

To open a cube file in Excel 2003, do the following:

1. Click File ➤ Open.

2. In the Files of Type list, select All Data Sources.

3. Browse to and select a file with the .cub file extension.

4. Click Open.

5. Create a PivotTable using the PivotTable Field List pane.

Alternatively, for Excel 2003, do the following:

1. Start Excel.

2. Click Data ➤ Import External Data ➤ New Database Query.

3. With the Use the Query Wizard to Create/Edit Queries check box selected and the OLAP Cubes tab selected, select the cube file's name (or click Browse, browse to and select the cube file, and click Open), and click OK. The PivotTable and PivotChart Wizard – Step 3 of 3 dialog box appears.

4. Click Finish.

5. Create a PivotTable using the PivotTable Field List pane.

Tip

To learn more about multidimensional databases, cubes, and a multidimensional data management methodology called *online analytical processing* (OLAP), see Chapter 6, "Analyzing Multidimensional Data with PivotTables," in my book *A Complete Guide to PivotTables: A Visual Approach* (Apress, 2004).

Try It

In this exercise you will use Excel 2003 to create a cube file. Later, you will use Excel 2007 or Excel 2003 to display the cube file's data in Excel.

Using Excel 2003, connect to the data that you will use to create the cube file:

1. Start Excel.

2. Click Data ➤ Import External Data ➤ New Database Query.

3. With the Use the Query Wizard to Create/Edit Queries check box selected and the Databases tab selected, click Excel Files, and click OK.

4. Browse to and select the ExcelDB_Ch01_05.xls file, and click OK.

5. Click Options.

6. Select the System Tables check box, and click OK.

7. In the Available Tables and Columns list, click Data$, click the right arrow (➤) button, and click Next.

8. Click Next two more times.

9. Select the Create an OLAP Cube from This Query option, and click Finish. The Welcome to the OLAP Cube Wizard page or the OLAP Cube Wizard Step 1 of 3 page appears.

Next, use Excel 2003 to create the cube file:

1. If the Welcome to the OLAP Cube Wizard page is displayed, click Next.

2. Clear the Year and Quarter check boxes, and click Next.

3. In the Source Fields list, click Country, and click the right arrow (➤) button.

4. In the Dimensions list, right-click the Country dimension, click Rename, type **Location**, and press Enter.

5. Drag District from the Source Fields list to Country in the Dimensions list.

6. In the Source Fields list, click Year, and click the right arrow button.

7. In the Dimensions list, right-click the Year dimension, click Rename, type **Time**, and press Enter.

8. Drag Quarter from the Source Fields list to Year in the Dimensions list.

9. In the Source Fields list, click Category, and click the right arrow button.

10. In the Dimensions list, right-click the Category dimension, click Rename, type **Product**, and press Enter.

11. Drag Price Point from the Source Fields list to Category in the Dimensions list.

In the Dimensions list, you should have a Location dimension with a Country member and a District member; a Time dimension with a Year member and a Quarter member; and a Product dimension with a Category member and a Price Point member. Compare your results with Figure 1-2.

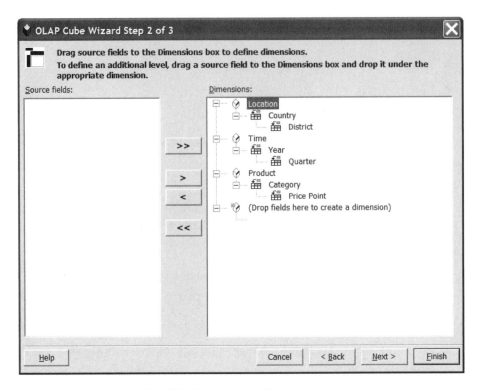

Figure 1-2. *The completed OLAP Wizard Step 2 of 3 page*

12. Click Next.

13. With the Save a Cube File Containing All Data for the Cube option selected, click Browse.

14. In the File Name list, type **ExcelDB_Ch01_05.cub**, and click Save.

15. Click Finish.

16. If the Save As dialog box appears to save the query, type **Excel_Ch01_05** in the File Name box, and click Save. The PivotTable and PivotChart Wizard — Step 3 of 3 dialog box appears.

Finally, display the cube file's data in Excel in 2003:

1. With the PivotTable and PivotChart Wizard — Step 3 of 3 dialog box displayed, click Finish.

In the PivotTable Field List pane, do the following:

2. Click Location, select Page Area in the Add To list, and click Add To.

3. Click Product, select Row Area in the Add To list, and click Add To.

4. Click Time, select Column Area in the Add To list, and click Add To.

5. Click Sum of Units Sold, select Data Area in the Add To list, and click Add To.

If you are using Excel 2007, connect to the ExcelDB_Ch01_05.cub file included in the Source Code/Download section of the Apress web site, `http://www.apress.com`, and use the PivotTable Field List pane to display the cube file's data, as follows:

1. Start Excel.

2. Click Data ➤ (Get External Data) From Other Sources ➤ From Microsoft Query.

3. With the OLAP Cubes tab selected, click <New Data Source>, and click OK.

4. In the What Name Do You Want to Give Your Data Source box, type **ExcelDB_Ch01_05**.

5. In the Select an OLAP Provider for the Database You Want to Access list, select Microsoft OLE DB Provider for OLAP Services 8.0.

6. Click Connect. The Multidimensional Connection dialog box appears.

7. Click the Cube File option.

8. Next to the File box, click the ellipsis (. . .) button.

9. Browse to and select the ExcelDB_Ch01_05.cub file, click Open.

10. Click Finish, and click OK.

11. In the Choose Data Source dialog box on the OLAP Cubes tab, select ExcelDB_Ch01_05.

12. Click OK. The Import Data dialog box appears.

13. Click OK. The PivotTable Field List pane appears.

14. In the PivotTable Field List pane, select the Sum of Units Sold, Location, Product, and Time check boxes.

15. Drag the Location icon from the Row Labels box to the Report Filter box.

16. Drag the Time icon from the Row Labels box to the Column Labels box.

1.6 Choose the Right Database Product

This chapter concludes with a list of considerations to help you decide whether to use Excel, Access, or SQL Server to address your specific data management needs. You may use Excel for some sets of data, while you may use Access or SQL Server for others.

Use Excel when

- You have a relatively small amount of data.

- Your data is stored in one data table or a relatively small number of tables, and your data tables do not have many complex relationships defined.

- You want to execute data calculations or formulas, perform statistical data analysis, or perform other unique computations on data for which Excel is particularly suited.

- You want to quickly print data without a lot of additional formatting work.

- You don't have any special requirements for data synchronization over multiple remote locations, advanced data backup and restore needs, or ongoing data logging and audit tracking requirements.

- You want to present a simple snapshot of your data over the Web.

Use Access when

- Your data exceeds Excel's operating limits.

- You have more than a few people, but not more than say a couple dozen people, who need simultaneous access to the data.

- You need to synchronize data over a few remote locations.

- You want to take advantage of more robust data entry, querying, and reporting solution options.

- You want to create a lightweight Web-based data entry and reporting solution without a lot of additional effort.

- You want to implement some degree of data security and data backup and restore, and you're willing to make a small time investment to do so.

Use SQL Server when

- Your data exceeds Access's operating limits.

- You have a large amount of multidimensional data.

- You have a large number of people that need simultaneous access to the data.

- You need to synchronize a large amount of data over a large number of remote locations.

- You need to perform a large number of transactions that can be rolled back as a group if certain conditions aren't met.

- You have advanced or unique needs for data storage; data backup, retrieval, and restore; and data logging and audit tracking.

- You have advanced or unique solution development needs such as data entry triggers and stored procedures.

- You want to import, export, or synchronize data across a wide array of database management systems.

- You want to create an end-to-end, Web-based solution to interact with and manage your data.

- You want to take advantage of more powerful computing resources for faster data access and data management.

For more information on Access and SQL Server, see the following:

- *Microsoft Office Access 2007*: http://office.microsoft.com/en-us/access/FX100487571033.aspx

- *Access 2003 Product Information*: http://www.microsoft.com/office/access/prodinfo

- *SQL Server 2005 Overview*: http://www.microsoft.com/sql/prodinfo/overview

■■■

CHAPTER 2

Define Your Data

Before you create your database's data tables and fill those tables with values, you should set aside some time for defining your data. You start defining your data by determining the goals, results, or outcomes that you want your data to help you achieve. Next, you determine the technical requirements for gathering, entering, storing, using, and analyzing your data. Equipped with this information, you can better select a suitable database management system and better design your tables, fields, and table relations.

2.1 Determine Your Goals, Results, or Outcomes

Many individuals and organizations start defining and designing a database by creating some data tables, relating the tables together, and filling them with values. These steps alone are not sufficient for a well-planned database definition and design. You should first determine the goals, results, or outcomes you need your data to help you achieve. You should then determine how collecting and analyzing data will help you achieve those goals, results, or outcomes. Doing so can help provide a broader view of the types of tables and relationships among those tables to better capture and analyze all of your data.

Quick Start

First, gather key folks who are involved in the designing of your database, those who collect, enter, and analyze your data, and finally those who make important decisions based on that data. Then, collect information from these people to help you better design your database.

How To

The key folks involved with your database and its data should be prepared to answer three questions:

Question #1: What are your goals, and what are the goals of our organization? This can be broken down into the following:

- What goals are we trying to achieve by collecting this data?

- What kinds of problems or issues are we facing that this data may help address?

- What are we trying to measure, track, or analyze with this data?

- From whom or from where are we collecting this data?

- How often are we collecting this data?

Question #2: What results are you looking for, and what result is our organization trying to achieve? This means the following:

- What do we need to do with this data once we have collected it?

- What results are we hoping to achieve by collecting, measuring, tracking, or analyzing this data?

Question #3: What would a successful outcome look like for you and for our organization?

- What would a successful outcome look like once we have collected, measured, tracked, or analyzed this data?

- How do we envision ultimately benefiting from successfully collecting, measuring, tracking, or analyzing this data?

Use the results of this information-gathering session to develop a plan to better design your database.

▪**Tip** Don't underestimate the power of clearly defining your and your organization's goals, results, and outcomes that your data will help you achieve. For example, clear goals can help you focus on collecting only the most important data to reach your desired results and outcomes. Focusing on collecting only the most important data can result in a less cluttered database design that is easier to use and consumes fewer computing resources.

Try It

The ExcelDB_Ch02_01.doc file in the Source Code/Download section of the Apress web site, http://www.apress.com, contains a version of the questions in the preceding "How To" section. You could use this file in helping determine your organization's goals, results, or outcomes you need your data to help you achieve.

2.2 Determine Requirements for Collecting, Storing, Analyzing, and Maintaining Your Data

After determining the overall goals, results, or outcomes for your data, you should choose a database management system to collect, store, analyze, and maintain your data. You should also determine whether you have any specific needs for remote users, Web-based users, security requirements, and so on. To choose the most appropriate database management system, you should first determine your technical requirements. From there, you should gather your other nontechnical organizational needs and requirements to help ensure the best possible database design. Doing this can keep you from wasting time and money later on, as you have a database management system and a database design that is able to handle your requirements as you go.

Quick Start

First, gather key folks who are involved in selecting and purchasing your database management system; designing your database; collecting, entering, and analyzing your data; and making important decisions based on your data. Second, gather both technical and nontechnical requirements from these folks to help you select the best database management system and better design your database.

How To

These key folks, working together as a team, should be prepared to answer the following questions:

- Who will be using the database? What data entry, data analysis, and decision-making tasks will they be expected to perform?

- Who will be providing technical support for the database? What data management and data maintenance tasks will technical support specialists be expected to perform and how often? What defects with the database will technical support specialists be expected to fix and how often?

- Can you estimate how many data tables, data fields, data records, and data table relationships you may be initially creating for the database?

- Can you estimate how many additional data tables, data fields, data records, and data table relationships you may be creating over time for the database?

- How often will the data be changed? Who will make these changes?

- What is the estimated greatest number of people who may need to access the database at the same time? In how many remote locations do these people exist?

- Do you need to support data transactions—grouping together related sets of data record additions, changes, and deletions, and committing or rolling back each of these transaction sets as a single data operation? How often are data transactions expected to take place, and how many data transactions are expected to occur at the same time?

- How many remote computers may need direct access to this database? How many remote computers could operate with a snapshot copy of this database? What is the longest amount of time that could pass before these remote snapshot data copies must be refreshed with the latest snapshot of the most accurate data?

- Do you need to import, export, or synchronize data across a wide array of database management systems, and if so, how many and by which software manufacturers?

- Do you have any special requirements for advanced data backup and restore needs, and if so, what are those requirements?

- Will data access be offered over an intranet, an extranet, or over the Web? If so, what levels of data access need to be supported?

- Do you have any special security needs, such as controlling who has access to view, change, and maintain the data? Do you have any ongoing data logging or audit tracking requirements?

- What computing resources are available? Is there a budget for increasing these resources?

Use the results of this information-gathering session to help you select and purchase your database management system, and also to help you better design your database.

Tip You can also use the guidance in "Section 1.6: Choose the Right Database Product" in Chapter 1 to help you select and purchase your database management system.

Try It

The ExcelDB_Ch02_02.doc file in the Source Code/Download section of the Apress web site, http://www.apress.com, contains a version of the questions in the preceding "How To" section. You could use this file in helping you select and purchase your database management system, and also to help you better design your database.

2.3 Design Your Data

Now you have determined what goals, results, or outcomes you need your data to help you achieve. You have determined your requirements for collecting, storing, analyzing, and maintaining your data. You have also selected a database format and a database management system. Now you are ready to design your data tables, data fields, and, where applicable, your data table relationships.

Quick Start

If you have selected a flat file database format, you can simply begin entering data values and data records. Similarly, if you have selected a nonrelational database format, you can simply begin entering data field names, and then enter data values and data records. If you have selected a relational database format, you should consider additional design considerations, such as defining primary keys, foreign keys, and data table relationships. For multidimensional database formats, even more design considerations (such as dimensions, levels, and members) should be considered.

How To

To design a relational database's tables, records, and fields, do the following:

Step 1: Examine your data to see if you can break it further into its most indivisible parts. For example, consider two record scenarios for real estate property listings. The first record scenario might contain the following:

- *Property address*: 123 Main Street Northwest, Mountain City, Idaho, 88812

- *Year house built*: 2002

- *Property owners*: John Doe and Jane Doe, a married couple

- *Property assessed value*: $225,000 in 2002; $230,000 in 2003; $235,000 in 2004; $237,000 in 2005; $240,000 in 2006

- *Property parcel number*: Lot 921, plat 47, parcel E2, as recorded in the year 2002 on page 114 of Springsville County Public Records

The second record scenario might contain the following:

- *Property address*: 234 Second Street Northwest, Mountain City, Idaho, 88812

- *Year house built*: 2003

- *Property owners*: John Q. Public and David Doe

- *Property assessed value*: $275,000 in 2003; $285,000 in 2004; $299,000 in 2005; $302,000 in 2006

- *Property parcel number*: Lot 919, plat 34, parcel E1, as recorded in the year 2003 on page 382 of Springsville County Public Records

In these two records, notice the following:

- The property address information could be divided into data fields such as street address, city, state, and postal code.

- The property owners could be listed by individual name.

- The property assessed value information could be divided into individual year and value data fields.

- The property parcel numbers could be divided into data fields such as lot, plat, parcel, year recorded, pages recorded, and volume recorded.

Step 2: Examine your data to see if you can group related information into individual data tables. In this example, you could create individual tables for the following:

- Property addresses

- Years that houses were built on the properties (e.g., if a house is rebuilt on a property due to remodeling or disaster)

- Property owners

- Property assessed values

- Property parcel numbers

Step 3: Begin adding data records to individual data tables. The property addresses data table could be presented with the records shown in Table 2-1.

Table 2-1. *Addresses Data Table*

Street_Address	City	State	Postal_Code
123 Main Street Northwest	Mountain City	Idaho	88812
234 Second Street Northwest	Mountain City	Idaho	88812

The table containing the years that the houses were built on the properties could contain the records shown in Table 2-2.

Table 2-2. *Years_Built Data Table*

Year_Built
2002
2003

The property owners table could be presented with the records shown in Table 2-3.

Table 2-3. *Owners Data Table*

Name
John Doe
Jane Doe
John Q. Public
David Doe

The table on property assessed values could be presented with the records shown in Table 2-4.

Table 2-4. *Assessments Data Table*

Year_Assessed	Assessed_Value
2002	$225,000
2003	$230,000
2004	$235,000
2005	$237,000
2006	$240,000
2003	$275,000
2004	$285,000
2005	$299,000
2006	$302,000

The table on property parcel numbers could be presented with the records shown in Table 2-5.

Table 2-5. *Parcels Data Table*

Lot	Plat	Parcel	Year_Recorded	Page	Volume
921	47	E2	2002	114	Springsville County Public Records
919	34	E1	2003	382	Springsville County Public Records

Step 4: Remove duplicate data records from each data table, creating additional data tables as needed for volatile duplicate data in portions of complete data records.

In the preceding data tables, there is some duplicate data: the cities, states, and postal codes in the Addresses data table; the years in the Assessments data table; and the volume in the Parcels data table.

The state names likely would never change, but the city names and postal codes may change depending on local governments' decisions. So the cities, states, and postal codes should probably be moved to a separate data table and changed in only one data record if needed. The extra instance of the city, state, and postal code would then be removed from the separate data table, leaving only one data record.

The years that the properties were assessed are historical facts, so there's probably no need to move that data to a separate data table.

The volume names could change if the county name ever were to change, so the volume names could be moved to a separate data table and changed in only one data record if needed. The extra instance of the data record would then be removed from the separate data table, leaving only one data record.

Step 5: For each one-to-many data record relationship between data tables, define those relationships using the unique identifiers from related records (a primary key that is cross-referenced from other data tables is known as a *foreign key*).

To keep things simple, within each data table, each data record could be assigned a unique number, starting at one (1) and increasing by one for each additional data record in that data table. For clarity in this example, each data record identification number will be unique across the entire database.

For consistency and readability, you could name the primary key data field after the primary data table name, followed by _PK for *primary key*. You could also name the foreign key data field after the related data table name, followed by _FK for *foreign key*. So the data tables shown in Tables 2-6 through 2-12 emerge.

Table 2-6. *Addresses Data Table*

Addresses_PK	Address_Cities_FK	Street_Address
1	3	123 Main Street Northwest
2	3	234 Second Street Northwest

Table 2-7. *Address_Cities Data Table*

Address_Cities_PK	City	State	Postal_Code
3	Mountain City	Idaho	88812

Table 2-8. *Years_Built Data Table*

Years_Built_PK	Addresses_FK	Year_Built
4	1	2002
5	2	2003

Table 2-9. *Owners Data Table*

Owners_PK	Addresses_FK	Name
6	1	John Doe
7	1	Jane Doe
8	2	John Q. Public
9	2	David Doe

Table 2-10. *Assessments Data Table*

Assessments_PK	Addresses_FK	Year_Assessed	Assessed_Value
10	1	2002	$225,000
11	1	2003	$230,000
12	1	2004	$235,000
13	1	2005	$237,000
14	1	2006	$240,000
15	2	2003	$275,000
16	2	2004	$285,000
17	2	2005	$299,000
18	2	2006	$302,000

Table 2-11. *Parcels Data Table*

Parcels_PK	Addresses_FK	Parcel_Volumes_FK	Lot	Plat	Parcel	Year_Recorded	Page
19	1	21	921	47	E2	2002	114
20	2	21	919	34	E1	2003	382

Table 2-12. *Parcel_Volumes Data Table*

Parcel_Volumes_PK	Volume
21	Springsville County Public Records

Step 6: Examine your database design to see if you can use the data table relationships, primary keys, and foreign keys to assemble a complete representative set of data records with no duplicated data.

Using the preceding data tables, here's the data you could gather for the property at 234 Second Street Northwest:

- *Property address*: 234 Second Street Northwest; Mountain City, Idaho 88812

- *Year house built*: 2003

- *Property owners*: John Q. Public and David Doe

- *Assessed property values*: $275,000 in 2003; $285,000 in 2004; $299,000 in 2005; $302,000 in 2006

- *Property parcel number*: Lot 919, plat 34, parcel E1, as recorded in the year 2003 on page 382 of Springsville County Public Records

Step 7: Confirm that if you need to change any of the records' volatile facts, you should only make changes in one record in one table, or add one record to a limited number of tables:

- If the government or the postal system needs to change a property address or the postal code you would only need to change one record in the Addresses data table or one record in the Address_Cities data table.

- If the city government needs to redraw city boundaries so that a property is now considered in a different city, or if the city government changes the city's name altogether, you would only need to change one record in the Addresses table and one record in the Address_Cities table.

- If a house on a property is to be torn down and rebuilt in 2007, you would only need to add one record in the Years_Built table.

- If property owners' names need to be changed, you would only need to add, remove, or change records in the Owners table.

- When a property is reassessed in 2007, you would only need to add one record to the Assessments table.

- If the local government needs to change a property parcel number, you would only need to change one record in the Parcels table.

- If the county government needs to redraw county boundaries so that a property is now considered in a different county, or if the county government changes the county's name altogether, you would only need to change one record in the Parcel_Volumes table.

To design a multidimensional database's structure, do the following:

Step 1: Identify the multidimensional database's dimensions, which are categories or groupings of similar facts and figures. In the preceding example, assuming you have a database full of tens of thousands or more property listings, you could create the following dimensions:

- Geographic Location

- Time

- Assessed Value

- Parcel Location

Step 2: Identify the multidimensional database's levels, which are further groupings of data in each dimension.

For the Geographic Location dimension, you could create the following levels:

- City

- County

- State

- Postal Code

For the Time dimension, you could create a Year level.

For the Assessed Value dimension, you could create a Value Point level.

For the Parcel Location dimension, you could create the following levels:

- Lot

- Plat

Step 3: Identify the multidimensional database's members, which are groupings of data in each level.

For the Geographic Location dimension, you could create the following members:

- Mountain City (for the City level)

- Springsville County (for the County level)

- Idaho (for the State level)

- 88812 (for the Postal Code level)

For the Time dimension, you could create one member per year (e.g., 2002 and 2003 for the Year level)

For the Parcel Location dimension, you could create the following members:

- 919 and 921 (for the Lot level)

- 34 and 47 (for the Plat level)

Step 4: Identify the multidimensional database's measures, which are the summarized data values. For example, you could create an Assessed Value measure to summarize the assessed house values by dimension, level, or member.

For many-to-many record relationships between data tables, you should create an intermediate table (known as an *intersection table*) containing foreign keys from those tables. For example, in Table 2-13, note that there is an inherent many-to-many data record relationship. Each boat can have many parts, and each part can be used in many different models of boats.

Table 2-13. *Boats Data Table*

Boat_Model	Part_Name
Starfish Cruiser	Propeller
Starfish Cruiser	Rudder
Starfish Cruiser	Mast
Starfish Cruiser	Sail
Starfish Cruiser	Propeller
Starfish Cruiser	Rudder
Starfish Cruiser	Mast
Starfish Cruiser	Sail
Barnacle Tug	Propeller
Barnacle Tug	Rudder
Barnacle Tug	Boiler
Barnacle Tug	Propeller
Barnacle Tug	Rudder
Barnacle Tug	Boiler

You could create the tables shown in Table 2-14 and Table 2-15 and an intermediate table as shown in Table 2-16.

Table 2-14. *Boat_Models Data Table*

Boat_Models_PK	Boat_Model
20	Starfish Cruiser
21	Barnacle Tug

Table 2-15. *Boat_Parts Data Table*

Boat_Parts_PK	Part_Name
30	Propeller
31	Rudder
32	Mast
33	Sail
34	Boiler

Table 2-16. *Models_Parts Data Table*

Models_Parts_PK	Boat_Models_FK	Boat_Parts_FK
1	20	30
2	20	31
3	20	32
4	20	33
5	20	30
6	20	31
7	20	32
8	20	33
9	21	30
10	21	31
11	21	34
12	21	30
13	21	31
14	21	34

Try It

The ExcelDB_Ch02_03.xls file in the download in the Source Code/Download section of the Apress web site, http://www.apress.com, contains two worksheets that you can use to practice database design principles. You can use the first worksheet, titled Survey Results, to practice designing a relational database. You can use the second worksheet, titled Units Produced, to practice designing a multidimensional database.

CHAPTER 3

■■■

Enter Data

So you've created a new database or opened an existing database in Excel. Now you'll likely want to add or change records and values in the database. Copying and moving data, filling a closely related series of data across many worksheet cells, entering data with a data form, referring to groups of cells using named ranges, formatting data, protecting data, inserting functions and formulas, validating data, and importing data are all important skills to master with your Excel database. This chapter teaches you these skills.

3.1 Copy and Move Data

Just about every software application provides the ability to copy or move data from one location to another. Excel lets you copy or move not only data in individual worksheet cells, but entire worksheet rows and columns, and even entire worksheets. This allows you to enter repeating data into an Excel database much quicker than entering it manually.

Quick Start

To copy or move data, do the following:

1. Select the worksheet cells that you want to copy or move.

2. To copy the selected worksheet cells, click Home ➤ (Clipboard) Copy (in Excel 2007) or click Edit ➤ Copy (in Excel 2003). To move the selected worksheet cells, click Home ➤ (Clipboard) Cut (in Excel 2007) or click Edit ➤ Cut (in Excel 2003).

3. Choose the destination for the selected worksheet cells.

4. In Excel 2007, click Home ➤ (Clipboard) Paste, and click a paste option such as Paste Special. In Excel 2003, click Edit ➤ Paste or Edit ➤ Paste Special.

How To

Table 3-1 shows different ways of selecting worksheet cells that you want to copy or cut and paste.

Table 3-1. *How to Select Worksheet Cells*

What to Select	How to Select
Text in a single worksheet cell	Either double-click the cell and select the text in the worksheet cell, or select the worksheet cell and select the text in the Formula Bar
A single worksheet cell	Click that worksheet cell
Multiple worksheet cells that are next to each other	Either click the first worksheet cell and drag to the last worksheet cell; or click the first worksheet cell, press and hold the Shift key, click the last worksheet cell, and then release the Shift key
Multiple worksheet cells that are not next to each other	Press and hold the Ctrl key, and click or drag all of the worksheet cells that you want to select
All cells on a worksheet	Click the Select All button in the worksheet's upper corner at the intersection of the row and column headings
All worksheet cells in a single row or column	Click the row heading or column heading
All worksheet cells in multiple rows or columns that are next to each other	Click the first row heading or column heading and drag to the last row heading or column heading; or click the first row heading or column heading, press and hold the Shift key, click the last row heading or column heading, and then release the Shift key
All worksheet cells in multiple rows or columns that are not next to each other	Press and hold the Ctrl key, and click or drag all of the row headings or column headings that you want to select

To copy the selected worksheet cells, do the following:

1. Click Home ➤ (Clipboard) Copy (in Excel 2007) or click Edit ➤ Copy (in Excel 2003). To move the selected worksheet cells, click Home ➤ (Clipboard) Cut (in Excel 2007) or click Edit ➤ Cut (in Excel 2003).

2. Select the destination for the selected worksheet cells.

3. To paste the copied worksheet cells, choose one of the following:

   - In Excel 2007, click Home ➤ (Clipboard) Paste to paste the selected worksheet cells along with any text formatting, formulas, and comments; to paste the selected worksheet cells in a special way, click Paste ➤ Paste Special.

   - In Excel 2003, click Edit ➤ Paste to paste the selected worksheet cells along with any text formatting, formulas, and comments. To paste the selected worksheet cells in a special way (e.g., to paste only the data and not any underlying text formatting or formulas), click Edit ➤ Paste Special, and complete the Paste Special dialog box.

To copy or move one or more entire worksheets, do the following:

1. Select the worksheet tab of the worksheet that you want to move or copy. To select multiple worksheets, press and hold the Ctrl key, select the worksheets, and release the Ctrl key.

2. In Excel 2007, right-click one of the selected worksheet tabs and click Move or Copy. In Excel 2003, click Edit ➤ Move or Copy Sheet.

3. In the To Book list, select the workbook you want to copy or move the selected worksheets to.

4. In the Before Sheet list, select the worksheet that you want to move your selected worksheets in front of.

5. Select the Create a Copy check box to copy the worksheets; or clear the Create a Copy check box to move the worksheets.

6. Click OK.

Try It

In this exercise, you will practice copying and pasting multiple worksheet cells and multiple rows and columns on worksheets. You will also practice copying and moving entire worksheets.

First, practice copying multiple worksheet cells:

1. Start Excel.

2. Click Office Button ➤ Open (in Excel 2007) or File ➤ Open (in Excel 2003).

3. Browse to and select the ExcelDB_Ch03_01-09.xls file, and click Open.

4. Click the SalesData worksheet tab, click cell B3, press and hold the Ctrl key, drag the mouse over cells B3 through D3, and release the mouse button.

5. With the Ctrl key still held, drag the mouse over cells B6 through D6, B9 through D9, and B10 through D10, releasing the mouse button between groups of cells.

6. In Excel 2007, click Home ➤ (Clipboard) Copy. In Excel 2003, click Edit ➤ Copy.

7. Click the Scratchpad worksheet tab, click cell A1, and in Excel 2007, click Home ➤ (Clipboard) Paste. In Excel 2003, click Edit ➤ Paste.

The selected cells are pasted to cells A1 through C4.

Next, practice copying multiple worksheet rows and columns as follows:

1. Click the SalesData worksheet tab, press the Esc key to deselect the previously selected cells, click the row header for row 4, press and hold the Ctrl key, and click the row headers for rows 7, 10, and 11.

2. In Excel 2007, click Home ➤ (Clipboard) Copy. In Excel 2003, click Edit ➤ Copy.

3. Click the Scratchpad worksheet tab, click cell A6, and in Excel 2007, click Home ➤ (Clipboard) Paste. In Excel 2003, click Edit ➤ Paste. The selected cells are pasted to cells A6 through H9.

4. On the SalesData worksheet, press the Esc key to deselect the previously selected cells, click the column header for column C, press and hold the Ctrl key, and click the column headers for columns D, E, G, and H.

5. In Excel 2007, click Home ➤ (Clipboard) Copy. In Excel 2003, click Edit ➤ Copy.

6. Click the Scratchpad worksheet tab, click cell J1, and then in Excel 2007, click Home ➤ (Clipboard) Paste. In Excel 2003, click Edit ➤ Paste.

The selected cells are pasted to cells J1 through N11.
Now, practice copying and moving worksheets:

1. Right-click the SalesData worksheet tab, and click Move or Copy.

2. In the Before Sheet list, select Move to End, and click OK. The SalesData worksheet is moved to the end of the worksheet tabs.

3. Right-click the SalesData worksheet tab again, and click Move or Copy.

4. In the Before Sheet list, select the Create a Copy check box, and click OK. A copy of the SalesData worksheet named SalesData (2) is created and moved to the beginning of the worksheet tabs.

3.2 Fill Data

You can use Excel's Fill menu command or Auto Fill Options button to copy or fill values across rows or down columns. This technique is helpful for quickly entering identical or closely related values in an Excel database.

Quick Start

To copy or fill data values, do the following:

1. Select the cells containing the values that you want to copy or fill.

2. Select the cells into which you want to copy the values or fill a series of closely related values.

3. Click Home ➤ (Editing) Fill (for Excel 2007) or click Edit ➤ Fill (for Excel 2003), and select one of the Fill submenu commands in order to specify a copy or fill method. Or drag the fill handle (the small box in the lowest right corner of the selected worksheet cells) to the worksheet cells for which you want to copy the selected values, and then release the mouse button; then click the Auto Fill Options button that appears, and specify a copy or fill method, as shown in Figure 3-1.

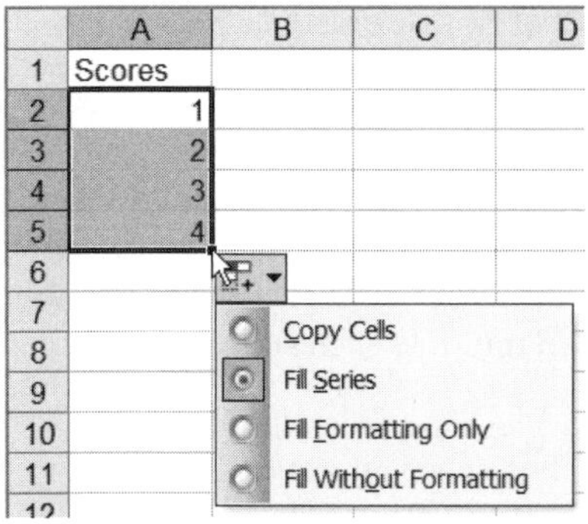

Figure 3-1. *Dragging the fill handle in Excel, clicking the Auto Fill Options button that appears, and specifying a copy or fill method*

How To

Select the worksheet cells that you want to copy or fill in, using one of the ways shown previously in Table 3-1.

Note Excel's fill features do not always work when multiple selected worksheet cells are not next to each other. You'll need to experiment to determine whether Excel will be able to fill based on the proximity of multiple worksheet cells that you select.

To copy or fill values, select the worksheet cells into which you want to copy the values or fill a series of closely related values. Click Home ➤ (Editing) Fill (for Excel 2007) or click Edit ➤ Fill (for Excel 2003), and select one of the Fill submenu commands in order to specify a copy or fill method. Or drag the fill handle (the small box in the lowest right corner of the selected worksheet cells) to the worksheet cells for which you want to copy the selected values, and then release the mouse button; then click the Auto Fill Options button that appears, and specify a copy or fill method.

You can use the Series dialog box (in Excel 2007, click Home ➤ (Editing) Fill ➤ Series; in Excel 2003, click Edit ➤ Fill ➤ Series) for greater control over the copy or fill method:

1. Select a Series In area option to fill the values by rows or by columns: select the Rows option to copy or fill the values across the selected rows, or the Columns option to copy or fill the values down the selected columns.

2. Select a Type area option to fill the data in an additive or multiplicative manner: select the Linear option to add the value in the Step Value box to the first starting data value and then to subsequent values, or select the Growth option to multiply the value in the Step Value box by the first starting data value and then multiply each subsequent value.

3. Select the Date option to fill date-based values, and then select an option in the Date Unit area to specify the date increment to use as the data fill value; you can increment by Day, Weekday, Month, or Year.

4. Select AutoFill to have Excel automatically guess and create a fill pattern.

5. Select the Trend check box if there is more than one starting value and you want Excel to create the fill trend.

6. In the Step Value box, type a value by which you want to increase the values.

7. In the Stop Value box, type a value by which you want to stop increasing the values.

You can fill values across worksheets by doing the following:

1. Select the worksheet that contains the data, and select the worksheets to which you want to copy the values.

2. Select the worksheet cells that contain the data you want to copy.

3. In Excel 2007, click Home ➤ (Editing) Fill ➤ Across Worksheets. In Excel 2003, click Edit ➤ Fill ➤ Across Worksheets.

Try It

In this exercise, you will practice filling data in a variety of ways. If the workbook from section 3.1 is not already open, do the following to open it:

1. Start Excel.

2. Click Office Button ➤ Open (in Excel 2007) or File ➤ Open (in Excel 2003).

3. Browse to and select the ExcelDB_Ch03_01-09.xls file, and click Open.

4. Click the DataFills worksheet tab.

Practice filling worksheet cells by month by clicking cell A2, dragging the fill handle (the small box in the lower right corner of cell A2) to cell A13, and then releasing the mouse button. The months January through December appear.

Practice filling worksheet cells by weekday:

1. Click cell B2, drag the fill handle to cell B11, and then release the mouse button.

2. Click the Auto Fill Options button, and click Fill Weekdays. The days Monday through Friday appear twice.

Practice filling worksheet cells by copying the same value repeatedly:

1. Click cell C2, press and hold the Shift key, and click cell C11.

2. In Excel 2007, click Home ➤ (Editing) Fill ➤ Down. In Excel 2003, click Edit ➤ Fill ➤ Down.

The number 1 appears ten times.
Practice filling worksheet cells by an additive series of one per subsequent cell:

1. Click cell D2, drag the fill handle to cell D12, and then release the mouse button.

2. Click the Auto Fill Options button, and click Fill Series. The numbers 10 through 20 appear.

Practice filling worksheet cells by an additive series of 100 per subsequent cell:

1. Click cell E2, press and hold the Shift key, and click cell E11.

2. In Excel 2007, click Home ➤ (Editing) Fill ➤ Series. In Excel 2003, click Edit ➤ Fill ➤ Series.

3. In the Step Value box, type **100**, and click OK. The numbers 100 through 1,000 appear.

Practice filling worksheet cells by an additive series of 500 per subsequent cell, not to exceed 4,000:

1. Click cell F2, press and hold the Shift key, and click cell F11.

2. In Excel 2007, click Home ➤ (Editing) Fill ➤ Series. In Excel 2003, click Edit ➤ Fill ➤ Series.

3. In the Step Value box, type **500**, and in the Stop Value box, type **4000**.

4. Click OK. The numbers 1,000 through 4,000 appear in cells F2 through F8 only. This is because once the number 4,000 is reached, Excel stops filling values in the remaining worksheet cells.

3.3 Enter Data with a Data Form

A *data form* is a simple, convenient way to enter one complete record on a worksheet without scrolling back and forth among records and fields. Many databases use data forms to facilitate entering records, and Excel is no exception.

Use a data form when a simple form with a list of field names and boxes in which to enter values is fine for your needs, or you have no more than 32 data fields in each record and you want all of the fields to fit on the screen at one time.

Quick Start

To create and use a data form, do the following:

1. Make sure data field names appear at the top of each worksheet column.

2. Select the data field names.

3. In Excel 2007, add the Form command to the Quick Access Toolbar, and then click the Form command. In Excel 2003, click Data ➤ Form.

■**Note** For instructions on how to add the Form command to the Quick Access Toolbar, see the instructions in the sidebar in this section.

---

4. Follow the onscreen instructions to create the data form.

5. Use the data form controls to add, delete, restore, or find data records.

How To

To create the form, do the following:

1. Before you can use it, the list of data records must have data field names at the top of each column.

2. Select the field names and any existing records under the data field names.

3. In Excel 2007, add the Form command to the Quick Access Toolbar, and then click the Form command. In Excel 2003, click Data ➤ Form. The form is shown in Figure 3-2.

Figure 3-2. *The Excel data form*

4. Follow the onscreen instructions to create the data form.

ADD THE FORM COMMAND TO THE QUICK ACCESS TOOLBAR

1. On the Quick Access Toolbar (by default, this toolbar is next to the Office Button), click Customize Quick Access Toolbar ➤ More Commands, as shown in the figure.

2. In the Choose Commands From list, select All Commands.

3. In the list below the Choose Commands From list, select Form.

4. Click Add.

5. Click OK. The Form command appears on the Quick Access Toolbar.

To add a data record using the data form, do the following:

1. Click the New button.

2. Type the data into the data field boxes.

3. Click the New button again.

To delete a data record using the data form, do the following:

1. Use the Find Prev, Find Next, or Criteria buttons to locate the data record that you want to delete.

2. Click the Delete button, and click OK.

To find specific data records using the data form, do the following:

1. Click the Criteria button.

2. Type text in any of the data field boxes for which you want to find matching data records.

3. Click the Find Next or Find Prev buttons to move back and forth through any matching data records.

4. To return to all of the data records, click the Criteria button, click the Clear button, and click the Form button.

Tip To restore a data record that is currently being changed back to its original data values using the data form, click the Restore button.

Try It

In this exercise, you will practice displaying a data form and entering and searching for data using the data form. If the practice workbook is not open from the previous exercise, do the following to open it:

1. Start Excel.

2. Click Office Button ➤ Open (in Excel 2007) or File ➤ Open (in Excel 2003).

3. Browse to and select the ExcelDB_Ch03_01-09.xls file, and click Open.

Display the data form:

1. Click the Contacts worksheet tab.

2. Select cells A1 through G1, and in Excel 2007, add the Form command to the Quick Access Toolbar, click the Form command, and click OK. In Excel 2003, click Data ➤ Form, and click OK.

Note For instructions on how to add the Form command to the Quick Access Toolbar, see the sidebar previously in this section.

Add data records to the worksheet using the data form, and move among the data records:

1. Type data in the First Name, Last Name, Street Address, City, State, Postal Code, and Home Phone boxes, pressing the Tab key after you type data in each box.

2. When you are finished typing data in each of the boxes, press the Enter key or click the New button.

3. Repeat steps 1 and 2 at least three times.

4. Click the Find Prev and Find Next buttons to move among the data records.

Find matching records using the data form:

1. Click the Criteria button.

2. In the City box, type a field value that matches one or more of the existing records.

3. Click Find Next to move to the first matching data record.

4. To clear the criteria, click the Criteria button, click Clear, and then click Form.

5. When you are done using the data form, click Close.

3.4 Define, Create, or Apply a Name

It can be difficult to remember worksheet cells by their row-and-column addresses. Names provide a more convenient and easier to remember way to refer to cells, especially in worksheet formulas. You can also use names as a shortcut for referring to a worksheet formula itself or a series of text characters.

The concept of names is uncommon in many database management systems. You will most likely use names very often for their convenience.

Quick Start

To define a name, do the following:

1. Select a single cell or a group of cells that you want to name. You can use the Shift key and the arrow keys or a mouse to quickly select cells that are next to each other. You can use the Ctrl key and a mouse to select cells that are not next to each other.

2. Do one of the following:

- In Excel 2007 or Excel 2003, click the Name Box as shown in Figure 3-3, type a name for the group of cells, and press Enter.

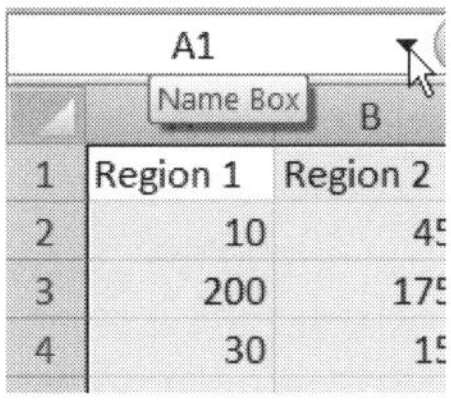

Figure 3-3. *The Excel Name Box*

- Or in Excel 2007, click Formulas ➤ (Defined Names) Define Name. Type a name in the Name Box, and click OK.

- Or in Excel 2003, click Insert ➤ Name ➤ Define, type a name in the Names in Workbook box, and click OK.

How To

To define a name for a group of one or more worksheet cells, a formula, or a series of text characters, do the following:

1. In Excel 2007, click Formulas ➤ (Defined Names) Define Name. In Excel 2003, click Insert ➤ Name ➤ Define.

2. In the Name Box, type a name that conveniently describes the cells, formula, or string of text characters.

3. In Excel 2007, in the Scope list, select a scope to which the name applies; for example, at the workbook level or at an individual worksheet level.

4. There are three different ways of defining a name in the Refers To box:

   - To define a name for a group of one or more worksheet cells, select the target worksheet cells, or type the target worksheet cells' reference.

   - To define a name for a formula, type the formula.

   - To define a name for a string of text characters, type the text string.

5. Click OK. The name is defined.

In Excel 2003 only, to instruct Excel to allow use of names in formulas, based on one or more row or column names for one or more data records in the same worksheet, do the following:

▨Note In Excel 2007, the ability to instruct Excel to allow the use of names in formulas, based on one or more row or column names for one or more data records in the same worksheet, has been removed for technical reasons.

---

1. Click Insert ➤ Name ➤ Label.

2. In the Add Label Range box, type or select one or more worksheet cells on one worksheet that contain the row or column names for one or more data records.

3. Select the Row Labels option if the selected worksheet cells contain a unique data record name for each data record, or select the Column Labels option if the selected worksheet cells contain a unique data field name for each data record.

4. Click OK. The label range is added.

▨Note In Excel 2003 only, to use worksheet label names instead of worksheet cell references in a worksheet's formulas, you must first click Tools ➤ Options, select the Accept Labels in Formulas check box on the Calculation tab, and click OK.

To define names based on one or more row or column names for one or more data records in one or more worksheets, do the following:

1. Select the group of worksheet cells that contain the records' field names, the record names if any, and the records' values if any.

2. In Excel 2007, click Formulas ➤ (Defined Names) Create from Selection. In Excel 2003, click Insert ➤ Name ➤ Create.

3. Select one or more of these check boxes:

   • Top Row, if you want to create a name for each data record field name as it appears in the top row of the selected worksheet cells.

   • Left Column, if you want to create a name for each data record name as the record appears in the left column of the selected worksheet cells.

   • Bottom Row, if you want to create a name for each data record field name as it appears in the bottom row of the selected worksheet cells.

   • Right Column, if you want to create a name for each data record name as it appears in the right column of the selected worksheet cells.

4. Click OK. A name is defined for each data record field name and data record name based on the check boxes selected.

To determine what one or more names refer to, do the following:

1. In Excel 2007, click Formulas ➤ (Defined Names) Name Manager. In Excel 2003, click Insert ➤ Name ➤ Define.

2. Click the target name in the list of names, and look at the contents of the Refers To box.

3. Select a blank area in the workbook that spans at least two blank columns. Click a worksheet cell in these two blank columns that represents the upper left corner of where the list will start.

4. In Excel 2007, click Formulas ➤ (Defined Names) Use in Formula ➤ Paste Names. In Excel 2003, click Insert ➤ Name ➤ Paste.

5. Click Paste List to list all of the names in the workbook and their definitions in the two selected blank columns.

To replace worksheet cell references in an individual worksheet's formulas with their defined names, if any, do the following:

1. Select the worksheet cells that contain formulas in which you want to replace worksheet cell references with names, or select a single worksheet cell to replace the references with names in all formulas on the worksheet.

2. In Excel 2007, click Formulas ➤ (Defined Names) Define Name ➤ Apply Names. In Excel 2003, click Insert ➤ Name ➤ Apply.

3. In the Apply Names box, click one or more names to replace any formulas that refer to the names' underlying cell references, and click OK.

Tip

To define a name for a collection of two or more worksheet cells spanning two or more contiguous worksheets, use the following syntax, referred to as a *3-D reference*:

```
='BeginningSheetName:EndingSheetName'!CellReference
```

For example, to define a name that refers to cells C2 through E5 on three contiguous worksheets named Sheet1, Sheet2, and Sheet3, use the following 3-D reference:

```
='Sheet1:Sheet3'!C2:E5
```

Note that the worksheet cells must be in the same location on all of the referenced worksheets, and the worksheet tabs must all be touching each other. For example, you cannot use a 3-D reference to define a name that refers collectively to cells C2 through E5 on Sheet1, cells A1 through B4 on Sheet2, and cells F6 through G11 on Sheet 3.

Try It

In this exercise, you will practice defining names and labels for a group of worksheet cells and two series of text characters. You will also practice adding two label ranges. You will then refer to these names and label ranges in a series of worksheet formulas. You will also list the names and their definitions in the workbook. If the practice workbook is not open from the previous exercise, open it:

1. Start Excel.

2. Click Office Button ➤ Open (in Excel 2007) or File ➤ Open (in Excel 2003).

3. Browse to and select the ExcelDB_Ch03_01-09.xls file, and click Open.

Define three named ranges:

1. Click the DefinedRanges worksheet tab, select cells A1 through D13, and in Excel 2007, click Formulas ➤ (Defined Names) Define Name. In Excel 2003, click Insert ➤ Name ➤ Define.

2. In the Name box, type **SalesData**, and click OK. The SalesData named range is defined.

3. Select cells B2 through B13, and in Excel 2007, click Formulas ➤ (Defined Names) Define Name. In Excel 2003, click Insert ➤ Name ➤ Define.

4. In the Name box, type **Ordered**, and click OK. The Ordered named range is defined.

5. Select cells D2 through D13, and in Excel 2007, click Formulas ➤ (Defined Names) Define Name. In Excel 2003, click Insert ➤ Name ➤ Define.

6. In the Name box, type **OnHand**. The OnHand named range is defined.

In Excel 2007 only, create two additional sets of named ranges:

1. Select cells A2 through D13, and then click Formulas ➤ (Defined Names) Create from Selection.

2. With only the Left Column check box selected, click OK. Names for rows 2 through 13 are created.

3. Select cells B1 through D13, and then click ➤ (Defined Names) Create from Selection.

4. With only the Top Row check box selected, click OK. Names for columns B through D are created.

In Excel 2003 only, create two label ranges as follows:

1. Select cells A2 through A13, and click Insert ➤ Name ➤ Label.

2. With the Row Labels option selected, click Add. Names for rows 2 through 13 are created.

3. Select cells B1 through D1, select the Column Labels option, and click Add. Names for columns B through D are created.

4. Click OK.

For Excel 2007 or Excel 2003, you can create formulas based on these names and labels as follows:

1. In cell E2 type =**January Quantity-January In_Stock** (for Excel 2007) or =**January Quantity-January In Stock** (for Excel 2003), and press the Enter key. The difference between cell B2 (the value 150, which is the intersection of the January row and the Quantity column) and cell D2 (the value 145, which is the intersection of the January row and the In Stock column) appears, which is the number 5.

■**Note** In Excel 2003 only, to use worksheet label names instead of worksheet cell references in a worksheet's formulas, you must first click Tools ➤ Options, select the Accept Labels in Formulas check box on the Calculation tab, and click OK.

---

2. For Excel 2003, in cell E2, drag the fill handle (the small black box in the lower right corner of the cell) to cell E13, and release the mouse button.

3. For Excel 2003, click the individual cells E3, E4, and so on, down to cell E13 to see the fill that Excel completed based on the formula defined in cell E2.

■**Note** In Excel 2007, you cannot drag the fill handle to AutoFill subsequent month names in this context. To work around this, you can type =**February Quantity-February In_Stock** in cell E3, =**March Quantity-March In_Stock** in cell E4, and so on down through cell E13.

Next, for Excel 2007 or Excel 2003, enter functions with cell references that will be replaced with defined names:

1. In cell B14, type =**SUM(B2:B13)**, and press the Enter key.

2. In cell D14, type =**SUM(D2:D13)**, and press the Enter key.

3. In Excel 2007, click Formulas ➤ (Defined Names) Define Name ➤ Apply Names. In Excel 2003, click Insert ➤ Name ➤ Apply.

4. In the Apply Names box, deselect all selected items, select Ordered and OnHand, and click OK.

5. Click the individual worksheet cells B14 and D14 to see that the cell references are replaced by names.

6. In cell E16, in Excel 2007, type **=SUM(SalesData Quantity)-SUM(SalesData In_Stock)**, and press the Enter key. In Excel 2003, type **=SUM(SalesData Quantity)-SUM(Sales-Data In Stock)**, and press the Enter key. The difference between the sum of the Quantity column in the SalesData named range and the sum of the In Stock column in the SalesData named range is displayed, which is the value 130.

7. In cell E17, type **=SUM(Ordered)-SUM(OnHand)**, and press the Enter key. Notice that the value of cell E17 is the same value as cell E16.

List the names in the workbook and their definitions:

1. Click cell G1, and in Excel 2007, click Formulas ➤ (Defined Names) Use in Formula ➤ Paste Names. In Excel 2003, click Insert ➤ Name ➤ Paste.

2. Click Paste List. In Excel 2007, the list of names and their corresponding definitions appear in cells G1 through H18. In Excel 2003, the list of names and their corresponding definitions appear in cells G1 through H3.

3.5 Format Data

Many database management systems provide robust access to data but not many robust features for displaying data in different visual formats. Excel provides a wide variety of options for presenting data visually in various formats.

Use Excel's data formatting options when you want to highlight specific values, change how values are displayed, or otherwise change the visual display of data in worksheets for easier data recognition visually, faster data analysis, and greater data precision.

Quick Start

To format a worksheet's values or the formatting of the worksheet's rows and columns, do the following:

1. Select the worksheet cells, rows, or columns containing the data values for which you want to change formatting.

2. Do one of these:

   - In Excel 2007, click Home, and click one of the menu commands in the Font, Alignment, Number, Styles, or Cells areas to format individual worksheet cells, rows, or columns, and follow the onscreen directions accordingly.

   - In Excel 2003, on the Format menu, click or point to one of the menu commands or submenus to format individual worksheet cells, rows, or columns, and follow the onscreen directions accordingly.

How To

There are different ways of formatting data.

To change the number formatting in specific worksheet cells, do the following:

1. Select the worksheet cells to change. (See Table 3-1 earlier in this chapter for directions on selecting cells.)

2. In Excel 2007, click Home ➤ (Number) Format Cells: Number. In Excel 2003, click Format ➤ Cells.

3. On the Number tab, in the Category list, select a number category.

4. Depending on the number category selected, set the controls to specify the number of decimal places, the thousands separator symbol, the currency symbol, how to represent negative numbers, and so on.

5. Click OK. The number formatting is changed for the selected worksheet cells.

To change the text alignment in specific worksheet cells (horizontally, vertically, etc.), do the following:

1. Select the worksheet cells to change.

2. In Excel 2007, click Home ➤ (Cells) Format ➤ Format Cells. In Excel 2003, click Format ➤ Cells.

3. On the Alignment tab, as shown in Figure 3-4, in the Text Alignment area, if you choose the Horizontal list, do the following:

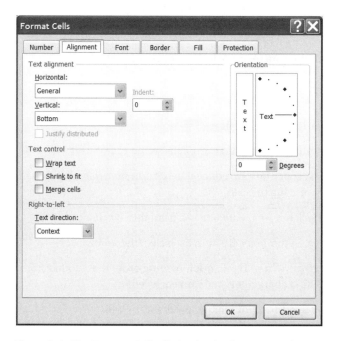

Figure 3-4. *The Format Cells dialog box's Alignment tab*

- Select General to let Excel decide how to position the data in the cells.

- Select Left (Indent) to indent data from the left sides of the cells. Also, use the Indent box's up and down buttons to specify how far you want to indent the data. (Type zero (0) in the Indent box to position the data near the left sides of the cells.)

- Select Center to position data in the center of the cells.

- Select Right (Indent) to indent data from the right sides of the cells. Also, use the Indent box's up and down buttons to specify how far you want to indent the data. (Type zero (0) in the Indent box to position the data near the right sides of the cells.)

- Select Fill to duplicate data values within cells to fill the entire cells' widths.

- Select Justify to position data equally from both sides of the cells.

- Select Center Across Selection to position data in the centers of the cells based on the selected cells' widths.

- Select Distributed (Indent) to indent data from both sides of the cells. Also, use the Indent box's up and down buttons to specify how far you want to indent the data on both sides.

- Select Distributed (Indent), as well as select the Justify Distributed check box, to indent data equally from both sides of the cells.

4. On the Alignment tab, in the Text Alignment area's Vertical list, select from the following options:

- Top, to position the data near the top edges of the cells.

- Center, to position the data in the center of the cells.

- Bottom, to position the data near the bottom edges of the cells.

- Justify or Distributed, to position the data equally from the top and bottom edges of the cells.

5. In the Text Control area, select one or more of the following:

- The Wrap Text check box, to wrap text vertically in the cells.

- The Shrink to Fit Text check box, to reduce the font size such that all data is displayed in each cell without resizing the cells.

- The Merge Cells check box, to create one cell from the selected cells.

6. In the Right-to-Left area, in the Text Direction list, select the following:

- Context, to set a left-to-right or right-to-left reading order that is consistent with the language of the first character typed into each cell.

- Left-to-Right, to set a left-to-right reading order for the cells.

- Right-to-Left, to set a right-to-left reading order for the cells.

7. In the Orientation area, in the Degrees box, click the up and down buttons to click a degree point, or drag the indicator to the angle you want. To display text vertically from top to bottom, click the vertical Text box.

8. Click OK. Excel applies the selected alignment options to the selected worksheet cells.

To change the font style, size, or color in specific worksheet cells, do the following:

1. Select the worksheet cells to change.

2. In Excel 2007, click Home ➤ (Font) Format Cells: Font. In Excel 2003, click Format ➤ Cells.

3. Go to the Font tab, and do the following:

   a. In the Font list, select the font name.

   b. In the Font Style list, select a special font style if desired, such as italic, bold, or italic and bold.

   c. In the Size list, select the font size in points.

   d. In the Underline list, select the underline style if desired, such as single underline or double underline.

   e. In the Color list, select the text color.

   f. Select the Normal Font check box to automatically select a standard font (such as Arial) in the Font list.

   g. In the Effects area, select one or more text effect check boxes if desired, such as Strikethrough, Superscript, or Subscript.

4. Click OK. Excel applies the selected font style, size, and color options to the selected worksheet cells.

To change specific worksheet cells' border styles or colors, do the following:

1. Select the worksheet cells to change.

2. In Excel 2007, click Home ➤ (Cells) Format ➤ Format Cells. In Excel 2003, click Format ➤ Cells.

3. Go to the Border tab, and do the following:

   a. In the Presets area, click the None, Outline, or Inside button to preselect a series of buttons in the Border area as desired to remove border lines, add border lines around the outer edge of the selected worksheet cells, or add border lines to the inner portions of the selected worksheet cells, respectively.

   b. In the Border area, click one or more of the eight buttons as desired to further customize the border lines to be added or removed from the selected worksheet cells.

   c. Go to the Line area, and in the Style box, click the desired border line style. In the Color list, select the desired border line color.

4. Click OK. Excel applies the selected border styles and color options to the selected worksheet cells.

To change specific worksheet cells' background colors or patterns, do the following:

1. Select the cells to change.

2. In Excel 2007, click Home ➤ (Cells) Format ➤ Format Cells, and then click the Fill tab. In Excel 2003, click Format ➤ Cells, and click the Patterns tab.

3. In the Background Color (in Excel 2007) or Color (in Excel 2003) area, click a color. In the Pattern Color and Pattern Style lists (in Excel 2007) or the Pattern list (in Excel 2003), click a pattern (and pattern style in Excel 2007).

4. Click OK. Excel applies the selected background colors and patterns to the selected worksheet cells.

To change specific worksheet rows' heights or visibility, select the rows to change. In Excel 2007, do the following:

1. To change the selected rows' heights, click Home ➤ (Cells) Format ➤ Row Height, type the rows' new height in the Row Height box, and click OK.

2. To change the selected rows' heights so that they fit the text in the rows' cells, click Home ➤ (Cells) Format ➤ AutoFit Row Height.

3. To hide the selected rows, click Home ➤ (Cells) Format ➤ Hide & Unhide ➤ Hide Rows.

4. To unhide specific hidden rows, select the rows on either side of the hidden rows, click Home ➤ (Cells) Format ➤ Hide & Unhide ➤ Unhide Rows.

In Excel 2003, do the following:

1. To change the selected rows' heights, click Format ➤ Row ➤ Height, type the rows' new height in the Row Height box, and click OK.

2. To change the selected rows' heights so that they fit the text in the rows' cells, click Format ➤ Row ➤ AutoFit.

3. To hide the selected rows, click Format ➤ Row ➤ Hide.

4. To unhide specific hidden rows, select the rows on either side of the hidden rows and click Format ➤ Row ➤ Unhide.

To change specific worksheet columns' width or visibility, select the columns to change. In Excel 2007, do the following:

1. To change the selected columns' widths, click Home ➤ (Cells) Format ➤ Column Width, type the columns' new width in the Column Width box, and click OK.

2. To change the selected columns' widths so that they fit the text in the columns' cells, click Home ➤ (Cells) Format ➤ AutoFit Column Width.

3. To hide the selected columns, click Home ➤ (Cells) Format ➤ Hide & Unhide ➤ Hide Columns.

4. To unhide specific hidden columns, select the columns on either side of the hidden rows, click Home ➤ (Cells) Format ➤ Hide & Unhide ➤ Unhide Columns.

In Excel 2003, do the following:

1. To change the selected columns' widths, click Format ➤ Column ➤ Width, type the columns' new width in the Column Width box, and click OK.

2. To change the selected columns' widths so that they fit the text in the columns' cells, click Format ➤ Column ➤ AutoFit Selection.

3. To hide the selected columns, click Format ➤ Column ➤ Hide.

4. To unhide specific hidden columns, select the columns on either side of the hidden columns and click Format ➤ Column ➤ Unhide.

To change a worksheet's name, visibility, background color, or tab color, select the worksheet to change.

In Excel 2007, do the following:

1. To change the worksheet's name, click Home ➤ (Cells) Format ➤ Rename Sheet, type the new worksheet name, and press the Enter key.

2. To hide the worksheet, click Home ➤ (Cells) Format ➤ Hide & Unhide ➤ Hide Sheet.

3. To unhide a specific hidden worksheet, click Home ➤ (Cells) Format ➤ Hide & Unhide ➤ Unhide Sheet, click the worksheet to unhide, and click OK.

4. To change the worksheet's background picture, click Page Layout ➤ (Page Setup) Background. Browse to and select an image file, and click Insert.

5. To change the worksheet's tab color, click Home ➤ (Cells) Format ➤ Tab Color, click a color, and click OK.

In Excel 2003, do the following:

1. To change the worksheet's name, click Format ➤ Sheet ➤ Rename, type the new worksheet name, and press the Enter key.

2. To hide the worksheet, click Format ➤ Sheet ➤ Hide.

3. To unhide a specific hidden worksheet, click Format ➤ Sheet ➤ Unhide, click the worksheet to unhide, and click OK.

4. To change the worksheet's background picture, click Format ➤ Sheet ➤ Background, browse to and select an image file, and click Insert.

5. To change the worksheet's tab color, click Format ➤ Sheet ➤ Tab Color, click a color, and click OK.

To apply predetermined formatting to one or more worksheet cells, do the following:

1. Select the worksheet cells for which you want to change formatting.

2. In Excel 2007, add the AutoFormat command to the Quick Access Toolbar, and then click the AutoFormat command. In Excel 2003, click Format ➤ AutoFormat.

ADD THE AUTOFORMAT COMMAND TO THE QUICK ACCESS TOOLBAR

1. On the Quick Access Toolbar (by default, this toolbar is next to the Office Button), click Customize Quick Access Toolbar ➤ More Commands.

2. In the Choose Commands From list, select All Commands.

3. In the list below the Choose Commands From list, select AutoFormat.

4. Click Add.

5. Click OK. The AutoFormat command appears on the Quick Access Toolbar.

3. Click a desired format style.

4. If there are any specific formats that you don't want to apply, click the Options button, and in the Formats to Apply area, clear any check boxes corresponding to any desired formats that you don't want to apply. By default, all of the check boxes are selected.

To copy formatting among worksheet cells, do the following:

1. Select the worksheet cells for which you want to copy formatting.

2. In Excel 2007, click Home ➤ (Clipboard) Format Painter. In Excel 2003, on the Standard toolbar, click the Format Painter button.

3. Select the worksheet cells for which you want to paste formatting. The formatting is copied.

Tip

To unhide all columns on a worksheet at the same time, click the Select All button, and then, in Excel 2007, click Home ➤ (Cells) Format ➤ Hide & Unhide ➤ Unhide Columns; in Excel 2003, click Format ➤ Column ➤ Unhide.

To unhide all rows on a worksheet at the same time, click the Select All button, and then, in Excel 2007, click Home ➤ (Cells) Format ➤ Hide & Unhide ➤ Unhide Rows; in Excel 2003, click Format ➤ Row ➤ Unhide.

To remove a worksheet's background picture, in Excel 2007, click Page Layout ➤ (Page Setup) Background; in Excel 2003, click Format ➤ Sheet ➤ Delete Background.

Try It

In this exercise, you will practice formatting data by changing number formatting, text alignment, text font, and display behavior for cells, rows, columns, and worksheets.

If the practice workbook is not open from the previous exercise, do the following to open it:

1. Start Excel.

2. Click Office Button ➤ Open (in Excel 2007) or File ➤ Open (in Excel 2003).

3. Browse to and select the ExcelDB_Ch03_01-09.xls file, and click Open.

First, practice formatting data:

1. Click the Formatting worksheet tab, and select cells A2 through A6.

2. In Excel 2007, click Home ➤ (Cells) Format ➤ Format Cells. In Excel 2003, click Format ➤ Cells.

3. Click the Number tab.

4. In the Category list, select Currency.

5. With the number 2 showing in the Decimal Places box, select an appropriate currency symbol in the Symbol list, select an appropriate display format in the Negative Numbers list, and click OK. The data format in cells A2 through A6 is changed.

Practice aligning text:

1. On the Formatting worksheet, select cells B2 through B13.

2. In Excel 2007, click Home ➤ (Cells) Format ➤ Format Cells. In Excel 2003, click Format ➤ Cells.

3. Click the Alignment tab.

4. In the Horizontal list, select Right (Indent).

5. In the Indent box, type **1**, and click OK. The text in cells B2 through B15 is aligned to the right side of each cell with a padding of one character.

6. In Excel 2007, click Home ➤ (Cells) Format ➤ Format Cells. In Excel 2003, click Format ➤ Cells.

7. Click the Alignment tab.

8. Select the Wrap Text check box, and click OK. The height of cells B11 through B13 increases to accommodate the text.

9. In Excel 2007, click Home ➤ (Cells) Format ➤ Format Cells. In Excel 2003, click Format ➤ Cells.

10. Click the Alignment tab.

11. Clear the Wrap Text check box, select the Shrink to Fit check box, and click OK. The font size of the text in cells B11 through B13 and the height of cells B11 through B13 decrease accordingly.

Practice changing font style, size, or color text font:

1. On the Formatting worksheet, select cells C2 through C10.

2. In Excel 2007, click Home ➤ (Cells) Format ➤ Format Cells. In Excel 2003, click Format ➤ Cells.

3. Click the Font tab.

4. In the Font list, select Courier New.

5. In the Color list, select the green color box.

6. Select the Strikethrough box, and click OK. The font in cells C2 through C10 changes accordingly.

Practice changing display behavior for cells:

1. On the Formatting worksheet, select cells D2 through D7.

2. In Excel 2007, click Home ➤ (Cells) Format ➤ Format Cells. In Excel 2003, click Format ➤ Cells.

3. Click the Border tab.

4. In the Presets area, click the None button.

5. Click the Fill tab (in Excel 2007) or Patterns tab (in Excel 2003).

6. In the Background Color list (in Excel 2007) or the Color list (in Excel 2003), click the yellow color box.

7. In the Pattern Style list (in Excel 2007) or the Pattern list (in Excel 2003), click any pattern, and click OK. The display behavior for cells D2 through D7 changes accordingly.

Practice changing display behavior for rows and columns:

1. On the Formatting worksheet, select rows 3 through 6.

2. In Excel 2007, click Home ➤ (Cells) Format ➤ Hide & Unhide ➤ Hide Rows. Rows 3 through 6 are hidden. In Excel 2003, click Format ➤ Row ➤ Hide. Rows 3 through 6 are hidden.

3. Select columns C and E.

4. In Excel 2007, click Home ➤ (Cells) Format ➤ Hide & Unhide ➤ Hide Columns. In Excel 2003, click Format ➤ Column ➤ Hide. Columns C and E are hidden.

5. Click the Select All button.

6. In Excel 2007, click Sheet ➤ (Cells) Format ➤ Hide & Unhide ➤ Unhide Rows. In Excel 2003, click Format ➤ Row ➤ Unhide. Rows 3 through 6 are visible.

7. In Excel 2007, click Sheet ➤ (Cells) Format ➤ Hide & Unhide ➤ Unhide Columns. In Excel 2003, click Format ➤ Column ➤ Unhide. Columns C and E are visible.

Practice changing display behavior for worksheets:

1. In Excel 2007, with the Formatting worksheet tab selected, click Home ➤ (Cells) Format ➤ Hide & Unhide ➤ Hide Sheet. In Excel 2003, click the Formatting worksheet tab, and click Format ➤ Sheet ➤ Hide. The Formatting worksheet is hidden.

2. In Excel 2007, right-click any worksheet tab, click Home ➤ (Cells) Format ➤ Hide & Unhide ➤ Unhide Sheet, click Formatting, and click OK. In Excel 2003, click Format ➤ Sheet ➤ Unhide, click Formatting, and click OK. The Formatting worksheet is visible.

3. In Excel 2007, with the Formatting worksheet tab selected, click Home ➤ (Cells) Format ➤ Tab Color, click the red color box, and click OK. In Excel 2003, click Format ➤ Sheet ➤ Tab Color, click the red color box, and click OK. The Formatting worksheet tab turns red.

3.6 Conditionally Format Data

A *conditional format* is a visual display format, such as cell shading or font color, that Excel automatically applies to cells if a specified condition is true. Many database management systems do not provide robust features for displaying data in different visual formats. Excel provides not only a wide variety of options for presenting data visually in various formats, but also the ability to change data formatting based on each worksheet cell's data value.

Quick Start

Select the worksheet cells to which you want to add conditional formatting.

In Excel 2007, click Home ➤ (Styles) Conditional Formatting, and then do one of the following:

- Click one of the options on the Highlight Cells Rules, Top/Bottom Rules, Data Bars, Color Scales, or Icon Sets menus respectively to highlight cell values. Specifically, you can highlight cell values that are greater than, less than, between, or equal to specific data values. You can also highlight cell values that are in the top, bottom, above average, or below average of a specified data value or percentage of all of the cell values. You can add to the cells some visual data bars whose lengths correspond to lower or higher data values. You can add to the cells some colors whose hues correspond to lower or higher data values. Or you can add to the cells some icons whose pictures correspond to lower or higher data values.

- Click Manage Rules to customize the behavior of any existing conditional formatting rule in the workbook; and click OK when you are done customizing conditional formatting rules.

In Excel 2003, click Format ➤ Conditional Formatting. The Conditional Formatting dialog box appears, as shown in Figure 3-5.

Figure 3-5. *The Excel 2003 Conditional Formatting dialog box*

1. Set the options in the Conditional Formatting dialog box to add the first conditional format rule.

2. Click Add if you want to create additional conditional format rules.

3. When you have finished creating your conditional format rules for the selected worksheet cells, click OK.

How To

To add conditional formatting to one or more worksheet cells, select the cells for which you want to add conditional formatting.

In Excel 2007, click Home ➤ (Styles) Conditional Formatting. Table 3-2 shows the conditional formatting options.

Table 3-2. *Excel 2007 Conditional Formatting Options*

Click	Conditional Formatting Rule
One of the options on the Highlight Cells Rules menu	Highlight cell values that are greater than, less than, between, or equal to specific data values; contain specific text; occur on a specific date; or contain unique or duplicate values. Complete the options in the dialog box that appears, and click OK.
One of the options on the Top/Bottom Rules menu	Highlight cell values that are in the top, bottom, above average, or below average of a specified data value or percentage of all of the cell values. Complete the options in the dialog box that appears, and click OK.
One of the options on the Data Bars menu	Add to the cells some visual data bars whose lengths correspond to lower or higher data values, and then click a data bar color.
One of the options on the Color Scales menu	Add to the cells some colors whose hues correspond to lower or higher data values, and then click a color scale.
One of the options on the Icon Sets menu	Add to the cells some icons whose pictures correspond to lower or higher data values, and then click an icon set.
Manage Rules	Customize the behavior of any existing conditional formatting rule in the workbook, and click OK when you are done customizing conditional formatting rules.

In Excel 2003, do the following:

1. Click Format ➤ Conditional Formatting.

2. In the far left list, you can select Cell Value Is to add a conditional format based on specific values that you type or specific values in one or more worksheet cells. In the list to the right of this list, select Between or Not Between to add a conditional format based on the values that you type (or worksheet cells that you select) for the two boxes to the right of the Between box. Alternatively, you can select Equal To, Not Equal To, Greater Than, Less Than, Greater Than or Equal To, or Less Than or Equal To to add a conditional format based on the value that you type (or worksheet cell that you select) for the box to the right of the Equal To, Not Equal To, Greater Than, Less Than, Greater Than or Equal To, or Less Than or Equal To box.

3. In the far left list, you can select Formula Is to add a conditional format based on the outcome of a formula that you type or select. If you select Formula Is, in the box to the right of this list, type the formula, or click the worksheet cell containing the formula.

4. Click the Format button.

5. Select the desired options on the Font, Border, and Patterns tabs to change the cells' formatting if the condition that you specified earlier evaluates to true, and then click OK. For information on how to select the desired options on these tabs, see section "3.5: Format Data," previously in this chapter.

6. To add up to two more conditional formats, click the Add button, and repeat steps 2 through 5.

7. Click OK.

To change a conditional format in Excel 2007, do the following:

1. Click Home ➤ (Styles) Conditional Formatting ➤ Manage Rules.

2. In the Show Formatting Rules For list, select Current Selection, This Worksheet, or a specific worksheet to which the desired conditional format applies.

3. Click the conditional format in the list of rules.

4. Click Edit Rule.

5. Change the conditional formatting rule, and click OK to apply the changes.

In Excel 2003, do the following:

1. Click Format ➤ Conditional Formatting.

2. Click the Format button for the condition that you want to change.

3. Select the desired options on the Font, Border, and Patterns tabs to change the cells' formatting, and then click OK.

4. Click OK again.

To remove conditional formatting in Excel 2007, do the following:

1. Click Home ➤ (Styles) Conditional Formatting ➤ Manage Rules.

2. In the Show Formatting Rules For list, select Current Selection, This Worksheet, or a specific worksheet to which the desired conditional format applies.

3. Click the conditional format in the list of rules.

4. Click Delete Rule.

5. Click OK.

In Excel 2003, do the following:

1. Click Format ➤ Conditional Formatting.

2. Click Delete.

3. Select one or more check boxes next to the conditions that you want to delete.

4. Click OK, and click OK again.

If more than one conditional format evaluates to true, Excel applies only the format of the first true condition, even if more than one condition evaluates to true.

To find all cells in a workbook that contain conditional formatting, in Excel 2007, click Home ➤ (Editing) Find & Select ➤ Conditional Formatting. In Excel 2003, click Edit ➤ Go To, click the Special button, click the Conditional Formats option, and click OK.

To copy conditional formats to other cells, select the cells that contain the conditional formats that you want to copy.

In Excel 2007, click Home ➤ (Clipboard) Format Painter. Then select the cells to which you want to apply the conditional format.

In Excel 2003, on the Standard toolbar, click Format Painter, and then select the cells to which you want to apply the conditional format.

To remove all formatting, including conditional formats, from one or more selected worksheet cells, select the cells, and in Excel 2007, click Home ➤ (Editing) Clear ➤ Clear Formats. In Excel 2003, click Edit ➤ Clear ➤ Formats.

Try It

In this exercise, you will practice conditionally formatting data that is above, equal to, or below a specified value.

If the practice workbook is not open from the previous exercise, open it first, and then click the ConditionalFormatting worksheet tab.

In Excel 2007, do the following:

1. Select cells B2 through B20, and then click Home ➤ (Styles) Conditional Formatting ➤ Highlight Cells Rules ➤ Less Than.

2. In the left box, type **=AVERAGE($B$2:$B$20)**.

3. In the right box, select Custom Format.

4. On the Fill tab, click the green box, click OK, and click OK again.

5. Click Home ➤ (Styles) Conditional Formatting ➤ Highlight Cells Rules ➤ Greater Than.

6. In the left box, type **=AVERAGE($B$2:$B$20)**.

7. In the right box, select Custom Format.

8. On the Fill tab, click the red box, click OK, and click OK again. The background color of cells B2 through B9 turns green because their data values are less than the average temperature value for all of the temperatures in cells B2 through B20, while the background color of cells B10 through B20 turns red because their data values are greater than the average temperature for all of the temperature value in cells B2 through B20.

In Excel 2003, do the following:

1. Select cells B2 through B20, and then click Format ➤ Conditional Formatting.

2. In the list to the right of the Cell Value Is box, select Less Than.

3. In the box to the right of the Less Than list, type **=AVERAGE($B$2:$B$20)**.

4. Click the Format button.

5. Click the Pattern tab, click the green box, and click OK.

6. Click the Add button.

7. In the list to the right of the Cell Value Is box, select Greater Than.

8. In the box to the right of the Greater Than list, type **=AVERAGE($B$2:$B$20)**.

9. Click the Format button.

10. Click the Pattern tab, click the red box, click OK, and click OK again. The background color of cells B2 through B9 turns green because their data values are less than the average temperature value for all of the temperatures in cells B2 through B20, while the background color of cells B10 through B20 turns red because their data values are greater than the average temperature for all of the temperature values in cells B2 through B20.

To remove the conditional formatting, select cells B2 through B20.
In Excel 2007, do the following:

1. Click Home ➤ (Styles) Conditional Formatting ➤ Manage Rules.

2. In the Show Formatting Rules For list, click This Worksheet.

3. Click the Cell Value > AVERAGE rule, and click Delete Rule.

4. Click the Cell Value < AVERAGE rule, and click Delete Rule.

5. Click OK. The conditional formatting is removed from the selected cells.

In Excel 2003, do the following:

1. Click Format ➤ Conditional Formatting.

2. Click the Delete button.

3. Select the Condition 1 and Condition 2 check boxes.

4. Click OK, and then click OK again. The conditional formatting is removed from the selected cells.

3.7 Protect Data

Excel allows you to protect individual worksheet cells, an entire worksheet, a chart sheet, or an entire workbook with a password. You can also restrict access to specific worksheet cells or an entire worksheet by a user's workgroup login name or network login name. These levels of protection are as good as, or better than, many other database management systems.

Quick Start

To protect individual worksheet cells but not others in a single worksheet, select the cells that you want others to be able to change (locked cells are protected by default when you protect a worksheet) and do the following:

- In Excel 2007, click Home ➤ (Cells) Format, and deselect Lock Cell. Then protect the worksheet.

- In Excel 2003, click Format ➤ Cells, click the Protection tab, clear the Locked check box, and click OK. Then protect the worksheet.

To protect an entire worksheet, do the following:

- In Excel 2007, click Review ➤ (Changes) Protect Sheet. Complete the Protect Sheet dialog box, and then click OK.

- In Excel 2003, click Tools ➤ Protection ➤ Protect Sheet, complete the Protect Sheet dialog box, and then click OK.

To protect an entire workbook, do the following:

- In Excel 2007, click Review ➤ (Changes) Protect Workbook. Select or clear one or more of the commands on the Protect Workbook menu.

- In Excel 2003, click Tools ➤ Protection ➤ Protect Workbook, complete the Protect Workbook dialog box, and then click OK.

To protect and share an entire workbook, do the following:

- In Excel 2007, click Review ➤ (Changes) Protect and Share Workbook, complete the Protect Shared Workbook dialog box, and then click OK.

- In Excel 2003, click Tools ➤ Protection ➤ Protect and Share Workbook, complete the Protect Shared Workbook dialog box, and then click OK.

How To

To protect an individual worksheet, do the following:

1. Click the worksheet tab of the worksheet that you want to protect.

2. If you want users to be able to change the contents of some worksheet cells but not others, select the cells that you want your users to be able to change:

   - In Excel 2007, click Home ➤ (Cells) Format, and deselect Lock Cell.

   - In Excel 2003, click Format ➤ Cells, click the Protection tab, clear the Locked check box, and click OK.

3. If you want to hide any formulas from users, select the cells with the formulas that you want to hide:

   - In Excel 2007, click Home ➤ (Cells) Format ➤ Format Cells. Click the Protection tab, select the Hidden check box, and click OK.

   - In Excel 2003, click Format ➤ Cells, click the Protection tab, select the Hidden check box, and click OK.

4. If you want users to be able to change the contents of some graphic objects on the worksheet but not others, press and hold the Ctrl key and click each object you want your users to be able to change, then:

- In Excel 2007, click (Drawing Tools) Format ➤ (Size) Size and Properties. Click the Properties tab, clear the Locked check box (and if present, clear the Lock Text check box), and click Close.

- In Excel 2003, click Format ➤ AutoShape (or Object, TextBox, Picture, Control, or WordArt, depending on the type of selected graphic object), click the Protection tab, clear the Locked check box (and if present, clear the Lock Text check box), and click OK.

5. In Excel 2007, click Review ➤ (Changes) Protect Sheet. In Excel 2003, click Tools ➤ Protection ➤ Protect Sheet.

6. Select the Protect Worksheet and Contents of Locked Cells to prevent users from making changes to cells that you locked before protecting the worksheet (unless you allowed a user to edit the locked cells in the Allow Users to Edit Ranges dialog box) as well as prevent users from viewing rows, columns, and formulas that you hid before protecting the worksheet.

7. In the Password to Unprotect Sheet box, type a password for the worksheet.

■**Caution** Although a password is not required, if you don't type a password, any user will be able to unprotect the worksheet and change any protected items on the worksheet. Also, type a password that you can easily remember. If you forget the password, there is no way to change the protected items on the worksheet.

---

8. In the Allow All Users of This Worksheet To list, select the check boxes next to the items that you want users to be able to change, as shown in Table 3-3.

Table 3-3. *Check Boxes for the Protect Sheet Dialog Box's Allow All Users of This Workbook To List*

Check Box	Description
Select Locked Cells	Select cells that were locked before the worksheet was protected
Select Unlocked Cells	Press the Tab key to move among the worksheet's unlocked cells
Format Cells	Change the options in the Format Cells and Conditional Formatting dialog boxes
Format Columns	Click Home ➤ Cells ➤ Format and format columns (in Excel 2007) or click Format ➤ Column and issue any of the Column submenu commands (in Excel 2003)
Format Rows	Click Home ➤ Cells ➤ Format and format rows (in Excel 2007) or click Format ➤ Row and issue any of the Row submenu commands (in Excel 2003)
Insert Columns	Click Home ➤ Cells ➤ Insert ➤ Insert Cells or Insert Sheet Columns (in Excel 2007) or click Insert ➤ Columns (in Excel 2003)

continued

Table 3-3. *Continued*

Check Box	Description
Insert Rows	Click Home ➤ Cells ➤ Insert ➤ Insert Cells or Insert Sheet Rows (in Excel 2007) or click Insert ➤ Rows (in Excel 2003)
Insert Hyperlinks	Click Insert ➤ Links ➤ Hyperlink (in Excel 2007) or click Insert ➤ Hyperlink (in Excel 2003)
Delete Columns	Select one or more columns and click Home ➤ Cells ➤ Delete ➤ Delete Cells or Delete Sheet Columns (in Excel 2007), or click Edit ➤ Delete (in Excel 2003), or right-click the column and then click Delete
Delete Rows	Select one or more rows and click Home ➤ Cells ➤ Delete ➤ Delete Cells or Delete Sheet Rows (in Excel 2007), or click Edit ➤ Delete (in Excel 2003), or right-click and click Delete
Sort	Click Data ➤ Sort & Filter ➤ Sort, or click any of the commands on the Home ➤ Editing ➤ Sort & Filter menu (in Excel 2007); or in Excel 2003, click Data ➤ Sort or, on the Standard toolbar, click the Sort Ascending and Sort Descending buttons
Use AutoFilter	Use the drop-down arrows to change the filter on one or more autofiltered cells
Use PivotTable reports	Format, change the layout, refresh, or otherwise change PivotTable reports and create new PivotTable reports
Edit Objects	Make changes to graphic objects that you did not lock before you protected a worksheet; make changes to embedded charts; and add and delete comments
Edit Scenarios	View hidden scenarios, make changes to scenarios to which you have prevented changes, and delete scenarios

▪**Note** If you run an Excel macro that tries to perform an action that's protected on the worksheet, the macro stops running, and a message appears.

9. Click OK.

10. Retype the password if asked, and click OK.

To protect an individual chart sheet (a special type of worksheet that contains only a chart), do the following:

1. In Excel 2007, click Review ➤ (Changes) Protect Sheet. In Excel 2003, click Tools ➤ Protection ➤ Protect Sheet.

2. In the Protect Worksheet area, select one or both of these check boxes:

   • Contents, to prevent users from making changes to chart items such as data series, axes, and legends

   • Objects, to prevent users from making changes to locked graphic objects

3. In the Password box, type a password for the chart sheet, and click OK.

To give specific users access to protected worksheet cells on a computer with Microsoft Windows 2000 or later installed and connected to a computer network, do the following:

1. Select the worksheet tab of the worksheet in which you want to allow specific users access to protected worksheet cells.

2. Unprotect the worksheet if it is protected. In Excel 2007, click Review ➤ (Changes) Unprotect Sheet. Type the worksheet's password, and click OK. In Excel 2003, click Tools ➤ Protection ➤ Unprotect Sheet, type the worksheet's password, and click OK.

3. In Excel 2007, click Review ➤ (Changes) Allow Users to Edit Ranges. In Excel 2003, click Tools ➤ Protection ➤ Allow Users to Edit Ranges.

4. Click New.

5. In the Title box, type a title for the group of one or more cells for which you're granting access.

6. In the Refers to Cells box, type an equal sign (=), and then type a cell reference or select the group of one or more cells.

7. In the Range Password box, type a password to access the selected group of one or more cells.

8. Click Permissions, and then click Add.

9. Select the users to whom you want to give access. (Press and hold the Ctrl key to select multiple users.)

10. Click OK two times, and retype the password.

11. Repeat steps 4 through 10 for each group of cells for which you want to give access to specific users.

12. Click the Protect Sheet button.

13. With the Protect Worksheet and Contents of Locked Cells check box selected, type a password for the worksheet, click OK, retype the password, and click OK.

To protect an entire workbook, do the following:

1. In Excel 2007, click Review ➤ (Changes) Protect Workbook ➤ Protect Structure and Windows. In Excel 2003, click Tools ➤ Protection ➤ Protect Workbook.

2. Select either of the following check boxes in the Protect Workbook For area:

- Structure, to ensure that the workbook's worksheets can't be moved, deleted, hidden, unhidden, or renamed, and ensure that new worksheets can't be inserted.

- Windows, to ensure that windows are in the same position and are the same size whenever the workbook is opened.

3. In the Password box, type a password to prevent others from removing workbook protection, click OK, retype the password, and click OK.

You can protect a shared workbook (a workbook that is set up to allow multiple users on a computer network to view and make changes at the same time). If the workbook is already shared, first unshare the workbook, and then have all users save and close the shared workbook.

In Excel 2007, click Review ➤ (Changes) Share Workbook, and then click the Editing tab. In Excel 2003, click Tools ➤ Share Workbook, and then click the Editing tab.

Make sure that you are the only person listed in the Who Has This Workbook Open Now list. Clear the Allow Changes by More Than One User at the Same Time check box.

■**Note** If the Allow Changes by More Than One User at the Same Time check box is not available, you must unprotect the workbook before clearing the check box. In Excel 2007, click OK, click Review ➤ (Changes) Unprotect Shared Workbook. Type the password, and click OK. Then click Review ➤ (Changes) Share Workbook, and click the Editing tab. In Excel 2003, click OK, click Tools ➤ Protection ➤ Unprotect Shared Workbook, type the password, and click OK. Then click Tools ➤ Share Workbook, and click the Editing tab.

---

1. Click OK. When prompted about the effects on other users, click Yes.

2. Set other types of protection if you want, according to the previous procedures in this section.

3. In Excel 2007, click Review ➤ (Changes) Protect Shared Workbook. In Excel 2003, click Tools ➤ Protection ➤ Protect and Share Workbook.

4. Select the Sharing with Track Changes check box.

5. In the Password box, type a password to prevent others from turning off the workbook's change history or remove the workbook from shared use, click OK, retype the password, and click OK.

6. If prompted, save the workbook.

To protect a workbook file from viewing or editing, do the following:

1. In Excel 2007, click Office Button ➤ Save As. In Excel 2003, click File ➤ Save As.

2. Click Tools ➤ General Options.

3. Do either of these:

   - In the Password to Open box, type a password to require others to type a password before they can view the workbook.

   - In the Password to Modify box, type a password to require others to type a password before they can save changes to the workbook.

4. Click OK. If prompted, retype your passwords.

5. Click Save.

6. If prompted, click Yes to replace the existing workbook.

Although you can use the procedures in the previous section to hide data and protect worksheets and passwords, these steps are not intended to be failsafe ways to protect secure or confidential information. Given enough time and skill, others can obtain and modify all of the data in a workbook, as long as they are able to access it. To help ensure that your data is protected, you can restrict others from accessing confidential information by storing workbooks in locations that you make available only to authorized users.

If you write computer programming code and attach it to a workbook, you can protect the code. In Excel 2007, show the Developer menu if it is not already visible by clicking Office Button ➤ Excel Options, clicking Popular, selecting the Show Developer Tab in the Ribbon check box, and clicking OK, as shown in Figure 3-6. Then click Developer ➤ (Code) Visual Basic. In the Visual Basic Editor, click Tools ➤ (*your project name*) Properties, select the desired options in the Project Properties dialog box's Protection tab, and then click OK.

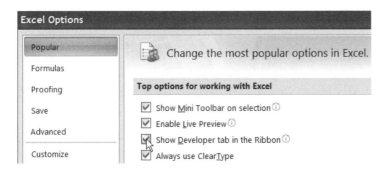

Figure 3-6. *Selecting the Show Developer Tab in the Ribbon check box in Excel 2007*

In Excel 2003, click Tools ➤ Macro ➤ Visual Basic Editor, then in the Visual Basic Editor, click Tools ➤ (*your project name*) Properties, select the desired options in the Project Properties dialog box's Protection tab, and then click OK.

Try It

In this exercise, you will practice protecting individual worksheet cells and other items in a worksheet, you will practice protecting an entire worksheet, and you will practice protecting the structure of an entire workbook.

If the practice workbook is not open from the previous exercise, open it first.

Practice protecting individual worksheet cells by clicking the ProtectData worksheet tab. Make sure that all of the worksheet cells on the ProtectData worksheet will be locked by default when the worksheet is protected.

To protect it, click the Select All button (the button in the upper left corner of the worksheet at the intersection of the row and column headings).

In Excel 2007, click Home ➤ (Cells) Format, and select Lock Cell if it is not already selected. In Excel 2003, click Format ➤ Cells, click the Protection tab, select the Locked check box, and then click OK.

Now unlock some cells so that they can be edited when the worksheet is protected. Select cells E4 through E6 and E8 through E10.

In Excel 2007, click Home ➤ (Cells) Format, and deselect Lock Cell. In Excel 2003, click Format ➤ Cells, click the Protection tab, clear the Locked check box, and then click OK.

Practice protecting other items in a worksheet.

In Excel 2007, click WordArt, and then click (Drawing Tools) Format ➤ (Size) Size and Properties. Click the Properties tab, clear the Locked and Lock Text check boxes, and click Close. In Excel 2003, right-click WordArt, click Format WordArt, click the Protection tab, clear the Locked check box, and click OK.

In Excel 2007, click a blank area of the chart, click (Chart Tools) Format ➤ (Size) Size and Properties. Click the Properties tab, make sure the Locked check box is selected, and click Close. In Excel 2003, right-click a blank area of the chart, click Format Chart Area, click the Properties tab, make sure the Locked check box is selected, and click OK.

Practice protecting an entire worksheet, and then attempt to edit individual data values and objects on the worksheet:

1. In Excel 2007, click Review ➤ (Changes) Protect Sheet. In Excel 2003, click Tools ➤ Protection ➤ Protect Sheet.

2. With the Protect Worksheet and Contents of Locked Cells check box selected, in the Password to Unprotect Sheet box, type **test**.

3. Clear the Select Locked Cells check box, and make sure the Select Unlocked Cells check box is selected. Also, make sure that all of the other check boxes below the Select Unlocked Cells check box are cleared.

4. Click OK.

5. In the Reenter Password to Proceed, type **test**, and click OK.

▓**Note** Notice that you now cannot select any cells other than cells E4 through E6 and E8 through E10. Notice that you can still select any of the cells E4 through E6 and E8 through E10 and change those cells' values.

Notice that you now cannot select the chart, but you can select and change the contents of the WordArt.

Notice also that many of the commands on insert- and format-related menus, for example, are not available.

---

6. Unprotect the worksheet. In Excel 2007, click Review ➤ (Changes) Unprotect Sheet. Type **test** in the Password box, and click OK. In Excel 2003, click Tools ➤ Protection ➤ Unprotect Sheet, type **test** in the Password box, and click OK.

▓**Note** Notice that you can now select and change any cell, the chart, and the WordArt on the worksheet.

Practice protecting an entire workbook's structure. In Excel 2007, click Review ➤ (Changes) Protect Workbook ➤ Protect Structure and Windows. Make sure the Structure check box is selected, type **test** in the Password box, click OK, type **test** again, and click OK. In Excel 2003, click Tools ➤ Protection ➤ Protect Workbook, make sure the Structure check box is selected, type **test** in the Password box, click OK, type **test** again, and click OK.

Notice that in Excel 2007, the Home ➤ (Cells) Insert ➤ Insert Sheet command is not available. In Excel 2003, the Insert ➤ Worksheet command and many of the commands on the Format ➤ Sheet menu are not available. Also notice that many of the commands are not available when you right-click any worksheet tab in the workbook.

To unprotect the workbook, in Excel 2007, click Review ➤ (Changes) Protect Workbook, and clear the Protect Structure and Windows command. Type **test** in the Password box, and click OK. Notice that the Home ➤ (Cells) Insert ➤ Insert Sheet command is now available. In Excel 2003, click Tools ➤ Protection ➤ Unprotect Workbook, type **test** in the Password box, and click OK. Notice that the Insert ➤ Worksheet command and that most of the commands on the Format ➤ Sheet menu are now available. Also notice for both Excel 2007 and Excel 2003 that all of the commands are available when you right-click any worksheet tab in the workbook.

3.8 Insert a Formula or Function

In Excel, a *formula* is an equation that performs a calculation and returns the result into the worksheet cell containing the formula. A formula begins with an equals sign (=) and is followed by a series of numbers, mathematical symbols, and cell references. For example, the formula =A1+A2 returns the sum of the data values in cells A1 and A2.

In Excel, a *function* is a formula with zero or more predefined input values (called *arguments* or *parameters*) to produce as output the result of a calculation based on those input values. For example the formula =SUM(A1,A2) returns the sum of the data values in cells A1 and A2.

Some database management systems don't provide formulas; most database management systems provide functions; and some database management systems provide advanced functions called *stored procedures*. In Excel, formulas and functions are simple to understand, easy to insert, and can be fast to run.

Quick Start

To insert a formula into a worksheet cell, press the F2 key or click the Formula Bar, type the formula, and press the Enter key.

To insert a function into a worksheet cell in Excel 2007, click Formulas ➤ (Function Library) Insert Function. Complete the Insert Function dialog box, click OK, complete the Function Arguments dialog box as necessary, and click OK again. In Excel 2003, click Insert ➤ Function, complete the Insert Function dialog box, click OK, complete the Function Arguments dialog box as necessary, and click OK again.

How To

To insert a formula into a worksheet cell, do the following:

1. Click the worksheet cell into which you want to insert the formula.

2. Press the F2 key or click the Formula Bar, as shown in Figure 3-7.

3. Type the formula. To add a cell reference to a formula, type the cell reference or select the corresponding cells.

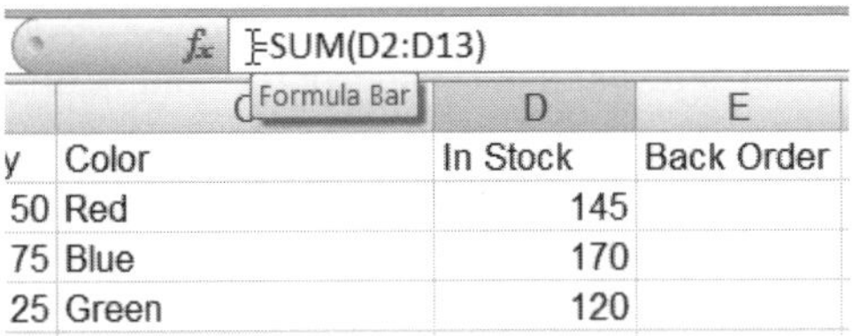

Figure 3-7. *The Excel Formula Bar*

4. Press the Enter key.

To insert a function, do the following:

1. Click the worksheet cell into which you want to insert the function.

2. In Excel 2007, click Formulas ➤ (Function Library) Insert Function. Or, next to the Formula Bar, click the Insert Function button. In Excel 2003, click Insert ➤ Function or, next to the Formula Bar, click the Insert Function button.

3. In the Insert Function dialog box, in the Search For a Function box, type the function's name or a brief description of the function, and then click the Go button. Or, in the Or Select a Category list, select a category of functions that contains the function for which you're looking.

4. In the Select a Function list, select the function for which you're looking.

5. Click OK.

6. Complete the options in the Function Arguments dialog box, if any, and click OK.

Tip If you need help with a function, click the Help on This Function link in the Insert Function or Function Arguments dialog boxes.

If you know a function's name, you do not have to use the Insert Function dialog box. You can simply do the following:

1. Select the desired worksheet cell.

2. Type an equals sign.

3. Type the function's name.

4. Type an opening parenthesis.

5. Type values for any function arguments separated by commas.

6. Type a closing parenthesis.

7. Press the Enter key.

Try It

In this exercise, you will practice inserting formulas and functions into worksheet cells. If the practice workbook is not open from the previous exercise, start Excel, click Office Button ➤ Open (in Excel 2007) or File ➤ Open (in Excel 2003). Browse to and select the ExcelDB_ Ch03_01-09.xls file, and click Open.

1. Click the FunctionsFormulas worksheet tab.

2. In cell D2, type **=B2+B10**, and press the Enter key. The sum of the data values in B2 and B10 is displayed in cell D2.

3. Click cell E2, type =, click cell B15, type -, click cell B7, and press the Enter key. The difference of the data values in B15 and B7 is displayed in cell E2.

4. Click cell F2 and, in Excel 2007, click Formulas ➤ (Function Library) Insert Function. In Excel 2003, click Insert ➤ Function.

5. In the Search For a Function box, type **Add cells' values**, and click the Go button.

6. In the Select a Function list, click SUM, and click OK.

7. Clear the contents of the Number1 box, select the Number1 box, select cells B2 through B16, and click OK. The sum of the data values in cells B2 through B16 is displayed in cell F2.

8. Click cell G2 and click the Insert Function button.

9. In the Or Select a Category list, select Statistical.

10. In the Select a Function list, click AVERAGE, and click OK.

11. Clear the contents of the Number1 box, type **B2:B16** in it, and click OK. The average of the data values in cells B2 through B16 is displayed in cell G2.

12. Click cell H2, type **=MAX(**, select cells B2 through B16, then type), and press the Enter key. The highest data value for the data values in cells B2 through B16 is displayed in cell H2.

13. Click cell I2, type **=MIN(B2:B16)**, and press the Enter key. The lowest data value for the data values in cells B2 through B16 is displayed in cell I2.

14. Click cell J2, type **=IF(AVERAGE(B2:B16)>1000, "Average > 1000", "Average < 1000")**, and press the Enter key. The text *Average > 1000* is displayed in cell J2 because the average of the data values in cells B2 through B16 is greater than 1,000.

3.9 Validate Data

To help ensure that users enter only expected data values into worksheet cells, Excel can compare data values to rules that you can define for specific cells. If those rules are broken, Excel can alert users that their data values are not acceptable and request users to enter acceptable data values. In some database management systems, creating these data validation rules takes a lot of knowledge and effort. Creating these rules in Excel is very straightforward and fast.

Quick Start

To create a data validation rule, do the following:

1. Select one or more worksheet cells to which the data validation rule will apply.

2. In Excel 2007, click Data ➤ (Data Tools) Data Validation. In Excel 2003, click Data ➤ Validation.

3. In the Data Validation dialog box, complete the Settings tab, and optionally the Input Message and Error Alert tabs, and then click OK. The data validation rule is created.

How To

To apply a data validation rule to one or more worksheet cells, do the following:

1. Select the worksheet cells for which you want to apply a data validation rule.

2. In Excel 2007, click Data ➤ (Data Tools) Data Validation. In Excel 2003, click Data ➤ Validation.

3. On the Settings tab, in the Validation Criteria area, select one of the items in the Allow list, as shown in Table 3-4.

Table 3-4. *Items in the Allow List*

Allow List Item	Restricts
Any Value	Any values
Whole Number	Only whole numbers (numbers without fractions)
Decimal	Only numbers with decimal symbols
List	Only a data value from a predefined list of data values
Date	Only date values
Time	Only time values
Text length	Only a specific number of alphanumeric characters
Custom	Data values conforming to a specific formula's results

4. In the Allow list, if you select Whole Number, Decimal, Date, Time, or Text Length, select one of the items in Table 3-5 from the Data list.

Table 3-5. *Items in the Data List*

Items in the Data List	Description
Between or Not Between	A value between or not between the values in the Minimum and Maximum boxes
Equal or Not Equal	A value equal or not equal to the value in the Value box or Length box
Greater Than or Greater Than or Equal To	A value greater than or greater than or equal to the value in the Minimum box
Less Than or Less Than or Equal To	A value less than or less than or equal to the value in the Maximum box

5. In the Allow list, if you select List, then in the Source box, type the list of allowed values separated by commas, or select the worksheet cells containing the list or allowed values.

6. In the Allow list, if you select Custom, then in the Formula box, type or select the formula by whose result you want to restrict the allowed data values in the selected worksheet cells.

■**Note** If you select Custom in the Allow list, in the Formula box, enter a formula that calculates a logical value. If the formula in the Formula box evaluates to true, then data values can be entered in the selected worksheet cells without displaying an error. If the formula in the Formula box evaluates to false, then an error appears whenever any data values are entered in the selected worksheet cells. For example, if you type **=AND(AVERAGE(H2:H11)>60)** in the Formula box, data values can only be entered into the selected worksheet cells if the formula in the Formula box evaluates to true (in this case, the average of the data values in cells H2 through H11 is greater than 60).

---

7. Select the Ignore Blank check box to not validate a selected cell containing no data against the data validation rule.

8. In the Allow list, if you select List, select the In-Cell Dropdown check box to allow others to select a data value from the list that appears when you click one of the selected worksheet cells.

9. On the Input Message tab, select the Show Input Message When Cell Is Selected check box if you want to display a dialog box whenever someone selects one of the worksheet cells for which the corresponding data validation rule applies. Also, in the When Cell Is Selected, Show This Input Message area, do the following:

   a. In the Title box, type a title for the dialog box that appears when others select one of the selected worksheet cells.

   b. In the Input message box, type the message that you want others to see in the dialog box when others select one of the selected worksheet cells.

10. On the Error Alert tab, select the Show Error Alert After Invalid Data Is Entered check box if you want to display a dialog box whenever someone types or enters a data value that violates the data validation rule for which one of the worksheet cells applies. Also, in the When User Enters Invalid Data, Show This Error Alert area, do the following:

   a. In the Style list, select Stop, Warning, or Information to display a stop icon, warning icon, or information icon in the dialog box that appears when someone types or enters a data value that violates the data validation rule.

   b. In the Title box, type a title for the dialog box that appears when someone types or enters a data value that violates the data validation rule.

   c. In the Error message box, type the message that appears in the dialog box when someone types or enters a data value that violates the data validation rule.

11. Click OK.

In the Data Validation dialog box's Settings tab, you can select the Apply These Changes to All Other Cells with the Same Settings check box when you are changing a validation rule, in order to apply the changes to all other worksheet cells that have the same validation rule defined.

To find all cells in a workbook that match a specific data validation rule, click a worksheet cell that has a known data validation rule for which you want to find matches. In Excel 2007, click Home ➤ (Editing) Find & Select ➤ Go To Special, click the Data Validation option, click the Same option, and click OK. In Excel 2003, click Edit ➤ Go To, click the Special button, click the Data Validation option, click the Same option, and click OK.

To find all cells in a workbook that contain data validation rules, in Excel 2007, click Home ➤ (Editing) Find & Select ➤ Go To Special, click the Data Validation option, click the All option, and click OK. In Excel 2003, click Edit ➤ Go To, click the Special button, click the Data Validation option, click the All option, and click OK.

Try It

In this exercise, you will practice validating data in various worksheet cells against data-entry criteria for whole numbers, dates, times, text string lengths, lists of data values, and formulas. If the practice workbook is not open from the previous exercise, start Excel, click Office Button ➤ Open (in Excel 2007) or File ➤ Open (in Excel 2003). Browse to and select the ExcelDB_Ch03_ 01-09.xls file, and click Open. Click the ValidateData worksheet tab.

Practice validating data for whole numbers:

1. Select cells A2 and A3, and in Excel 2007, click Data ➤ (Data Tools) Data Validation. In Excel 2003, click Data ➤ Validation.

2. Click the Settings tab.

3. In the Allow list, select Whole Number.

4. In the Data list, select Between.

5. In the Minimum box, type **0**.

6. In the Maximum box, type **10**.

7. Click the Input Message tab.

8. With the Show Input Message When Cell Is Selected check box selected, in the Title box, type **Whole Numbers Only**.

9. In the Input Message box, type **Enter a whole number between 0 and 10**.

10. Click the Error Alert tab.

11. With the Show Error Alert After Invalid Data Is Entered check box selected, in the Title box, type **Invalid Number**.

12. In the Error Message box, type **Only whole numbers between 0 and 10 are allowed**, and click OK.

13. Click cell A2, type **7**, and press the Enter key.

14. Click cell A3, type 15, and press the Enter key. An error message appears because the data value is not between 0 and 10.

15. Click Retry, type **2**, and press the Enter key.

Next, practice validating data for dates:

1. Select cells B2 and B3, and in Excel 2007, click Data ➤ (Data Tools) Data Validation. In Excel 2003, click Data ➤ Validation.

2. Click the Settings tab.

3. In the Allow list, select Date.

4. In the Data list, select Greater Than or Equal To.

5. In the Start Date box, type **01/01/2006**, and click OK.

6. Click cell B2, type **12/04/2006**, and press the Enter key.

7. Click cell B3, type **10/09/2004**, and press the Enter key. An error message appears because the data value is not greater than or equal to the date 01/01/2006.

8. Click Retry, type **10/09/2007**, and press the Enter key.

Practice validating data for times:

1. Select cells C2 and C3, and in Excel 2007, click Data ➤ (Data Tools) Data Validation. In Excel 2003, click Data ➤ Validation.

2. Click the Settings tab.

3. In the Allow list, select Time.

4. In the Data list, select Less Than.

5. In the End Time box, type **14:00**, and click OK.

6. Click cell C2, type **8:35**, and press the Enter key.

7. Click cell C3, type **8:35 PM**, and press the Enter key. An error message appears because the data value is not earlier than 2:00 PM.

8. Click Retry, type **8:35 AM**, and press the Enter key.

Next, practice validating data for text string lengths:

1. Select cells D2 and D3, and in Excel 2007, click Data ➤ (Data Tools) Data Validation. In Excel 2003, click Data ➤ Validation.

2. Click the Settings tab.

3. In the Allow list, select Text Length.

4. In the Data list, select Not Equal To.

5. In the Length box, type **5**.

6. Click the Input Message tab.

7. With the Show Input Message When Cell Is Selected check box selected, in the Title box, type **Text Length Restricted**.

8. In the Input Message box, type **Do not enter any text strings containing five characters**.

9. Click the Error Alert tab.

10. With the Show Error Alert After Invalid Data Is Entered check box selected, in the Title box, type **Invalid Text String Length**.

11. In the Error Message box, type **Only text strings with lengths other than five are allowed**, and click OK.

12. Click cell D2, type **Banana**, and press the Enter key.

13. Click cell D3, type **Fruit**, and press the Enter key. An error message appears because the text string length is five characters in length.

14. Click Retry, type **Orange**, and press the Enter key.

Practice validating data for lists of data values:

1. Select cells E2 and E3, and in Excel 2007, click Data ➤ (Data Tools) Data Validation. In Excel 2003, click Data ➤ Validation.

2. Click the Settings tab.

3. In the Allow list, select List.

4. With the Ignore Blank and In-Cell Dropdown check boxes selected, in the Source box, type **Low,Medium,High**, and click OK.

5. Click cell E2, click the arrow, and select Low from the list.

6. Click cell E3, type **Mediocre**, and press the Enter key. An error message appears because the text is not one of the values Low, Medium, or High.

7. Click Cancel, click the arrow, and select Medium from the list.

8. In cells J1 through J4, type the words **Red**, **Yellow**, **Blue**, and **Green** respectively.

9. Select cells F2 and F3, and in Excel 2007, click Data ➤ (Data Tools) Data Validation. In Excel 2003, click Data ➤ Validation.

10. Click the Settings tab.

11. In the Allow list, select List.

12. With the Ignore Blank and In-Cell Dropdown check boxes selected, click the Source box, select cells J1 through J4, and click OK.

13. Click cell F2, click the arrow, and select Blue from the list.

14. Click cell F3, type **Purple**, and press the Enter key. An error message appears because the text is not one of the values Red, Yellow, Blue, or Green.

15. Click Cancel, click the arrow, and select Green from the list.

Last, practice validating data for formulas:

1. Select cell G2, and in Excel 2007, click Data ➤ (Data Tools) Data Validation. In Excel 2003, click Data ➤ Validation.

2. Click the Settings tab.

3. In the Allow list, select Custom.

4. Click the Formula box, type **=AND(AVERAGE(H2:H11)>60)**, and click OK.

5. Click cell G2, type some text, and press the Enter key. An error message appears because the average of the values in cells H2 through H11 is not greater than 60.

6. Click Cancel.

7. Select cell G2, and in Excel 2007, click Data ➤ (Data Tools) Data Validation. In Excel 2003, click Data ➤ Validation.

8. Click the Settings tab.

9. Click the Formula box, change the formula to **=AND(AVERAGE(H2:H11)>50)**, and click OK.

10. Click cell G2, type some text, and press the Enter key. No error message appears because the average of the values in cells H2 through H11 is greater than 50.

3.10 Import Data

As an alternative to typing or copying multiple data values into worksheet cells, you can import the data values into an Excel workbook. Importing data values into other database management systems can take a lot of effort, can be error-prone, and may require you to purchase additional expensive software add-ons. Excel can import data from many popular data sources quickly and with very few steps.

Quick Start

To import data values into an Excel workbook, in Excel 2007, click Data, click Get External Data, and then click one of the available commands. In Excel 2003, click Data ➤ Import External Data ➤ Import Data. Follow the onscreen steps to finish importing the data.

How To

To import data values into an Excel workbook, do the following:

1. Click the location in the worksheet into which you want to import the data.

▓**Note** You should choose a blank worksheet into which to import the data to prevent existing data values in the workbook from being overwritten.

---

2. In Excel 2007, click Data, click Get External Data, and then click one of the available commands. In Excel 2003, click Data ➤ Import External Data ➤ Import Data.

3. In Excel 2007, follow the onscreen steps to finish importing the data. In Excel 2003, do one of the following:

   • In the Select Data Source dialog box, browse to and select an available data source, and then click Open.

   • In the Select Data Source dialog box, click New Source. In the Data Connection Wizard, in the What Kind of Data Source Do You Want to Connect To list, choose a type of data source to connect to, and then click Next.

4. Depending on the type of data source that you want to connect to, complete the rest of the steps to finish importing your data.

Tip

If you want to import only a portion of the data values based on criteria that you specify; sort the data values before importing them into Excel; or bring together data values from separate data tables into a single Excel worksheet, you should use Microsoft Query, which is included with Excel. In Excel 2007, click Data ➤ Get External Data ➤ From Other Sources ➤ From Microsoft Query. In Excel 2003, click Data ➤ Import External Data ➤ New Database Query.

For more information about importing data using the Excel 2007 From Microsoft Query and the Excel 2003 New Database Query commands, see Chapter 5.

Try It

In this exercise, you will practice importing data values from the Northwind sample database that is included with Microsoft Access 2003 and Access 2007. To complete this exercise, if you are using Excel 2007, you must have Access 2003 or Access 2007 installed. If you are using Excel 2003, you must have Access 2003 installed. First, if it's not installed already, install the Northwind sample database. If you have Access 2007 installed, do the following in Access 2007:

1. Start Access 2007.

2. Click the Microsoft Office Access Help icon.

3. In the Type Words to Search For box, type **Northwind**, and press Enter.

4. In the Results list, click Northwind 2007. The Microsoft Office Online web site appears.

5. Follow the steps to download the Northwind sample database, and then return to Access 2007.

6. In the Template Categories pane, click either Local Templates or Sample, click the Northwind 2007 icon in the Local Templates or Sample pane, and then complete the items on the far right side of the screen to create an instance of the Northwind 2007 sample database. The Northwind 2007 sample database should appear.

7. Quit Access.

If you have Access 2003 installed, do the following:

1. Start Access 2003.

2. Click Help ➤ Sample Databases ➤ Northwind Sample Database. The Northwind sample database should appear. If you don't see the Northwind Sample Database command, you must install it by running Microsoft Office 2003 Setup.

3. Quit Access.

If the practice workbook is not open from the previous exercise, start Excel, click Office Button ➤ Open (in Excel 2007) or File ➤ Open (in Excel 2003), and browse to and select the ExcelDB_Ch03_01-09.xls file, and click Open.

Click the ImportData worksheet tab, and then in Excel 2007, do the following:

1. Click Data ➤ Get External Data ➤ From Access.

2. Browse to and select either the Access 2007 version of this file, Northwind 2007.accdb, in the location that you created earlier, or the Access 2003 version of the Northwind sample database file, Northwind.mdb (this file is usually installed into the <drive>:\ Program Files\Microsoft Office\OFFICE11\SAMPLES directory). Then click Open.

3. In the Select Table dialog box, click the Current Product List table, and then click OK twice. Excel imports the Current Product List table's data values into the worksheet.

In Excel 2003, do the following:

1. Click Data ➤ Import External Data ➤ Import Data.

2. Click the New Source button. The Data Connection Wizard appears.

3. In the What Kind of Data Source Do You Want to Connect To list, select ODBC DSN, and then click Next.

4. In the ODBC data sources list, select MS Access Database, and then click Next.

5. Browse to and select the Northwind.mdb file (for Access 2003, this file is usually installed into the <drive>:\Program Files\Microsoft Office\OFFICE11\SAMPLES directory), and then click OK. The Select Database and Table page appears.

6. With the Connect to a Specific Table check box selected, select the Current Product List table, and then click Finish.

7. Click Open, and then click OK. Excel imports the Current Product List table's data values into the worksheet.

CHAPTER 4

∎∎∎

Find Data

After you enter data into Excel, you will need a way to find specific data values later. In this chapter, you will learn how to find data by using Excel features and techniques such as worksheet cell references, the Find and Replace and Go To dialog boxes, cell offsets, the Lookup Wizard, and worksheet functions such as LOOKUP, HLOOKUP, VLOOKUP, INDEX, and MATCH.

4.1 Use Cell References

Excel uses fives types of references to refer to worksheet cells: absolute, relative, mixed, 3-D, and R1C1, defined in the following list. Understanding these types of references is critical when you try to locate or reference cells in worksheet formulas and functions. Using the wrong type of cell reference can yield unintended results.

An *absolute cell* reference is a cell reference that doesn't change when you copy formulas containing the cell reference across rows or down columns. Absolute cell references take the format *RowColumn* ($B$8, for example).

A *relative cell* reference is a cell reference that changes when you copy formulas containing the cell reference across rows or down columns. Absolute cell references take the format *RowColumn* (E12, for example). By default, new formulas use relative references.

A *mixed cell* reference is a cell reference in which the absolute portion of the cell reference doesn't change, but the relative portion of the cell reference changes when you copy formulas containing the cell reference across rows or down columns. Mixed cell references take the format *$RowColumn* or *Row$Column*, ($C3 or F$7, for example).

A *3-D cell* reference is a reference to a cell on one or more worksheets. 3-D cell references take the format *'FirstWorksheet:LastWorksheet'!CellReference* (for example, 'Sheet3:Sheet6'!G4 to refer to cell G4 on worksheets Sheet3 through Sheet6 inclusive).

An *R1C1 cell* reference is a cell reference in which all rows and columns are defined by numbers. R1C1 references take the format R*Row*C*Column* (for example, R3C5 to refer to cell E3). You can also use left square brackets and right square brackets along with positive and negative numbers to indicate cell references relative to the current cell, for example, R[2]C[3] to indicate a cell two rows below and three columns to the right of the current cell, or R[-2]C[-3] to indicate a cell two rows above and three columns to the left of the current cell.

Tip

To turn the R1C1 cell reference style on or off, do one of the following:

- In Excel 2007, click Office Button ➤ Excel Options. In the left pane, click Formulas. In the Working with Formulas area, select or clear the R1C1 Reference Style check box, and click OK.

- In Excel 2003, click Tools ➤ Options, and on the General tab, select or clear the R1C1 Reference Style check box.

Quick Start

By default, formulas use relative cell references, such as D4.

To create an absolute cell reference, preface the row numbers and column identifiers with the $ symbol, such as $D$4.

To create a 3-D cell reference, preface the cell reference with the corresponding worksheet name, such as 'Sheet2'!D4 or 'Sheet1:Sheet3'!$D$4.

To create an absolute R1C1 cell reference, use the format R2C6 to refer to cell F2. To create a relative cell reference, use the format R[2]C[-6] to refer to a cell two rows down and six cells to the left of the current cell.

For mixed cell references, use a combination of relative and absolute cell references, such as D$4, $D4, 'Sheet1:Sheet3'!$D4, or R[-2]C3.

How To

To create an absolute cell reference, precede the row number and column identifier with the $ symbol—for example, $F$4 to refer to cell F4. This cell reference will not change when you copy formulas containing the cell reference across rows or down columns.

To create a relative cell reference, simply type the cell reference—for example, **F4** to refer to cell F4. This cell reference will change when you copy formulas containing the cell reference across rows or down columns.

To create a mixed cell reference, precede the absolute row number or column identifier portion of the cell reference with the $ symbol—for example, $F4 or F$4 to refer to cell F4. The absolute portion of the cell reference will not change when you copy formulas containing the cell reference across rows or down columns, but the relative portion of the cell reference will change.

To create a 3-D cell reference, precede an absolute, relative, or mixed cell reference with the worksheet references—for example, 'Sheet2:Sheet4'!H$8 to refer to cell H8 on worksheets Sheet2 through Sheet4 inclusive.

To create an absolute R1C1 cell reference, use the letter *R*, followed by the row number, followed by the letter *C*, followed by the column identifier—for example, R4C2 to refer to cell B4. To create a relative R1C1 cell reference, use left square brackets and right square brackets along with positive and negative numbers to indicate cell references relative to the current cell—for example, R[2]C[3] to indicate a cell two rows below and three columns to the right of the current cell, or R[-2]C[-3] to indicate a cell two rows above and three columns to the left of the current cell. You can also create a mixed R1C1 cell reference by using a combination of bracketed and nonbracketed numbers—for example, R3C[-2] to indicate a cell on row 3, two columns above the current cell.

Try It

In this exercise, you will practice creating absolute, relative, mixed, 3-D, and R1C1 cell references. You will also see what happens to these cell references when you copy them to different worksheet cells.

First, open the ExcelDB_Ch04_01-05.xls file:

1. Start Excel.

2. Click Office Button ➤ Open (in Excel 2007) or File ➤ Open (in Excel 2003).

3. Browse to and select the ExcelDB_Ch04_01-05.xls file, and click Open.

Next, create and copy relative cell references:

1. Click the CellReferences worksheet tab.

2. In cell E2, type the formula =**A2*B2**, and press Enter.

3. Drag the fill handle (the small, square black box in the lower right corner of the cell) of cell E2 to cell E10. Notice that the results match column C.

Next, create and copy absolute cell references:

1. In cell F2, type the formula =**$A$2*$B$2**, and press Enter.

2. Drag the fill handle of cell F2 to cell F10. Notice that cells F3 through F10 are the same as cell F2 because you created an absolute cell reference in cell F2.

Create and copy mixed cell references:

1. In cell G2, type the formula =**$A2*$B2**, and press Enter.

2. Drag the fill handle of cell G2 to cell G10. Notice that the column identifier does not change, but the row number in each cell's formula increments by one for each subsequent cell.

Create and copy 3-D cell references:

1. In cell H2, type the formula =**A2*'3-DCellReferences'!F2**, and press Enter.

2. Drag the fill handle of cell H2 to cell H10. Notice that the results match column C, although the Units Sold were taken from column F on the 3-DCellReferences worksheet tab.

Create and copy R1C1 cell references:

1. In Excel 2007, click Office Button ➤ Excel Options. In the left pane, click Formulas. In the Working with Formulas area, select the R1C1 Reference Style check box, and click OK.

   In Excel 2003, click Tools ➤ Options, click the General tab, select the R1C1 Reference Style check box, and click OK.

2. In the cell at the intersection of row 2 and column 9, type the formula **=RC[-8]*RC[-7]**, and press Enter.

▨**Tip** Typing the formula **=RC[-8]*RC[-7]** is the same as typing the formula **=R[0]C[-8]*R[0]C[-7]**.

---

3. Drag the fill handle of the cell at the intersection of row 2 and column 9 to the cell at the intersection of row 10 and column 9. Notice that the results match column 3.

4. In Excel 2007, click File ➤ Excel Options. In the left pane, click Formulas. In the Working with Formulas area, clear the R1C1 Reference Style check box, and click OK.

   In Excel 2003, click Tools ➤ Options, click the General tab, clear the R1C1 Reference Style check box, and click OK.

4.2 Find, Replace, or Go To Data

As their names imply, the Find command allows you to find specific data values in specific cells, and the Replace command allows you to replace data values in specific cells. The Go To command allows you to select data values in specific cells or select cells with specific characteristics.

Quick Start

To find data values in specific cells, in Excel 2007, click Home ➤ (Editing) Find & Select ➤ Find. In Excel 2003, click Edit ➤ Find. Complete the options in the Find and Replace dialog box's Find tab, and click Find All or Find Next as desired.

   To replace data values in specific cells, in Excel 2007, click Home ➤ (Editing) Find & Select ➤ Replace. In Excel 2003, click Edit ➤ Replace. Complete the options in the Find and Replace dialog box's Replace tab, and click Replace All, Replace, Find All, or Find Next as desired.

   To go to or select data values in specific cells or cells with specific characteristics, in Excel 2007, click Home ➤ (Editing) Find & Select ➤ Go To. In Excel 2003, click Edit ➤ Go To. Complete the options in the Go To dialog box, and click OK.

How To

To find data values in specific cells:

1. In Excel 2007, click Home ➤ (Editing) Find & Select ➤ Find. In Excel 2003, click Edit ➤ Find.

2. In the Find and Replace dialog box, on the Find tab, in the Find What box, type the data value that you want to find.

■Tip In the Find What box, you can use a question mark (?) to match any single text character, or an asterisk (*) to match any string of text characters. For example, **state?** finds *states* and *stated*, and **custom*** finds *customer* and *customers*.

---

3. Click the Options button to display advanced find options (as shown in Figure 4-1), and do one or more of the following:

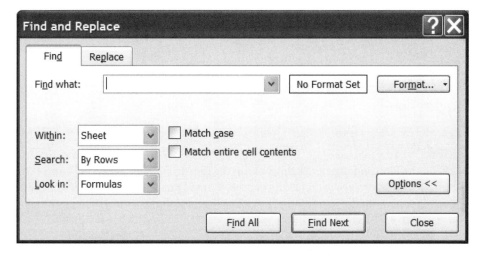

Figure 4-1. *The Find and Replace dialog box's Find tab with advanced find options displayed*

- Click the Format button to display the Find Format dialog box, which allows you to include cell formatting as part of the find options. If you click the down arrow in the Format button and click Choose Format from Cell, you can click a cell that meets the cell formatting that you want to include as part of the find options. If you click the arrow in the Format button and click Clear Find Format, all previous cell formatting find options are removed.

- In the Within list, select Sheet to limit your find options to the current worksheet. Select Workbook to broaden find options to include all worksheet sheets in the workbook.

- In the Search list, select By Rows to search for data values going to the right across the rows. Select By Columns to search for data values going down the columns from top to bottom.

■**Tip** To change the direction to search up the columns for data or to the left across rows, hold down the Shift key and click the Find Next button.

- In the Look In list, select Formulas to look for data values only in formulas, select Values to look for data values in cell values, or select Comments to look for data values in comments attached to cells.

- Select the Match Case check box to match the combination of uppercase and lowercase text characters as specified in the Find What box.

- Select the Match Entire Cell Contents check box to limit find options to an exact match of the text characters as specified in the Find What box.

4. Click the Find All button to find all instances of the search criteria in your document.

5. Click the Find Next button to find the next instance of the text characters specified in the Find What box. To find the previous instance, hold down the Shift key and click Find Next.

6. Click the Close button to close the Find or Replace dialog box.

To replace data values in specific cells, do the following:

1. In Excel 2007, click Home ➤ (Editing) Find & Select ➤ Replace. In Excel 2003, click Edit ➤ Replace.

2. In the Find and Replace dialog box, on the Replace tab (as shown in Figure 4-2), type, click, or select, according to the controls named identically to those in the previous Find tab, with the exception of the following additional controls:

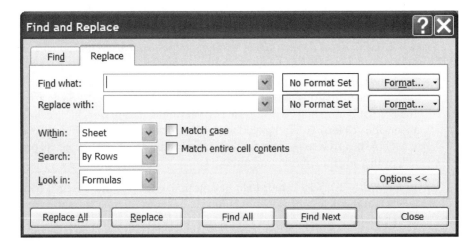

Figure 4-2. *The Find and Replace dialog box's Replace tab with advanced replace options displayed*

a. In the Replace With box, type the replacement text characters that you want to use to replace the text characters in the Find What box. To delete the text characters in the Find What box from your worksheet or workbook, leave the Replace With box blank.

b. Click the Replace All button to replace all instances of the found data in the worksheet or workbook.

c. Click the Replace button to replace the selected instance of the text characters in the Find What box, find the next instance, and then stop.

To go to or to select worksheet cells containing specific data values or specific characteristics, do the following:

1. In Excel 2007, click Home ➤ (Editing) Find & Select ➤ Go To. In Excel 2003, click Edit ➤ Go To.

2. To go to a group of cells that are tagged with a name (known as a *named range*), click the named range in the Go To box, and click OK.

3. To go to a specific cell reference, type the cell reference in the Reference box, and click OK.

4. To go to other types of worksheet cells, click the Special button, and do one of the following:

   • Click the Comments option to select cells that have attached comments.

   • Click the Constants option to select cells that contain text characters and not formulas, functions, or data values resulting from formulas or functions.

   • Click the Formulas option to select cells that contain formulas. Select the Numbers check box to select cells that contain number-related formulas; select the Text check box to select cells that contain text-related formulas; select the Logicals check box to select cells that contain logical-related (for example, true or false) formulas; or select the Errors check box to select cells that contain formulas returning errors.

   • Click the Blanks option to select blank cells in a selection of cells that contains blank cells surrounded by a combination of blank and nonblank cells.

   • Click the Current Region option to select the currently selected cells along with all adjacent cells up to the first row or column containing empty cells.

   • Click the Current Array option to select an entire array if the currently selected cell is contained in an array.

   • Click the Objects option to select buttons, charts, images, and similar graphics on the worksheet and inside of text boxes.

   • Click the Row Differences option to select from all selected cells in a row that are different from the currently selected cell in that row.

   • Click the Column Differences option to select from all selected cells in a column that are different from the currently selected cell in that column.

- Click the Precedents option to select cells that are referenced by the formula in the currently selected cell. If visible, click the Direct Only option to select cells that are directly referenced by the formula in the currently selected cell; or click the All Levels option to select cells that are either directly or indirectly referenced by the formula in the currently selected cell.

- Click the Dependents option to select cells with formulas that reference the currently selected cell. If visible, click the Direct Only option to select cells that are directly referenced by the formula in the currently selected cell; or click the All Levels option to select cells that are either directly or indirectly referenced by the formula in the currently selected cell.

- Click the Last Cell option to select the last cell that contains data values or cell formatting.

- Click the Visible Cells Only option to select visible cells as long as at least one row or column is hidden.

- Click the Conditional Formats option to select cells containing conditional formatting. If visible, click the All option to select all cells containing conditional formatting; or click the Same option to select cells containing the same conditional formatting as the currently selected cell.

- Click the Data Validation option to select cells containing data validation rules. If visible, click the All option to select all cells containing data validation rules; click the Same option to select all cells containing the same data validation rules as the currently selected cell.

5. Click OK.

Try It

In this exercise, you will use the Find and Replace commands to find and replace data values in specific cells. You will also use the Go To command to select cells with specific characteristics.

First, open the ExcelDB_Ch04_01-05.xls file:

1. Start Excel.

2. Click Office Button ➤ Open (in Excel 2007) or File ➤ Open (in Excel 2003).

3. Browse to and select the ExcelDB_Ch04_01-05.xls file, and click Open.

Next, practice finding data values using the Find command:

1. Select the FindReplaceGoTo worksheet tab.

2. In Excel 2007, click Home ➤ (Editing) Find & Select ➤ Find. In Excel 2003, click Edit ➤ Find.

3. In the Find What box, type **North***.

4. Click Find All. The values North, Northeast, and Northwest are displayed below the Find All button.

5. Click each of the find results to go to each result in the worksheet.

6. Click the Options button to display the find options.

7. Clear the contents of the Find What box.

8. Click Format.

9. Click the Choose Format from Cell button, and click cell D7.

10. Click Find All. The cells matching the cell formatting in cell D7 are displayed below the Final All button.

11. Click each of the find results to go to each result in the worksheet, and then click Close.

Next, practice replacing data values using the Replace command:

1. In Excel 2007, click Home ➤ (Editing) Find & Select ➤ Replace. In Excel 2003, click Edit ➤ Replace.

2. Click the down arrow in the Format button in the Find What row, and then click Clear Find Format.

3. Click the Format button in the Find What row, click the Font tab, and in the Font Style list, select Bold Italic. Then click OK.

4. In the Replace With box, type **Bold Italic Text**.

5. Click the Replace All button, and then click OK. The contents of all five cells with bold italic text are replaced with the text ***Bold Italic Text***.

6. With the Find and Replace dialog box still visible, on the Replace tab, click the down arrow in the Format button in the Find What row, and then click Clear Find Format.

7. Clear the contents of the Replace With box.

8. Click the Format button in the Find What row, click the Font tab, and in the Size box, select 12. Then click OK.

9. Click the Format button in the Replace With row, click the Font tab, and in the Size box, select 8, then click OK.

10. Click the Replace All button, and then click OK. The contents of all three cells with 12-point text are reduced to 8-point text.

11. Click OK, and then click Close.

Practice selecting specific cells using the Go To command:

1. Select cells B1 through B16, and in Excel 2007, click Home ➤ (Editing) Find & Select ➤ Go To, and click Special. In Excel 2003, click Edit ➤ Go To, and click Special.

2. Click the Blanks option, and click OK. Empty cell B8 is selected.

3. Select cells B1 through B16 again, and in Excel 2007, click Home ➤ (Editing) Find & Select ➤ Go To, and click Special. In Excel 2003, click Edit ➤ Go To, and click Special.

4. Click the Current Region option, and click OK. Cells A1 through D16, the region bounding cells B1 through B16, are selected.

5. Select cells B1 through B16 again, hold down the Ctrl key and select cell B2, and in Excel 2007, click Home ➤ (Editing) Find & Select ➤ Go To, and click Special. In Excel 2003, click Edit ➤ Go To, and click Special.

6. Select the Column Differences option, and click OK. Cells B3, B5, and B9 through B16 are selected as they are different from the value in cell B2.

4.3 Use the OFFSET Worksheet Function

There will come a time when you need to reference cells' locations from a worksheet function, but you know that the cells' exact addresses will change as rows or columns are inserted or deleted. You can use the OFFSET worksheet function in these situations to help create location-neutral worksheet functions that will still work as cell locations frequently change. Use the OFFSET worksheet function when you know that the target cells are a specified number of cells to the left, right, above, or below the originating cell containing the worksheet function.

The OFFSET worksheet function returns a reference to a range of cells that is a specified number of rows and columns from a cell or range of cells. The reference that is returned can be a single cell or a range of cells. You can specify the number of rows and the number of columns to be returned.

The OFFSET worksheet function takes the arguments *reference*, *rows*, *cols*, *height*, and *width*:

The required *reference* argument is the cell reference from which you want to determine the offset.

The required *rows* argument specifies the number of rows above (negative number) or rows below (positive number) the reference argument that you want the upper left cell to refer to.

The required *cols* argument specifies the number of columns to the right of (positive number) or columns to the left of (negative number) the reference argument that you want the upper left cell to refer to.

The optional positive *height* argument specifies the number of rows from which you want the returned reference.

The optional positive *width* argument specifies the number of columns that you want for the returned reference.

▓**Note** The cells referred to in the reference argument must be a single cell or a range of contiguous cells. Otherwise, the OFFSET worksheet function returns a #VALUE! error value. Also, if the *rows* or *cols* arguments return references that go past the edges of the worksheet, the OFFSET worksheet function returns a #REF! error value. If the *height* and *width* arguments are not included, the OFFSET worksheet function uses the same height and width as provided in the reference argument. The OFFSET worksheet function doesn't move any cells or change any selected cells.

Try It

In this exercise, you will practice using the OFFSET worksheet function to locate data values that are a specified distance away from originating cells and use them in sales inventory calculations.

Open the ExcelDB_Ch04_01-05.xls file:

1. Start Excel.

2. Click Office Button ➤ Open (in Excel 2007) or File ➤ Open (in Excel 2003).

3. Browse to and select the ExcelDB_Ch04_01-05.xls file, and click Open.

4. Click the Lookups worksheet tab.

In cells B10 through B13, enter variations of the OFFSET worksheet function to calculate the sales inventory for the number of vehicles in cells B2 through B5 multiplied by the vehicles' sales prices in cells E2 through E5, as follows:

In cell B10, type the following, and press Enter: **=OFFSET(A1,1,1)*OFFSET(D1,1,1)**. This formula can be interpreted as follows:

- Starting with cell A1, move one cell down and one cell to the right (cell B2), and store the data value in that cell (12,995).

- Starting with cell D1, move one cell down and one cell to the right (cell E2), and use the data value in that cell (100).

- Multiply the data values in cell B2 and E2 (1,299,500).

Select the fill handle (the small black box in the lower right corner) in cell B10 and drag it to cell B13. Offsets are calculated for the remaining vehicle types.

4.4 Use the LOOKUP, HLOOKUP, VLOOKUP, INDEX, and MATCH Worksheet Functions

In addition to the Find and Go To commands and the OFFSET function, you can also use the LOOKUP, HLOOKUP, VLOOKUP, INDEX, and MATCH worksheet functions to find specific data values:

Use the LOOKUP function to return a data value from a group of cells across a single row or down a single column.

Use the HLOOKUP function to return a data value in a single column of a group of cells based on a matching data value in the first row of the group of cells and a row number in the matching data value's corresponding column.

Use the VLOOKUP function to return a data value in a group of cells based on a matching data value in the first column of the group of cells and a column number in the matching data value's corresponding row.

Use the INDEX function to return a data value in a group of cells based on the intersection of a row number and column number.

Use the MATCH function to return the position of a data value in a group of cells.

The LOOKUP Function

The LOOKUP function returns a data value from a group of cells across a single row or down a column.

The *vector* (a group of cells across a single row or down a single column) form of the LOOKUP function takes three arguments: *lookup_value*, *lookup_vector*, and *result_vector*:

The required *lookup_value* argument is the data value that you want to find in the vector. The data value can be a number, a string of text characters, the data values False or True, or a cell reference that refers to a data value.

The required *lookup_vector* argument is the reference to a group of cells across a single row or down a single column. The referenced cells can contain numbers, strings of text characters, or the values False or True. The values must appear in ascending order.

■Note If the LOOKUP function can't find the data value specified in the *lookup_value* argument, it matches the largest value in the *lookup_vector* argument that is less than or equal to the data value specified in the *lookup_value* argument. If the data value specified in the *lookup_value* argument is smaller than the smallest data value specified in the *lookup_vector* argument, the LOOKUP function returns the #N/A error value.

The required *result_vector* argument is a corresponding group of cells across a single row or down a single column. This group of cells must have the same number of cells as the cells referenced in the *lookup_vector* argument.

■Tip There is another version of the LOOKUP function called the *array* form of the LOOKUP function, but using the HLOOKUP or VLOOKUP functions (described next) is generally preferred over using the array form of the LOOKUP function.

The HLOOKUP Function

The HLOOKUP function returns a data value in a single column of a group of cells based on a matching data value in the first row of the group of cells and a row number in the matching data value's corresponding column.

The HLOOKUP function takes four arguments: *lookup_value*, *table_array*, *row_index_num*, and *range_lookup*:

The required *lookup_value* argument specifies the data value to be found in the cell group's first row. The data value can be a number, a cell reference, or a string of text characters.

■Note If the value specified in the *lookup_value* argument is smaller than the smallest value in the first row of the group of cells, the HLOOKUP function returns the #N/A error value.

The required *table_array* argument is a reference to a group of cells, by using either a cell reference or a reference to a named range. The data values in the first row of the group of cells must be numbers, strings of text characters, or the values False or True.

The required *row_index_num* argument is the row number in the group of cells from which the matching data value will be returned.

■Note If the value of the *row_index_num* argument is less than 1, the HLOOKUP function returns the #VALUE! error value; if the value of the *row_index_num* argument is greater than the number of rows in the group of cells, the HLOOKUP function returns the #REF! error value.

The optional *range_lookup* argument specifies whether the HLOOKUP function uses an exact match or an approximate match to find the matching data value specified in the *lookup_value* argument, and takes the values True or False. If True is specified or omitted, an approximate match of the next largest value that is less than the data value specified in the *lookup_value* argument is used, and the data values in the cell group must be placed in ascending order. If False is specified, an exact match must be found or the #N/A error value is returned, and the data values in the cell group do not need to be sorted first.

The VLOOKUP Function

The VLOOKUP function returns a data value in a group of cells based on a matching data value in the first column of the group of cells and a column number in the matching data value's corresponding row.

The VLOOKUP function takes four arguments: *lookup_value, table_array, col_index_num*, and *range_lookup*:

The required *lookup_value* argument specifies the data value to be found in the cell group's first column. The data value can be a number, a cell reference, or a string of text characters.

■**Note** If the value specified in the *lookup_value* argument is smaller than the smallest value in the first column of the group of cells, the VLOOKUP function returns the #N/A error value.

The required *table_array* argument is a reference to a group of cells, by using either a cell reference or a reference to a named range. The data values in the first row of the group of cells must be numbers, strings of text characters, or the values False or True.

The required *col_index_num* argument is the column number in the group of cells from which the matching data value will be returned.

■**Note** If the value of the *col_index_num* argument is less than 1, the VLOOKUP function returns the #VALUE! error value; if the value of the *col_index_num* argument is greater than the number of columns in the group of cells, the VLOOKUP function returns the #REF! error value.

The optional *range_lookup* argument specifies whether the VLOOKUP function uses an exact match or an approximate match to find the matching data value specified in the *lookup_value* argument, and takes the values True or False. If True is specified or omitted, an approximate match of the next largest value that is less than the data value specified in the *lookup_value* argument is used, and the data values in the cell group must be placed in ascending order. If False is specified, an exact match must be found or the #N/A error value is returned, and the data values in the cell group do not need to be sorted first.

■**Note** If the VLOOKUP function can't find the data value specified in the *lookup_value* argument, and the value of the *range_lookup* argument is False, the VLOOKUP function returns the #N/A value.

The INDEX Function

The INDEX function returns a data value in a group of cells based on the intersection of a row number and column number.

The INDEX function takes two to five arguments depending on how you call it, and these arguments include *reference, array, row_num, column_num*, and *area_num*:

The *reference* argument is required if you are specifying more than one group of cells, and it specifies two or more cell references or a reference to two or more named cell ranges.

The *array* argument is required if you are specifying a single group of cells, and it specifies a cell reference or a reference to a named cell range.

The *row_num* argument is required if the group of cells contains more than one row, and it specifies the desired row number.

The *column_num* argument is required if the group of cells contains more than one column, and it specifies the desired column number.

■**Note** If the values of the *row_num* or the *column_num* arguments are not valid for the specified group of cells, the INDEX function returns the #REF! error value.

The *area_num* argument is required if the reference argument is specified, and it specifies the group of cells to use in calculating the intersection or the *row_num* and *column_num* arguments. The first cell group is numbered 1, the second is 2, and so on. If the *area_num* argument is omitted, the INDEX function uses cell group 1. For example, if the *area_num* argument specifies cell groups (B2:C4,D2:E5,F1:H3), then *area_num* 1 is the cell group B2:C4, *area_num* 2 is the cell group D2:E5, and *area_num* 3 is the cell group F1:H3.

The MATCH Function

The MATCH function returns the position of a data value in a group of cells.

The MATCH function takes three arguments: *lookup_value*, *lookup_array*, and *match_type*:

The required *lookup_value* argument is the data value you want to find in a group of cells. The data value can be a number, a string of text characters, the values True or False, a cell reference, or a reference to a named group of cells.

The required *lookup_array* argument is the group of cells in which you want to look.

The optional *match_type* argument is the number -1, 0, or 1, and specifies how the MATCH function finds the specified data value:

- If the *match_type* argument is set to 1 (or the *match_type* argument is omitted), the MATCH function finds the largest data value that is less than or equal to the specified data value, and the data values must appear in ascending order.

- If the *match_type* argument is set to 0, the MATCH function finds the data value that is exactly equal to the specified data value, but the data values can appear in any order.

- If the *match_type* argument is set to -1, the MATCH function finds the smallest data value that is greater than or equal to the specified data value, and the data values must appear in descending order.

■**Note** If the MATCH function cannot find a match, it returns the #N/A error value.

Tip

You can look up a value in a range that isn't sorted by using a combination of the INDEX and MATCH functions:

=INDEX(A1:B5, MATCH("Trucks", A1:A5, 0), MATCH("Price Each", A1:B1, 0))

For example, the preceding formula can be interpreted as follows:

The first occurrence of the MATCH function searches for the first occurrence in an unsorted list of data values (specified by the MATCH function's third argument of 0) of the exact string Trucks in cells A1 through A5. It then returns a number corresponding to the relative position of the cell with the string Trucks in that list of data values.

The second occurrence of the MATCH function searches for the first occurrence in an unsorted list of data values of the exact string Price Each in cells A1 through B1. It then returns a number corresponding to the relative position of the cell with the string Price Each in that list of data values.

The INDEX function then returns the data value in cells A1 through B5 at the intersection of the row with Trucks and the column with Price Each (the data value 32,950).

You can look up a value in a range of an unknown size that isn't sorted by using a combination of the OFFSET and MATCH functions:

=OFFSET(A1, MATCH("Trucks", A:A, 0), MATCH("Price Each", 1:1, 0) - 1)

For example, the preceding formula can be interpreted as follows:

The first occurrence of the MATCH function searches for the first occurrence in an unsorted list of data values (specified by the MATCH function's third argument of 0) of the exact string Trucks in column A. It then returns a number corresponding to the relative position of the cell with the string Trucks in that column.

The second occurrence of the MATCH function searches for the first occurrence in an unsorted list of data values of the exact string Price Each in row 1. It then returns a number corresponding to the relative position of the cell with the string Price Each in that row. The number 1 is subtracted from the number that the MATCH function returns in this case to account for the first column offset.

The OFFSET function then returns the data value by starting with cell A1, goes down the number of rows specified by the number returned by the first occurrence of the MATCH function, and then goes across the number of columns specified by the number returned by the second occurrence of the MATCH function (the data value 32,950).

Table 4-1 shows a representation of the data for additional context.

Table 4-1. *Vehicle Types and Prices Used in the Preceding INDEX/MATCH and OFFSET/MATCH Examples*

	A	B
1	Vehicle Type	Price Each
2	Cars	12995
3	Trucks	32950
4	Vans	22985
5	Minivans	18995

Try It

In this exercise, you will practice using the LOOKUP, HLOOKUP, VLOOKUP, INDEX, and MATCH worksheet functions to locate specific data values and use them in sales inventory calculations.

Open the ExcelDB_Ch04_01-05.xls file:

1. Start Excel.

2. Click Office Button ➤ Open (in Excel 2007) or File ➤ Open (in Excel 2003).

3. Browse to and select the ExcelDB_Ch04_01-05.xls file, and click Open.

4. Click the Lookups worksheet tab.

In cells E10 through E13, enter variations of the LOOKUP worksheet function to calculate the sales inventory for the number of vehicles in cells B2 through B5 multiplied by the vehicles' sales prices in cells E2 through E5.

In cell E10, type this formula, and press Enter: **=LOOKUP("Cars", $A$2:$A$5, $B$2:$B$5) *LOOKUP("Cars", $D$2:$D$5, $E$2:$E$5)**.

This formula can be interpreted as follows:

- Find the cell containing the word *Cars* in cells A2 through A5, and use the data value in the adjacent cell from cells B2 through B5 (cell B2 with the data value of 12,995).

- Find the cell containing the word *Cars* in cells D2 through D5, and use the data value in the adjacent cell from cells E2 through E5 (cell E2 with the data value of 100).

- Multiply the data values in cells B2 and E2 (1,299,500).

Type the following corresponding formulas in cells E11, E12, and E13 respectively, pressing Enter after typing each formula:

- **=LOOKUP("Trucks", $A$2:$A$5, $B$2:$B$5)*LOOKUP("Trucks", $D$2:$D$5, $E$2:$E$5)**

- **=LOOKUP("Vans", $A$2:$A$5, $B$2:$B$5)*LOOKUP("Vans", $D$2:$D$5, $E$2:$E$5)**

- **=LOOKUP("Minivans", $A$2:$A$5, $B$2:$B$5)*LOOKUP("Minivans", $D$2:$D$5, $E$2:$E$5)**

Results are calculated for the remaining vehicle types.

In cells B18 through B21, enter variations of the VLOOKUP worksheet function to calculate the sales inventory for the number of vehicles in cells B2 through B5 multiplied by the vehicles' sales prices in cells E2 through E5.

In cell B18, type this formula, and press Enter: **=VLOOKUP("Cars", Prices, 2, FALSE)** ***VLOOKUP("Cars", InStock, 2, FALSE)**.

This formula can be interpreted as follows:

- In the Prices named cell range (cells A1 through B5), find the word *Cars* in that named range's first column and use the data value in the named range's second column (cell B2).

- In the InStock named cell range (cells D1 through E5), find the word *Cars* in that named range's first column and use the data value in the named range's second column (cell E2).

- Multiply the data values in cells B2 and E2 (1,299,500).

Type the following corresponding formulas in cells B19, B20, and B21 respectively, pressing Enter after typing each formula:

- **=VLOOKUP("Trucks", Prices, 2, FALSE)*VLOOKUP("Trucks", InStock, 2, FALSE)**

- **=VLOOKUP("Vans", Prices, 2, FALSE)*VLOOKUP("Vans", InStock, 2, FALSE)**

- **=VLOOKUP("Minivans", Prices, 2, FALSE)*VLOOKUP("Minivans", InStock, 2, FALSE)**

Results are calculated for the remaining vehicle types.

In cells E18 through E21, enter variations of the HLOOKUP worksheet function to calculate the sales inventory for the number of vehicles in cells B2 through B5 multiplied by the vehicles' sales prices in cells E2 through E5.

In cell E18, type this formula, and press Enter: **=HLOOKUP("Price Each", Prices, 2, FALSE)** ***HLOOKUP("In Stock", InStock, 2, FALSE)**.

This formula can be interpreted as the following:

- In the Prices named cell range (cells A1 through B5), find the words *Price Each* in that named range's first row and use the data value in the Price Each column's second cell down (cell B2).

- In the InStock named cell range (cells D1 through E5), find the words *In Stock* in that named range's first row and use the data value in the In Stock column's second cell down (cell E2).

- Multiply the data values in cells B2 and E2 (1,299,500).

Type these corresponding formulas in cells E19, E20, and E21 respectively, pressing Enter after typing each formula:

- **=HLOOKUP("Price Each", Prices, 3, FALSE)*HLOOKUP("In Stock", InStock, 3, FALSE)**

- **=HLOOKUP("Price Each", Prices, 4, FALSE)*HLOOKUP("In Stock", InStock, 4, FALSE)**

- **=HLOOKUP("Price Each", Prices, 5, FALSE)*HLOOKUP("In Stock", InStock, 5, FALSE)**

Results are calculated for the remaining vehicle types.

In cells B26 through B29, enter variations of the INDEX worksheet function to calculate the sales inventory for the number of vehicles in cells B2 through B5 multiplied by the vehicles' sales prices in cells E2 through E5.

In cell B26, type this formula, and press Enter: **=INDEX(Prices, 2, 2)*INDEX(InStock, 2, 2)**. This formula can be interpreted as follows:

- In the Prices named cell range (cells A1 through B5), use the data value at the intersection of that named range's second row and second column (cell B2).

- In the InStock named cell range (cells D1 through E5), use the data value at the intersection of that named range's second row and second column (cell E2).

- Multiply the data values in cells B2 and E2 (1,299,500).

Type these corresponding formulas in cells B27, B28, and B29 respectively, pressing Enter after typing each formula:

- **=INDEX(Prices, 3, 2)*INDEX(InStock, 3, 2)**

- **=INDEX(Prices, 4, 2)*INDEX(InStock, 4, 2)**

- **=INDEX(Prices, 5, 2)*INDEX(InStock, 5, 2)**

Results are calculated for the remaining vehicle types.

In cells E26 through E29, enter variations of the MATCH worksheet function to calculate the relative position of specific vehicle types in the list of available vehicle types in cells A1 through A5.

In cell E26, type this formula, and press Enter: **=MATCH("Cars",A1:A5,0)**. This formula can be interpreted as follows:

- In cells A1 through A5, find the cell with the word *Cars* and note its relative position in those cells (2).

Type these corresponding formulas in cells E27, E28, and E29 respectively, pressing Enter after typing each formula:

- **=MATCH("Trucks",A1:A5,0)**

- **=MATCH("Vans",A1:A5,0)**

- **=MATCH("Minivans",A1:A5,0)**

Relative positions are calculated for the remaining vehicle types.

4.5 Use the Lookup Wizard

You can use Excel's Lookup Wizard to create a lookup formula that returns the value at the intersection of a given row and column, provided there is a group of worksheet cells that have both row and column labels. The Lookup Wizard uses a combination of the INDEX and MATCH worksheet functions to create the formula.

Quick Start

To use the Lookup Wizard, in Excel 2007, click Formulas ➤ (Solutions) Lookup. In Excel 2003, click Tools ➤ Lookup. Follow the instructions in the wizard.

■**Note** If the Lookup command is not available, see the sidebar in the "How To" section for how to make the command visi ble.

How To

To use the Lookup Wizard, in Excel 2007, click Formulas ➤ (Solutions) Lookup. In Excel 2003, click Tools ➤ Lookup.

1. In the wizard's Step 1 of 4 page, in the Where Is the Range to Search, Including Row and Column Labels box, type the cell reference or select the cells to search. Then click Next.

2. In the wizard's Step 2 of 4 page, in the Select the Column Label list, select the column label reference.

3. In the Select the Row Label list, select the row label reference. Then click Next.

4. In the wizard's Step 3 of 4 page, click the Copy Just the Formula to a Single Cell option to return the formula into a specific cell, or click the Copy the Formula and Lookup Parameters option to return the result and the lookup parameters into specific cells. Then click Next.

MAKE THE LOOKUP COMMAND VISIBLE

If the Lookup command is not visible in the Formulas ➤ (Solutions) group (in Excel 2007) or on the Tools menu (in Excel 2003), you can add it by doing the following in Excel 2007:

1. Click Office Button ➤ Excel Options.

2. In the left pane, click Add-Ins.

3. In the Manage list toward the bottom of the screen, with the Excel Add-Ins selection visible, click the Go button.

4. In the Add-Ins Available list, select the Lookup Wizard check box, and click OK.

In Excel 2003, do the following:

1. Click Tools ➤ Add-Ins.

2. Select the Lookup Wizard check box, and click OK.

5. If you clicked the Copy Just the Formula to a Single Cell option in the previous step 4 of this list, in the wizard's Step 4 of 4 page, type the cell reference or select the cell to return the formula. Then click Finish.

If you clicked the Copy the Formula and Lookup Parameters option in step 4 of this list, do the following:

   a. In the wizard's Step 4 of 6 page, in the Type or Select a Cell and Then Click Next box, type the cell reference or click the cell into which you want to return the first parameter. Then click Next.

   b. In the wizard's Step 5 of 6 page, in the Type or Select a Cell and Then Click Next box, type the cell reference or click the cell into which you want to return the second parameter. Then click Next.

   c. In the wizard's Step 6 of 6 page, in the Type or Select a Cell and Then Click Finish box, type the cell reference or click the cell into which you want to return the formula. Then click Finish. The formula—and parameters, if you selected that option earlier—are returned into the specified cells.

Try It

In this exercise, you will use the Lookup Wizard to locate specific data values and use them in sales inventory calculations.

Open the ExcelDB_Ch04_01-05.xls file, and click the Lookups worksheet tab.

In cells H10 through J13, use the Lookup Wizard to calculate the sales inventory for the number of vehicles in cells B2 through B5 multiplied by the vehicles' sales prices in cells E2 through E5, as follows:

1. In Excel 2007, click Formulas ➤ (Solutions) Lookup. In Excel 2003, click Tools ➤ Lookup.

2. Click the Where Is the Range to Search, Including the Row and Column Labels box, select cells A1 through B5, and click Next.

3. In the Select the Column Label list, select Price Each.

4. In the Select the Row Label list, select Cars, and click Next.

5. Click Next again.

6. Click the Type or Select a Cell and Then Click Finish box, click cell H10, and click Finish.

7. Repeat steps 1 through 6 for cells H11 through H13, respectively, specifying the following values in the Lookup Wizard:

   • For cell H11, search cells A1 through B5, and use the Price Each column and Trucks row labels.

   • For cell H12, search cells A1 through B5, and use the Price Each column and Vans row labels.

   • For cell H13, search cells A1 through B5, and use the Price Each column and Minivans row labels.

8. Repeat steps 1 through 6 for cells I10 through I13, respectively, specifying the following values in the Lookup Wizard:

- For cell I10, search cells D1 through E5, use the In Stock column and Cars row labels.

- For cell I11, search cells D1 through E5, use the In Stock column and Trucks row labels.

- For cell I12, search cells D1 through E5, use the In Stock column and Vans row labels.

- For cell I13, search cells D1 through E5, use the In Stock column and Minivans row labels.

Now, calculate the subtotals for cells H10 through I13:

1. Click cell J10, type **=PRODUCT(H10:I10)**, and press Enter.

2. Drag the fill handle (the small black box in the lower right corner of cell J10) to cell J13.

CHAPTER 5

■ ■ ■

Connect to Other Databases

You can use Excel to connect to any external database for which you have an accompanying ODBC driver or OLE DB provider (software translation programs that allow Excel to connect to external data). Once you have connected to an external database, you can use most if not all of Excel's built-in features for viewing, finding, refreshing, and analyzing the data associated with that database.

Some of the ODBC drivers and OLE DB providers that ship with Excel include the following:

- Microsoft Office Excel
- Microsoft Office Access
- Microsoft SQL Server
- Microsoft Windows SharePoint lists and document libraries
- Microsoft Business Solutions
- Microsoft Visual FoxPro
- dBASE
- Oracle
- Paradox
- Text file databases

This chapter describes how to establish connections from Excel to other external Excel databases as well as Access databases, SQL Server databases, and OLAP databases hosted in SQL Server Analysis Services. For information on how to connect to other database types, contact the specific database's manufacturer.

5.1 Create a Reusable Connection to External Data

If you find yourself connecting repeatedly from several Excel workbooks to data in a specific database, you can create a reusable connection to that data. Over time, this approach is more efficient than specifying the same connection information each time you want to connect to the same data.

Quick Start

To create a reusable connection to external data, do the following:

1. In Excel 2007 click Data ➤ Get External Data ➤ Existing Connections, and then click Browse for More. In Excel 2003, click Data ➤ Import External Data ➤ Import Data.

2. Click New Source.

3. Follow the onscreen directions to import the data into the current Excel workbook and create the connection file during the import operation. This connection file can be reused during subsequent import operations.

How To

To create a reusable connection, do the following:

1. In Excel 2007 click Data ➤ Get External Data ➤ Existing Connections, and then click Browse for More. In Excel 2003, click Data ➤ Import External Data ➤ Import Data.

2. Click New Source.

3. In the What Kind of Data Source Do You Want to Connect To list, make one of these selections:

   - If you select Microsoft SQL Server, Microsoft SQL Server OLAP Services, or Microsoft Data Access – OLE DB Provider for Oracle (in Excel 2007) or Oracle (in Excel 2003), Excel will ask you to provide the server name and logon credentials. Excel will then ask you for additional connection information based on the selected database type.

   - If you select Microsoft Business Solutions, Excel will ask you to provide the computer name or URL to where the accompanying *data retrieval service* (a Web service installed on Windows SharePoint Services for connecting to and retrieving data) is located. Excel will then ask you for additional connection information based on the selected computer name or URL.

   - If you select ODBC DSN, Excel will ask you to select an available ODBC driver type or data source name such as dBASE files, Excel files, or MS Access Database. Once you select an available ODBC driver type or data source name, the Data Connection Wizard will ask you for additional connection information depending on the selected ODBC driver type or data source name.

   - If you select Other/Advanced, Excel will ask you to select an available OLE DB provider. Once you select an available OLE DB provider on the Data Link Properties dialog box's Provider tab, click Next. The Data Link Properties dialog box will ask you for additional connection information on the Connection tab depending on the selected OLE DB provider.

4. After you supply Excel with the requested connection details, click OK or Next depending on the displayed dialog box. The Save Data Connection File and Finish page appears.

5. In the File Name box, type a name for the connection file. Click Browse to save the connection file to a specified location.

6. Depending on the selected data source, Excel may ask for additional connection information, or Excel may ask you to import the associated data directly into the current workbook.

After you finish importing the data, the connection information is saved as a reusable connection with the file extension .odc.

Once you create a reusable connection, reusing the connection file is straightforward:

1. In Excel 2007, click Data ➤ Get External Data ➤ Existing Connections. In Excel 2003, click Data ➤ Import External Data ➤ Import Data.

2. Browse to and select the connection file, and click Open.

3. Follow the onscreen directions to finish importing the external data into the current Excel workbook.

Try It

In this exercise, you will practice creating a reusable connection to a Microsoft Office Access database file. You will use the connection file to connect to the same Access database from two separate Excel worksheets.

Create the reusable connection file:

1. Start Excel.

2. With a new blank worksheet visible, in Excel 2007, click Data ➤ Get External Data ➤ Existing Connections, and then click Browse for More. In Excel 2003, click Data ➤ Import External Data ➤ Import Data.

3. Click New Source.

4. In the What Kind of Data Source Do You Want to Connect To, select ODBC DSN, and click Next.

5. In the ODBC Data Sources list, select MS Access Database, and click Next.

6. Browse to and select the ExcelDB_Ch05_01_04.mdb file, and click OK.

7. Clear the Connect to a Specific Table check box, and click Next.

8. In the Description box, type **Alaska Fish Counts and World Populations**.

9. In the Search Keywords box, type **Alaska fish counts world populations**, and click Finish.

10. Click Cancel.

Use the connection file to connect to the same Access database from two separate Excel worksheets:

1. With the Sheet1 worksheet tab of the new blank worksheet selected, in Excel 2007, click Data ➤ Get External Data ➤ Existing Connections. In Excel 2003, click Data ➤ Import External Data ➤ Import Data.

2. Select the ExcelDB_Ch05_01_04 connection file, and click Open.

3. In the Select Table dialog box, select AlaskaFishCounts, and click OK.

4. With the Existing worksheet option selected, click OK.

5. Click the Sheet2 worksheet tab, and in Excel 2007, click Data ➤ Get External Data ➤ Existing Connections. In Excel 2003, click Data ➤ Import External Data ➤ Import Data.

6. Select the ExcelDB_Ch05_01_04 connection file, and click Open.

■**Note** In Excel 2007, make sure to select the ExcelDB_Ch05_01_04 connection file listed in the Connection Files on This Computer section. If you select the ExcelDB_Ch05_01_04 connection file listed in the Connections in This Workbook section, you will not be able to complete the next step.

---

7. In the Select Table dialog box, select WorldPopulations, and click OK.

8. With the Existing worksheet option selected, click OK.

5.2 Adjust External Data While Importing

Before you connect to data in an external database, you may want to adjust the amount of data that Excel imports from that database during the import operation, either by importing specific data rows or data columns, by presorting the data, or by joining separate data tables together. To do this, you use a tool included with Excel named Microsoft Query.

■**Note** To use Microsoft Query in conjunction with an external database, you must first install that database's ODBC driver on the same computer that Excel is installed. ODBC drivers for Access, Excel, SQL Server, Microsoft Visual FoxPro, dBASE, Oracle, Paradox, and text file databases are included with Excel. For ODBC drivers for other database types, contact that database's manufacturer.

Quick Start

To use Microsoft Query to adjust external data while importing, do the following:

1. In Excel 2007, click Data ➤ Get External Data ➤ From Other Sources ➤ From Microsoft Query. In Excel 2003, click Data ➤ Import External Data ➤ New Database Query.

2. In the Choose Data Source dialog box, click the Databases tab, and click one of the available database types.

3. With the Use the Query Wizard to Create/Edit Queries check box selected, click OK.

4. Depending on the database type, complete the onscreen directions to finish importing the data into the current Excel workbook, start Microsoft Query and perform more advanced data filtering operations before importing the data into the current Excel workbook, or create an offline cube file from the imported data.

How To

To use Microsoft Query to adjust external data while importing it into the current Excel workbook, do the following:

1. In Excel 2007, click Data ➤ Get External Data ➤ From Other Sources ➤ From Microsoft Query. In Excel 2003, click Data ➤ Import External Data ➤ New Database Query.

2. In the Choose Data Source dialog box, click the Databases tab, and click one of the available database types.

3. With the Use the Query Wizard to Create/Edit Queries check box selected, click OK.

4. Depending on the database type, complete the onscreen directions to specify the database file or database connection details.

5. Select the newly created database connection entry, and click OK.

6. In the Query Wizard – Choose Columns page, in the Available Tables and Columns list, select the desired data columns to include in the incoming data, and click the arrow key to move the selected data columns to the Columns in Your Query list. Then click Next.

7. In the Query Wizard – Filter Data page, in the Column to Filter list, select any desired data columns by which to filter the incoming data. For each selected data column, in the Only Include Rows Where area, specify the filter criteria. Then click Next.

8. In the Query Wizard – Sort Order page, in the Sort By and Then By lists, select any desired data columns by which to sort the incoming data. Also click the Ascending or Descending options as desired. Then click Next.

9. In the Query Wizard – Finish page, do one of these options:

- Select the Return Data to Microsoft Office Excel option to import the data into the current Excel workbook.

- Select the View Data or Edit Query in Microsoft Query option to start Microsoft Query and perform more advanced data filtering operations before importing the data into the current Excel workbook.

- In Excel 2003 only, select the Create an OLAP Cube From This Query option to start the OLAP Cube Wizard and create an offline cube file from the imported data. Excel uses the offline cube file's contents to display the imported data.

10. If desired, click the Save Query button to save the data filtering details that you specified in the Query Wizard to a query file with the file extension .dqy. Provide the query file name and location in the Save As dialog box, and then click Save.

▓**Note** .dqy files can be reused on subsequent data import operations. In Excel 2007, click Data ➤ Get External Data ➤ From Other Sources ➤ From Microsoft Query, and then click the Queries tab. In Excel 2003, click Data ➤ Import External Data ➤ New Database Query, and then click the Queries tab.

---

11. Click Finish, and complete the onscreen directions to finish importing the data into the current Excel workbook; start Microsoft Query and perform more advanced data filtering operations before importing the data into the current Excel workbook; or in Excel 2003 create an offline cube file from the imported data.

Try It

In this exercise, you will practice using Microsoft Query to filter data in a text file as you are importing it into the current Excel workbook. You will also practice changing the data in the text file and refreshing the changed data in the Excel workbook.

Use Microsoft Query to filter data in the text file as you are importing it:

1. Start Excel.

2. With a new blank worksheet visible, in Excel 2007, click Data ➤ Get External Data ➤ From Other Sources ➤ From Microsoft Query. In Excel 2003, click Data ➤ Import External Data ➤ New Database Query.

3. In the Choose Data Source dialog box, with the Databases tab selected, click <New Data Source>, and click OK.

4. In the What Name Do You Want to Give Your Data Source, type **Alaska Fish Counts Text File**.

5. In the Select a Driver for the Type of Database You Want to Access list, select Microsoft Text Driver (*.txt; *.csv).

6. Click the Connect button.

7. Clear the Use Current Directory check box, and click the Select Directory button.

8. Browse to the folder containing the ExcelDB_Ch05_02.csv file, and click OK.

9. Click OK three more times in Excel 2007, and two more times in Excel 2003.

10. In the Choose Data Source dialog box, with the Databases tab selected, click Alaska Fish Counts Text File, and click OK.

Instruct the Query Wizard to only display rows where the city name contains the word *Creek* as follows:

1. In the Query Wizard – Choose Columns page, in the Available Tables and Columns list, select ExcelDB_Ch5_02.csv, click the right arrow (>) button, and click Next.

2. In the Query Wizard – Filter Data page, in the Column to Filter list, click City.

3. In the Only Include Rows Where list, in the top left list, select Contains.

4. In the top right box, type **Creek**, then click Next.

5. Since the results will already be sorted by city name, in the Query Wizard – Sort Order page, click Next.

6. In the Query Wizard – Finish page, click the Save Query button.

7. In the File Name box, type **Alaska Fish Counts Text File Query**, and click Save.

8. With the Return Data to Microsoft Excel option selected, click Finish.

9. With the Existing Worksheet option selected, click OK. Excel displays data records for six cities with the word *Creek* in their city names.

Change the data in the text file and refresh the changed data in the Excel workbook:

1. Using Windows Notepad, open the ExcelDB_Ch05_02.csv file.

2. Find the following line of text in the file: Alexander Creek,1,0,0.

3. Insert a blank line beneath this line and type the following text: **Alexandria Creek South,42,79,99**.

4. Save the file, and then return to Excel.

5. With the six cities visible in the worksheet, click any single cell inside the data, and then click Data (Connections) ➤ Refresh All (in Excel 2007) or click Data ➤ Refresh Data (in Excel 2003). The text *Alexandria Creek South,42,79,99* appears as a seventh matching data record.

6. Change the text in the worksheet from Alexandria Creek South to Alexander Creek North, and then click Data ➤ (Connections) Refresh All (in Excel 2007) or click Data ➤ Refresh Data (in Excel 2003).

The text changes back to *Alexandria Creek South*, because this is the text that is refreshed from the original connected text file.

5.3 Connect to Excel Data in Other Workbooks

In most circumstances, you will want to simply open an Excel workbook directly rather than import the workbook's data into another workbook. But there are some scenarios in which you might want to import a portion of an external workbook's data. For example, you may not want to risk modifying the data in the external workbook, so you decide to view, modify, and analyze a copy of the data from another workbook. You can refresh the copied data with the data values in the other workbook if you decide you ever want to start over with the original data values. Similarly, perhaps the data in the external workbook is updated frequently. You don't want to interrupt the data updating process, so you decide to view and analyze the constantly updating data from another workbook. You can refresh the data from the other workbook if you need to view and analyze the most up-to-date data.

Quick Start

To connect to Excel data in a workbook other than the current workbook, do the following:

1. In Excel 2007, click Data ➤ Get External Data ➤ Existing Connections, and then click Browse for More. In Excel 2003, click Data ➤ Import External Data ➤ Import Data.

2. With the Files of Type list displaying All Files, browse to and select the desired connection file or Excel workbook file, and click Open.

3. Complete the onscreen directions to finish importing the workbook's data into the current workbook.

How To

To connect to Excel data in a workbook other than the current workbook, do the following:

1. In Excel 2007, click Data ➤ Get External Data ➤ Existing Connections, and then click Browse for More. In Excel 2003, click Data ➤ Import External Data ➤ Import Data.

2. With the Files of Type list displaying All Files, browse to and select the desired connection file or Excel workbook file, and click Open.

3. In the Select Table dialog box, click the desired worksheet in the workbook, and click OK.

4. Go to the Import Data dialog box and do the following:

   a. In Excel 2007 only, click the Table, PivotTable Report, PivotChart and PivotTable Report, or Only Create Connection option to view the data as a data table, a Pivot-Table, or a PivotChart and PivotTable, or to create a reusable connection file, respectively.

   b. Click the Properties button to modify the default data refresh, formatting, and layout options.

c. In Excel 2003 only, click the Edit Query button to start the Query Wizard and adjust the data as it is being imported into the current workbook.

d. Click Existing Worksheet to import the data into the current worksheet, starting with the current worksheet cell.

e. Click New Worksheet to create a new worksheet in the current workbook and import the data into the newly created worksheet.

f. In Excel 2003 only, click Create a PivotTable Report to create a PivotTable in the current worksheet or a newly created worksheet.

■Note The preceding procedures assume that you want to import all of the data on the selected worksheet into the current Excel workbook. If you want to filter the imported data during the import operation, use Microsoft Query. For more information, see section "5.2: Adjust External Data While Importing."

Try It

In this exercise, you will practice importing data from an external Excel workbook into a new blank workbook:

1. Start Excel.

2. With a new blank worksheet visible, in Excel 2007, click Data ➤ Get External Data ➤ Existing Connections, and then click Browse for More. In Excel 2003, click Data ➤ Import External Data ➤ Import Data.

3. With the Files of Type list displaying All Files, browse to and select the ExcelDB_Ch05_03.xls file, and then click Open.

4. In the Select Table dialog box, click the Production$ worksheet, and click OK.

5. Click OK again to finish importing the worksheet's data into the current worksheet, beginning with the selected worksheet cell.

5.4 Connect to Microsoft Office Access Data

Although Access has a number of powerful features for working with data, Excel has a number of additional tools to complement these features for viewing, finding, and analyzing data. You can use Excel to import data from Access and then use Excel's tools to perform additional data analysis.

Quick Start

To connect to Access data, do the following:

1. In Excel 2007, click Data ➤ Get External Data ➤ From Access. In Excel 2003, click Data ➤ Import External Data ➤ Import Data.

2. With the Files of Type list displaying Access Databases, browse to and select the desired Access database file, and click Open.

3. Complete the onscreen directions to finish importing the desired Access data table or data query results into the current workbook.

How To

To connect to Access data, do the following:

1. In Excel 2007, click Data ➤ Get External Data ➤ From Access. In Excel 2003, click Data ➤ Import External Data ➤ Import Data.

2. While the Files of Type list is displaying Access Databases, browse to and select the desired Access database file, and click Open.

3. In the Select Table dialog box, click the desired data table or data query in the database file, and click OK.

4. In the Import Data dialog box, do the following:

   a. In Excel 2007 only, click the Table, PivotTable Report, PivotChart and PivotTable Report, or Only Create Connection option to view the data as a data table, a Pivot-Table, or a PivotChart and PivotTable, or to create a reusable connection file, respectively.

   b. Click the Properties button to modify the default data refresh, formatting, and layout options.

   c. In Excel 2003 only, click the Edit Query button to start the Query Wizard and adjust the data as it is being imported into the current workbook.

   d. Click Existing Worksheet to import the data into the current worksheet, starting with the current worksheet cell.

   e. Click New Worksheet to create a new worksheet in the current workbook and import the data into the newly created worksheet.

   f. In Excel 2003 only, click Create a PivotTable report to create a PivotTable in the current worksheet or a newly created worksheet.

Note The preceding procedures assume that you want to import all of the data in the selected data table or the data query results into the current Excel workbook. If you want to filter the imported data during the import operation, use Microsoft Query. For more information, see section "5.2: Adjust External Data While Importing."

Try It

In this exercise, you will practice importing data from an Access database into a blank Excel workbook:

1. In Excel 2007, click Data ➤ Get External Data ➤ From Access. In Excel 2003, click Data ➤ Import External Data ➤ Import Data.

2. With the Files of Type list displaying Access Databases, browse to and select the ExcelDB_Ch05_01_04.mdb file, and then click Open.

3. In the Select Table dialog box, click the WorldPopulations data table, and then click OK.

4. Click OK again to finish importing the table's data into the current worksheet, beginning with the selected worksheet cell.

5.5 Connect to Microsoft SQL Server Data

Although SQL Server is a powerful database management system, it doesn't have the range of built-in data analysis tools that Excel does. You can use Excel to import data from SQL Server and then use Excel's wide variety of tools to perform rich data analysis.

Quick Start

To connect to SQL Server data, do the following:

1. In Excel 2007, click Data ➤ Get External Data ➤ From Other Sources ➤ From SQL Server. In Excel 2003, click Data ➤ Import External Data ➤ Import Data. Then, with the Files of Type list displaying All Files, browse to and select the desired SQL Server connection file, or click New Source.

2. Complete the onscreen directions to finish importing the desired SQL Server data table or data view into the current workbook.

How To

To connect to SQL Server data, do the following:

1. In Excel 2007, click Data ➤ Get External Data ➤ From Other Sources ➤ From SQL Server. In Excel 2003, click Data ➤ Import External Data ➤ Import Data. Then, with the Files of Type list displaying All Files, browse to and select the desired SQL Server connection file, or click New Source.

2. If you are using Excel 2007, or you click New Source in Excel 2003, do the following, otherwise skip to step 3:

   a. In Excel 2003 only, in the What Kind of Data Source Do You Want to Connect To list, select Microsoft SQL Server, and click Next.

   b. In Excel 2007 and Excel 2003, in the Server Name box, type the desired SQL Server instance name.

   c. In the Log on Credentials area, do one of the following:

      • Click the Use Windows Authentication option if the SQL Server is set up to accept your Windows login name and password to determine the data tables to which you can connect.

      • Click the Use the Following User Name and Password option if the SQL Server is set up to accept a specific user name and password to determine the data tables to which you can connect. Type the specific user name and password in the User Name and Password boxes.

   d. Click Next.

   e. In the Select the Database That Contains the Data You Want list, select the desired database on the SQL Server.

   f. In the list of data tables and data views, select the desired data table or data view, and then click Next.

   g. On the Save Connection File and Finish page, specify the reusable connection file name and location and optionally a description and search keywords. Then click Finish.

   h. In Excel 2003 only, in the Select Data Source dialog box, select the newly created connection file, and click Open.

3. In the Import Data dialog box, do one or more of the following:

   • In Excel 2007 only, click the Table, PivotTable Report, PivotChart and PivotTable Report, or Only Create Connection option to view the data as a data table, a PivotTable, or a PivotChart and PivotTable, or to create a reusable connection file, respectively.

   • Click the Properties button to modify the default data refresh, formatting, and layout options.

   • In Excel 2003 only, click the Edit Query button to start the Query Wizard and adjust the data as it is being imported into the current workbook.

- Click Existing Worksheet to import the data into the current worksheet, starting with the current worksheet cell.

- Click New Worksheet to create a new worksheet in the current workbook and import the data into the newly created worksheet.

- In Excel 2003 only, click Create a PivotTable Report to create a PivotTable in the current worksheet or a newly created worksheet.

■**Note** The preceding procedures assume that you want to import all of the data in the selected data table or the data view into the current Excel workbook. If you want to filter the imported data during the import operation, use Microsoft Query. For more information, see section "5.2: Adjust External Data While Importing."

Try It

In this exercise, you will practice importing data from a Microsoft SQL Server 2005 Express Edition database table into a new blank Excel workbook.

■**Note** This exercise was written using Microsoft SQL Server 2005 Express Edition, SQL Server Management Studio Express, and the AdventureWorks sample databases installed. To install these components, see Microsoft SQL Server 2005 Express Edition "Download Now!" at `http://msdn.microsoft.com/vstudio/express/sql/download`. If you have an edition of SQL Server 2005 that is greater than Express Edition, some of these steps will differ slightly.

Verify that the AdventureWorks sample database is available from SQL Server 2005 Express Edition:

1. Start SQL Server Management Studio Express (click Start ➤ All Programs ➤ Microsoft SQL Server 2005 ➤ SQL Server Management Studio Express).

2. In the Connect to Server dialog box, do the following:

   a. In the Server Name list, select the server instance name on which the Adventure-Works sample database should be installed.

   b. In the Authentication list, select Windows Authentication or SQL Server Authentication, depending on how you set up the SQL Server to authenticate logins. If you select SQL Server Authentication, enter the user name and password in the User Name and Password boxes.

3. Click Connect.

4. In the Object Explorer pane (if the Object Explorer pane is not visible, click View ➤ Object Explorer), expand the server instance name on which the AdventureWorks sample database should be installed, and expand Databases. A node named AdventureWorks should be visible.

If you do not see an AdventureWorks node, you likely have not yet attached the AdventureWorks sample database to SQL Server 2005 Express Edition, and you will not be able to successfully import the data into Excel until you attach the sample database. You can attach the AdventureWorks sample database to SQL Server 2005 Express Edition by doing the following:

1. In the Object Explorer pane, right-click the Databases folder under the server instance name on which the AdventureWorks sample database should be installed, and click Attach.

2. Click the Add button.

3. In the Select the File list, browse to and select the AdventureWorks_Data.mdf file (this file is typically available in the *<drive>*:\Program Files\Microsoft SQL Server\MSSQL.1\ MSSQL\Data folder), and click OK.

4. Click OK again. The AdventureWorks node appears in the Object Explorer pane.

5. Quit SQL Server Management Studio Express.

Import data from the AdventureWorks sample database into a new blank Excel workbook by doing the following:

1. In Excel 2007, click Data ➤ Get External Data ➤ From Other Sources ➤ From SQL Server, and skip directly to the next step. In Excel 2003, click Data ➤ Import External Data ➤ Import Data. Click the New Source button. Then, in the What Kind of Data Source Do You Want to Connect To list, select Microsoft SQL Server, and click Next.

2. In the Server Name box, type the server instance name on which the AdventureWorks sample database is installed.

3. In the Log on Credentials area, do one of the following:

- Click the Use Windows Authentication option if the SQL Server is set up to accept your Windows login name and password to determine the data tables to which you can connect.

- Click the Use the Following User Name and Password option if the SQL Server is set up to accept a specific user name and password to determine the data tables to which you can connect. Type the specific user name and password in the User Name and Password boxes.

4. Click Next.

5. In the Select the Database That Contains the Data You Want list, select Adventure-Works.

6. Clear the Connect to a Specific Table check box, and then click Next.

7. On the Save Connection File and Finish page, in the Description box, type **SQL Server AdventureWorks Sample Database Connection.**

8. In the Search Keywords box, type **AdventureWorks**, and then click Finish.

9. In Excel 2003 only, in the Select Data Source dialog box, with the reusable connection file ending in AdventureWorks.odc selected, click Open.

10. In the Select Table dialog box, select the Product table, and click OK.

11. Click OK again to finish importing the table's data into the current worksheet, beginning with the selected worksheet cell.

5.6 Connect to OLAP Data in Microsoft SQL Server Analysis Services

You can use Microsoft SQL Server Analysis Services to summarize data originating in large data warehouses. The summarized data is typically stored in one or more cubes or cube files. You can use Excel to view the summarized data in these cubes and cube files.

■**Note** For more information about cube files, see section "1.5: Learn About Multidimensional Databases" in Chapter 1.

Quick Start

In Excel, to open and work with the data in a cube or cube file, do the following:

1. In Excel 2007, click Data ➤ Get External Data ➤ From Other Sources ➤ From Microsoft Query. In Excel 2003, click Data ➤ Import External Data ➤ New Database Query.

2. In the Choose Data Source dialog box, on the OLAP Cubes tab, do the following if the desired cube or cube file is not visible; otherwise, skip to step 3:

    a. With the <New Data Source> item selected, click OK.

    b. Complete the options in the Create New Data Source dialog box, and then click OK.

3. Select the cube or cube file on the OLAP Cubes tab, and then click OK.

4. Complete the options in the Import Data dialog box, and then click OK.

5. Use the PivotTable Field List to create and work with a PivotTable and optionally a PivotChart.

How To

In Excel, to open and work with the data in a cube or cube file, do the following:

1. In Excel 2007, click Data ➤ Get External Data ➤ From Other Sources ➤ From Microsoft Query. In Excel 2003, click Data ➤ Import External Data ➤ New Database Query.

2. In the Choose Data Source dialog box, on the OLAP Cubes tab, do the following if the desired cube or cube file is not visible; otherwise, skip to step 3:

   a. With the <New Data Source> item selected, click OK.

   b. In the Create New Data Source dialog box, in the What Name Do you Want to Give Your Data Source, type a name for the cube or cube file data source.

   c. In the Select an OLAP Provider for the Database You Want to Access list, select the appropriate OLAP provider, depending on the cube or cube file's data format.

   d. Click the Connect button.

   e. Go to the Multidimensional Connection dialog box, and do the following:

      • If the cube is stored in a SQL Server Analysis Services server, with the Analysis Server option selected, in the Server box, type the server name on which the cube is stored (and if needed, type the appropriate user name in the User ID box and password in the Password box); click Next; specify the database on which the cube is stored; and then click Finish.

      • If the cube file is stored in a file with the .cub extension, click the Cube File option, and type the full path to the cube file; or click the ellipsis (. . .) button, browse to and select the desired cube file, click Open, and then click Finish.

   f. In the Create New Data Source dialog box, click OK.

3. Select the desired cube or cube file on the OLAP Cubes tab, and then click OK.

4. Complete the options in the Import Data dialog box to create a PivotTable, a PivotTable and PivotChart, or a connection file only, and put the data on an existing worksheet or new worksheet, and then click OK.

5. Use the PivotTable Field List to create and work with a PivotTable (and optionally a PivotChart).

Try It

In this exercise, you will use Excel to connect to and view data in a cube stored on a Microsoft SQL Server Analysis Services server.

INSTALLING SQL SERVER AND THE SAMPLE DATA

This exercise was written using Microsoft SQL Server 2005 Standard Edition and Microsoft SQL Server 2005 Analysis Services installed, with the AdventureWorksDW sample database, Analysis Services Tutorial sample Analysis Services database, and Analysis Services Tutorial sample cube deployed accordingly. For more information, see the following:

- For more information on SQL Server 2005 Standard Edition see `http://www.microsoft.com/sql/editions/standard`.

- For more information on SQL Server 2005 Analysis Services see `http://www.microsoft.com/sql/technologies/analysis`.

- To install the AdventureWorksDW sample database on SQL Server 2005, search the Microsoft Download Center at `http://www.microsoft.com/downloads` using the **AdventureWorks** keyword, and then click the SQL Server 2005 Samples and Sample Databases link.

- For more information on creating and deploying the Analysis Services Tutorial sample database and sample cube, see the SQL Server 2005 Analysis Services Tutorial in SQL Server 2005 Books Online. To install SQL Server 2005 Books Online, search the Microsoft Download Center at `http://www.microsoft.com/downloads` using **SQL Server 2005 Books Online** as the search text, and then click the resulting SQL Server 2005 Books Online link.

To connect to the Analysis Services Tutorial cube on the Analysis Services server, do the following:

1. With Excel started and a blank workbook visible, in Excel 2007, click Data ➤ Get External Data ➤ From Other Sources ➤ From Microsoft Query. In Excel 2003, click Data ➤ Import External Data ➤ New Database Query.

2. Go to the Choose Data Source dialog box, on the OLAP Cubes tab, and do the following:

   a. With the <New Data Source> item selected, click OK.

   b. In the Create New Data Source dialog box, in the What Name Do You Want to Give Your Data Source, type **AdventureWorksCube**.

   c. In the Select an OLAP Provider for the Database You Want to Access List, select Microsoft OLE DB Provider for Analysis Services 9.0.

   d. Click the Connect button.

3. In the Multidimensional Connection 9.0 dialog box, do the following:

   a. With the Analysis Server option selected, in the Server box, type the server name on which the cube is stored (and if needed, type the appropriate user name in the User ID box and password in the Password box), and then click Next.

   b. In the Database list, select Analysis Services Tutorial, and then click Finish.

4. In the Create New Data Source dialog box, in the Select the Cube That Contains the Data You Want list, select Analysis Services Tutorial, and then click OK.

5. In the Choose Data Source dialog box, on the OLAP Cubes tab, select Adventure-WorksCube, and then click OK.

6. In Excel 2007, in the Import Data dialog box, with the PivotTable Report option and Existing Worksheet option selected, click OK. A PivotTable is created on the current blank worksheet and the PivotTable Field List is displayed. In Excel 2003, in the Pivot-Table and PivotChart Wizard – Step 3 of 3 dialog box, with the Existing Worksheet option selected, click Finish. A PivotTable is created on the current blank worksheet and the PivotTable Field List is displayed.

To view the data with the PivotTable, do the following:

1. In Excel 2007, in the PivotTable Field List (shown in Figure 5-1), in the Choose Fields to Add to Report list, select the following:

    a. Sales Amount check box (in the Internet Sales section)

    b. State Province Name – Geography check box (in the Customer section)

    c. OrderDate.CalendarYear – CalendarSemester – CalendarQuarter – EnglishMonthName – FullDateAlternateKey check box (in the Order Data section)

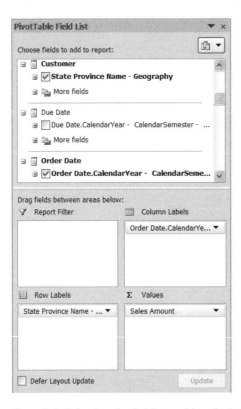

Figure 5-1. *Selecting the fields to add to the PivotTable in Excel 2007*

2. In Excel 2003, in the PivotTable Field List, click the following:

    a. Click the Sales Amount field near the bottom of the list; make sure that Data Area is showing in the Add To list, and click the Add To button (as shown in Figure 5-2).

    b. Click the State Province Name field; make sure that Row Area is showing in the Add To list, and click the Add To button.

    c. Click the OrderDate.CalendarYear – CalendarSemester – CalendarQuarter – EnglishMonthName – FullDateAlternateKey field, select Column Area in the Add To list, and click the Add To button.

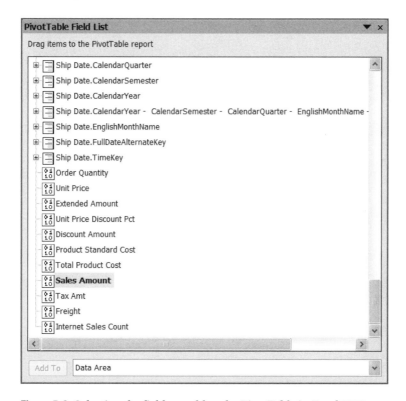

Figure 5-2. *Selecting the fields to add to the PivotTable in Excel 2003*

CHAPTER 6

■■■

Analyze Data

Excel provides a rich set of tools to enable you to analyze your data to help you make important decisions based on the outcome of that analysis. Excel data analysis techniques such as sorting, filtering, and subtotaling data; creating data tables; consolidating data; grouping and outlining data; creating tables/lists; creating scenarios; goal seeking; using Solver; creating PivotTables and PivotCharts; and performing statistical data analysis are covered in this chapter.

6.1 Sort Data

Excel can sort data values in a group of data records in ascending order (smallest to largest, 0 to 9, A to Z) or descending order (largest to smallest, 9 to 0, Z to A). For example, you could sort a series of political vote totals by voting district according to the candidate who received the most votes down to the candidate who received the least votes.

Quick Start

To sort a group of cells in an Excel worksheet, do the following:

1. Select a single cell (preferably a data column heading in the first row) within the group of cells that you want to sort.

2. In Excel 2007, click Home ➤ (Editing) Sort & Filter, and then click one of the sorting commands. In Excel 2003, click Data ➤ Sort, complete the options in the Sort dialog box, and then click OK.

How To

To sort a group of cells in an Excel worksheet, select a single cell (preferably a data column heading in the first row) within the group of cells that you want to sort.

In Excel 2007, do the following:

1. Click Home ➤ (Editing) Sort & Filter, and then do one of these:

- Click Sort A to Z, Sort Z to A, Sort Smallest to Largest, or Sort Largest to Smallest, to sort text in ascending order, to sort text in descending order, to sort numbers in ascending order, or to sort numbers in descending order, respectively.

- Click Custom Sort to display the Sort dialog box and specify a custom sort order. In the Sort dialog box, click Add Level, Delete Level, or Copy Level to add, delete, or copy the selected custom sort clause; click the up arrow or the down arrow to move the selected custom sort clause up or down in the list; or click the Options button to specify additional options. If you click the Options button, select the Case Sensitive check box if the column values should be sorted by case-sensitive order; in the Orientation area, click the Sort Top to Bottom or Sort Left to Right option to indicate whether the group of cells should be sorted from top to bottom or left to right, respectively.

2. Click OK to return to the Sort dialog box.

3. For each custom sort clause, do the following:

   a. In the Column column, specify the column by which to sort.

   b. In the Sort On column, specify whether to sort based on data values, cell color, font color, or cell icon.

   c. In the Order column, specify additional criteria based on the option specified in the Sort On column.

4. Click OK to sort the data.

In Excel 2003, do the following:

1. Click Data ➤ Sort to display the Sort dialog box.

2. In the Sort By area's box, select the first data column header by which you want to sort.

3. To the right of the Sort By area's box, click the Ascending option or Descending option.

4. In the Then By area's box, select the second data column header by which you want to sort.

5. To the right of the Then By area's box, click the Ascending or Descending option.

6. In the next Then By area's box, select the third data column header by which you want to sort.

7. To the right of the next Then By area's box, click the Ascending option or Descending option.

8. In the My Data Range Has area, click the Header Row or No Header row option to indicate whether the group of cells has column headers.

9. When you click the Options button to display the Sort Options dialog box, do the following steps:

    a. In the First Key Sort Order list, select one of the predefined sort orders, for example, you can select days of the week or months of the year.

    b. Select the Case Sensitive check box if the column values should be sorted by case-sensitive order.

    c. In the Orientation area, click the Sort Top to Bottom or Sort Left to Right option to indicate whether the group of cells should be sorted from top to bottom or left to right, respectively.

    d. Click OK to return to the Sort dialog box.

When you are done, click OK. The cell group is sorted in ascending or descending order.

Try It

In this exercise, you will practice sorting a set of data records in ascending and descending order:

1. Start Excel.

2. Click Office Button ➤ Open (in Excel 2007) or click File ➤ Open (in Excel 2003), browse to and select the ExcelDB_Ch06_01-05.xls file, and click Open.

First, sort the data records in ascending order by population. Click one of the column headings in the first row on the Counties worksheet tab, such as State, County_ID, or County_Name.

In Excel 2007, do the following:

1. Click Home ➤ (Editing) Sort & Filter ➤ Custom Sort.

2. In the first clause's Column column, in the Sort By list, select Population.

3. With the Sort On column set to Values, and the Order column set to Smallest to Largest, select any other clauses and click the Delete Level button for each clause, so that the Sort by Population clause is the only remaining clause visible.

When you are done, click OK. The data records are sorted in ascending population order (from 0 upward).

In Excel 2003, do the following:

1. Click Data ➤ Sort.

2. In the Sort By area's list, select Population. The Ascending option to the right of the list should already be selected.

When you are done, click OK. The data records are sorted in ascending population order (from 0 upward).

Next, sort the data records by state in ascending order and then in descending order by county land area.

In Excel 2007, do the following:

1. Click Home ➤ (Editing) Sort & Filter ➤ Custom Sort.

2. In the first clause's Column column, in the Sort By list, select State.

3. With the Sort On column set to Values, and the Order column set to A to Z, click the Add Level button.

4. In the second clause's Column column, in the Then By list, select Land_Area.

5. With the Sort On column set to Values, in the Order column, select Largest to Smallest.

6. Click OK. The data records are sorted in ascending order by state (AK to IL) and then in descending order by county land area within each state (for example, in AK from 9,052.7 to 1.2).

In Excel 2003, do the following:

1. Click Data ➤ Sort.

2. In the Sort By area's list, select State. The Ascending option to the right of the list should already be selected.

3. In the Then By list, select Land_Area, and click the Descending option.

When you are done, click OK. The data records are sorted in ascending order by state (AK to IL), and then in descending order by county land area within each state (for example, in AK, the values are sorted from 9,052.7 to 1.2).

6.2 Filter Data with AutoFilter

You can use Excel's AutoFilter feature to quickly show only those data records that match the criteria you specify. For example, you could show only sales data records that pertain to sales transactions in an eastern sales territory in the month of September that deal with more than 100 units of product.

Quick Start

To filter data in a group of cells in an Excel worksheet, do the following:

1. Select a single cell (preferably a data column heading in the first row) within the group of cells that you want to sort.

2. In Excel 2007, click Home ➤ (Editing) Sort & Filter ➤ Filter. In Excel 2003, click Data ➤ Filter ➤ AutoFilter.

3. Click one of the AutoFilter buttons (the buttons with the downward pointing arrows inside of the cells), and select one of the commands in the AutoFilter list. Only the data records matching the AutoFilter criteria are displayed.

How To

To filter data in a group of cells in an Excel worksheet, do the following:

1. Select a single cell (preferably a data column heading in the first row) within the group of cells that you want to filter.

2. In Excel 2007, click Home ➤ (Editing) Sort & Filter ➤ Filter. In Excel 2003, click Data ➤ Filter ➤ AutoFilter.

When you click one of the AutoFilter buttons (a button showing the down arrow in each of the heading row's cells), choose one of the commands in the AutoFilter list:

- Select Sort A to Z or Sort Smallest to Largest (in Excel 2007) or Sort Ascending (in Excel 2003) to sort the data records in ascending order according to the data values for that particular data field.

- Select Sort Z to A or Sort Largest to Smallest (in Excel 2007) or Sort Descending (in Excel 2003) to sort the data records in descending order according to the data values for that particular data field.

- Select Clear Filter From (in Excel 2007) or (All) (in Excel 2003) to remove AutoFilter criteria for that particular data field.

- Select Number Filters ➤ Top 10 (for number-based data fields in Excel 2007) or (Top 10 . . .) (in Excel 2003) to show up to the top or bottom 500 items or a percentage of the top or bottom data values for that particular data field. In the Top 10 AutoFilter dialog box, in the Show area, in the left box, select Top or Bottom. In the middle box select a number from 1 to 500. In the right box select Items or Percent. Then click OK.

- Select Text Filters ➤ Custom Filter or Number Filters ➤ Custom Filter (in Excel 2007) or (Custom . . .) (in Excel 2003) to show data records that match specific criteria.

- Select one of the data values in the list to show only data records with matching data values.

- If applicable, select (Blanks) to show only data records that have a blank cell for that particular data field.

- If applicable, select (NonBlanks) to show only data records that have a data value for that particular data field.

- To sort by color, click Sort by Color (Excel 2007 only).

- To display data records by color, click Filter by Color (Excel 2007 only).

- To display data records that match one of a selected list of specific data values, select the check box next to each specific data value (Excel 2007 only).

Tip You can apply additional AutoFilter criteria to multiple data fields. For example, let's pretend that you apply AutoFilter criteria to column B to show only data records with the data value North in column B. Of the records that are still showing, you could then apply an additional AutoFilter criteria to column E to show only data records with data values that are less than 100 in column E.

Each column that has AutoFilter criteria applied will display a blue downward pointing area in the AutoFilter button. To remove AutoFilter criteria for a single column, click the AutoFilter button, and then click Clear Filter From (in Excel 2007) or (All) (in Excel 2003). To remove AutoFilter criteria for all columns, click Home ➤ (Editing) Sort & Filter ➤ Clear (in Excel 2007) or Data ➤ Filter ➤ AutoFilter (in Excel 2003).

If you select Text Filters ➤ Custom Filter or Number Filters ➤ Custom Filter (in Excel 2007) or (Custom . . .) (in Excel 2003), do the following:

1. In the top left list, select one of the following choices:

   - Select Equals or Does Not Equal to specify data values that are equal to or not equal to the data value specified in the list to the right.

   - Select Is Greater Than or Is Greater Than or Equal To to specify data values that are greater than or greater than or equal to the data value specified in the list to the right.

   - Select Is Less Than or Is Less Than or Equal To to specify data values that are less than or less than or equal to the data value specified in the list to the right.

   - Select Begins With or Does Not Begin With to specify data values that begin with or do not begin with the data value specified in the list to the right.

   - Select End With or Does Not End With to specify data values that end with or do not end with the data value specified in the list to the right.

   - Select Contains or Does Not Contain to specify data values that contain or do not contain the data value specified in the list to the right.

2. In the top right list, type the data value to which you want to evaluate the condition in the top left list.

Note You can use the question mark (?) character to represent any single character. You can use the asterisk (*) character to represent any series of characters. For example, you can use **Southe??** or **Southe*** to match the data values Southend or Southern.

3. To apply an additional criteria, click the Add option or the Or option to apply an inclusive or exclusive filter criteria, respectively. Then repeat steps 1 and 2 for the bottom left list and bottom right list, respectively. Then click OK.

Try It

In this exercise, you will practice using the AutoFilter feature on a portion of United States census data to show data records matching specific criteria.

If the Excel workbook file is not open from the previous exercise, open it:

1. Start Excel.

2. Click Office Button ➤ Open (in Excel 2007) or File ➤ Open (in Excel 2003), browse to and select the ExcelDB_Ch06_01-05.xls file, and click Open.

Show data records only from counties in the state of Florida where the population and housing units both exceed 100,000:

1. On the Counties worksheet tab, click any single cell in row 1 on the Counties worksheet tab in columns A through G.

2. In Excel 2007, click Home ➤ (Editing) Sort & Filter ➤ Filter. In Excel 2003, click Data ➤ Filter ➤ AutoFilter.

3. Click the AutoFilter button in cell A1, and then show data records only from Florida counties. In Excel 2007, clear the (Select All) check box, select the FL check box, and then click OK. In Excel 2003, select FL.

4. Click the AutoFilter button in cell D1, and then in Excel 2007, click Number Filters ➤ Custom Filter. In Excel 2003, select (Custom . . .).

5. In the Custom AutoFilter dialog box, in the top left list, select Is Greater Than.

6. In the right box, type **100000**, and then click OK. Only data records from Florida counties with populations greater than 100,000 are shown.

7. Click the AutoFilter button in cell E1, and then in Excel 2007, click Number Filters ➤ Custom Filter. In Excel 2003, select (Custom . . .).

8. In the Custom AutoFilter dialog box, in the top left list, select Is Greater Than.

9. In the right box, type **100000**, and then click OK. Only data records from Florida counties with populations greater than 100,000 and housing units greater than 100,000 are shown.

10. Remove the AutoFilter criteria. In Excel 2007, click Home ➤ (Editing) Sort & Filter ➤ Filter or Home ➤ (Editing) Sort & Filter ➤ Clear. In Excel 2003, click Data ➤ Filter ➤ AutoFilter.

6.3 Filter Data with Advanced Criteria

Excel allows you to filter data with more advanced criteria then you can specify using the AutoFilter cell buttons or the AutoFilter dialog box. For example, with the AutoFilter feature, you could show only sales data records that pertain to sales transactions in an eastern sales territory in the month of September that deal with more than 100 units of product, while with advanced criteria, you could show only sales data records that pertain to sales transactions in eastern or western sales territories in the months of September or October that deal with between 100 and 500 units of product.

Quick Start

To apply advanced filter criteria to a group of cells, do the following:

1. Insert at least three blank rows above the group of cells that you want to filter. There must be at least one blank row between the advanced filter criteria and the group of cells that you want to filter, and both the advanced filter criteria's first row and the cell group's first row must contain data field labels.

2. Type the advanced filter criteria in the blank rows.

3. In Excel 2007, click Data ➤ (Sort & Filter) ➤ Advanced. In Excel 2003, click Data ➤ Filter ➤ Advanced Filter.

4. Complete the Advanced Filter dialog box, and click OK.

How To

To apply advanced filter criteria to a group of cells, do the following:

1. Insert at least three blank rows above the group of cells that you want to filter. You will use these blank rows to specify your advanced filter criteria. There must be at least one blank row between the advanced filter criteria and the group of cells that you want to filter, and both the advanced filter criteria's first row and the cell group's first row must contain data field labels.

2. Type the advanced filter criteria in the blank rows (see the examples in Tables 6-1 through 6-4). Place inclusive filter criteria ("and") on the same row. Place exclusive filter criteria ("or") on separate rows.

3. In Excel 2007, click Data ➤ (Sort & Filter) ➤ Advanced. In Excel 2003, click Data ➤ Filter ➤ Advanced Filter.

In the Advanced Filter dialog box, do the following:

1. In the Action area, select the Filter the List, In-Place option to display only data records that match the specified criteria. Select the Copy to Another Location option to copy to another location the data records that match the specified criteria.

2. In the List Range box, type or select the group of cells that you want to filter.

3. In the Criteria Range box, type or select the group of cells that contain the advanced filter criteria.

4. If you select the Copy to Another Location option, in the Copy To box, type or select the cell location to which you want to start copying the data records that match the specified criteria.

When you are done, click OK to apply the specified advanced filter criteria to the target cell group.

■**Note** For information on the Unique Records Only check box, see section "6.4: Filter for Unique Data."

Table 6-1 shows some example data to which advanced filter criteria are applied in Table 6-2.

Table 6-1. *Example Data Records to Apply Advanced Filter Criteria*

Sales Date	Product Name	Units Sold
1-Jan	Widgets	50
1-Jan	Gaskets	75
1-Jan	Gears	150
2-Jan	Widgets	125
2-Jan	Gaskets	100
2-Jan	Gears	250
3-Jan	Widgets	150
3-Jan	Gaskets	125
3-Jan	Gears	325

See Table 6-2 for an example of showing only data records that match these advanced filter criteria: sales dates after January 2, product names beginning with the letter G, and units sold in excess of 100.

Table 6-2. *Advanced Filter Criteria for Data Records*

Sales Date	Product Name	Units Sold
>1-Jan	="G*"	>100
Sales Date	**Product Name**	**Units Sold**
2-Jan	Gears	250
3-Jan	Gaskets	125
3-Jan	Gears	325

Table 6-3 shows an example of data records that match these advanced filter criteria: sales dates on January 1 or January 3, and number of units sold less than 150.

Table 6-3. *Advanced Filter Criteria and Results for Data Records*

Sales Date	Units Sold	
1-Jan	<150	
3-Jan	<150	
Sales Date	**Product Name**	**Units Sold**
1-Jan	Widgets	50
1-Jan	Gaskets	75
3-Jan	Gaskets	125

Table 6-4 shows an example of showing only data records that match these advanced filter criteria: sales dates of January 2, units sold of less than 150, and product names ending in the letters *ets*.

Table 6-4. *Advanced Filter Criteria and Results for Data Records*

Sales Date	Product Name	Units Sold
2-Jan		<150
	*ets	
Sales Date	**Product Name**	**Units Sold**
1-Jan	Widgets	50
1-Jan	Gaskets	75
2-Jan	Widgets	125
2-Jan	Gaskets	100
3-Jan	Widgets	150
3-Jan	Gaskets	125

■**Tip** To remove advanced filter criteria, clear the Home ➤ (Editing) Sort & Filter ➤ Clear command (in Excel 2007) or click Data ➤ Filter ➤ Show All (in Excel 2003).

Try It

In this exercise, you will practice using advanced filter criteria on a portion of United States census data to show matching data records.

If the Excel workbook file is not open from the previous exercise, open it:

1. Start Excel.

2. Click Office Button ➤ Open (in Excel 2007) or File ➤ Open (in Excel 2003), browse to and select the ExcelDB_Ch06_01-05.xls file, and click Open.

First, display data records for counties in the state of Florida with the words *North* or *South* in the county name and a land area of more than 500:

1. Insert four blank rows between the top of the Counties worksheet and the data records.

2. Type the advanced filter criteria shown in Table 6-5 in cells A1 through C3.

Table 6-5. *Advanced Filter Criteria for the Counties Worksheet*

State	County_Name	Land_Area
FL	North	>500
FL	South	>500

3. Click cell A5, and then in Excel 2007, click Data ➤ (Sort & Filter) ➤ Advanced. In Excel 2003, click Data ➤ Filter ➤ Advanced Filter.

4. In the Advanced Filter dialog box, with the List Range box showing the cell reference of cells A5 through G5409, click the Criteria Range list, select cells A1 through C3, and click OK. Three matching records are displayed.

5. In Excel 2007, click Home ➤ (Editing) Sort & Filter ➤ Clear. In Excel 2003, click Data ➤ Filter ➤ Show All.

Now, display data records for counties in the states of California or Colorado with populations between 200,000 and 300,000 and housing units of more than 100,000:

1. With the four rows between the top of the worksheet and the data records, replace the contents of cells A1 through C3 with the advanced filter criteria shown in Table 6-6 in cells A1 through D3.

Table 6-6. *More Advanced Filter Criteria for the Counties Worksheet*

State	Population	Population	Housing_Units
CA	>200000	<300000	>100000
CO	>200000	<300000	>100000

2. Click cell A5, and in Excel 2007, click Data ➤ (Sort & Filter) ➤ Advanced. In Excel 2003, click Data ➤ Filter ➤ Advanced Filter.

3. In the Advanced Filter dialog box, with the List Range box showing the cell reference of cells A5 through G5409, clear the contents of the Criteria Range list, select cells A1 through D3, and click OK. Three matching records are displayed.

4. Remove the advanced filter criteria from the worksheet before moving on to the next section. In Excel 2007, click Home ➤ (Editing) Sort & Filter ➤ Clear. In Excel 2003, click Data ➤ Filter ➤ Show All. Make sure also to delete the first four rows of the worksheet containing the advanced filter criteria.

6.4 Filter for Unique Data

You can filter data records not only to find specific data records, but you can also filter data records to show only one occurrence of each set of identical data records. For example, you may have several identical shipping records entered by a receiving clerk, a forklift operator, and a billing clerk, and you want to see only one occurrence of the particular shipping record.

How To

To filter for unique data records, do the following:

1. Select a single cell (preferably a data column heading in the first row) within the group of cells for which you want to display only unique data records.

2. In Excel 2007, click Data ➤ (Sort & Filter) ➤ Advanced. In Excel 2003, click Data ➤ Filter ➤ Advanced Filter.

3. In the Advanced Filter dialog box, select the Unique Records Only check box, and then click OK.

Tip To show all of the data records, clear the Home ➤ (Editing) Sort & Filter ➤ Clear command (in Excel 2007) or click Data ➤ Filter ➤ Show All (in Excel 2003).

Try It

In this exercise, you will practice showing only unique records for genders and age ranges in a demographic survey by population. In this example, each survey result data record must be validated by two auditors. You want to make sure that there are no records that differ only in the survey audit results.

If the Excel workbook file is not open from the previous exercise, open it:

1. Start Excel.

2. Click Office Button ➤ Open (in Excel 2007) or File ➤ Open (in Excel 2003), browse to and select the ExcelDB_Ch06_01-05.xls file, and click Open.

On the Demographics worksheet tab, notice that most of the data record pairs are identical, which means that the auditors appear to agree in their survey results. Confirm this by showing only unique data records:

1. Select cell A1.

2. In Excel 2007, click Data ➤ (Sort & Filter) ➤ Advanced. In Excel 2003, click Data ➤ Filter ➤ Advanced Filter. If a message appears asking if you want the first row of the selection or list used as labels and not data, click OK.

3. In the Advanced Filter dialog box, select the Unique Records Only check box, and then click OK.

4. Notice that rows 68 and 69 stick out because they differ in their survey results (the Surveyed data field values for these data records do not match), and these data records should be brought to the auditors' attention.

6.5 Subtotal Data

Excel can calculate subtotals for groups of related data records. For example, you may want to quickly determine the sum of products sold by a particular sales geography without having to manually insert multiple instances of the SUM worksheet function when each sales location changes.

After you subtotal the data records, you can use Excel's outline buttons in the subtotaled worksheet's left margin to show or hide individual data records in order to display fewer or more details along with the subtotals.

Quick Start

To subtotal data for a group of cells in an Excel worksheet, do the following:

1. Select a single cell (preferably a data column heading in the first row) within the group of cells that you want to subtotal.

2. In Excel 2007, click Data ➤ (Outline) ➤ Subtotal. In Excel 2003, click Data ➤ Subtotals.

3. Complete the Subtotal dialog box, and then click OK.

How To

To subtotal data for a group of cells in an Excel worksheet, do the following:

1. Select a single cell (preferably a data column heading in the first row) within the group of cells that you want to subtotal.

2. In Excel 2007, click Data ➤ (Outline) ➤ Subtotal. In Excel 2003, click Data ➤ Subtotals.

While you are in the Subtotal dialog box, do the following:

1. In the At Each Change In list, select the data field by which you want to insert subtotals at each change in a data value. For example, for a given sales geography, you want to insert a subtotal when the geography changes from North to East, then East to South, and so on.

▩**Tip** Subtotals work best in Excel when you sort or group similar data values in the data field that you select in the At Each Change In list.

---

2. In the Use Function list, select the function by which you want to subtotal.

3. In the Add Subtotal To list, select the data fields for which you want to display the selected subtotal. For example, at each change in a given sales geography, you may want to display the sum of all of the quarterly sales and the average number of sales transactions per sales outlet for that particular geography.

4. Select the Replace Current Subtotals check box to overwrite any existing subtotals for the cell group.

5. Select the Page Break Between Groups check box to have Excel insert a page break between each subtotal.

6. Select the Summary Below Data check box to have Excel display subtotals below the subtotaled rows. If this box is unchecked, Excel displays subtotals above the subtotaled rows.

7. Click the Remove All button to remove all subtotals from the cell group.

8. Click the OK button to subtotal the data according to the Subtotal dialog box's selections.

Try It

In this exercise, you will practice applying subtotals to a portion of United States census data. If the Excel workbook file is not open from the previous exercise, open it:

1. Start Excel.

2. Click Office Button ➤ Open (in Excel 2007) or File ➤ Open (in Excel 2003), browse to and select the ExcelDB_Ch06_01-05.xls file, and click Open.

First, display the average land area per state:

1. On the Counties worksheet tab, click cell A1 if it isn't already selected.

2. In Excel 2007, click Data ➤ (Outline) ➤ Subtotal. In Excel 2003, click Data ➤ Subtotals.

3. In the Subtotal dialog box, with the At Each Change In list showing State, in the Use Function list, select Average.

4. In the Add Subtotal To list, select the Land_Area check box, and make sure all of the list's other check boxes are cleared.

5. With the Replace Current Subtotals and the Summary Below Data check boxes selected, click OK.

6. In the three outline buttons toward the top of the left margin (the area to the left of the row number indicators), click the button with the number 2 on it. The average land area per state is displayed.

Now, display the average housing units and population per state:

1. In Excel 2007, click Data ➤ (Outline) ➤ Subtotal. In Excel 2003, click Data ➤ Subtotals.

2. In the Subtotal dialog box, with the At Each Change In list still showing State, and with the Use Function list still showing Average, in the Add Subtotal To list, select the Population and the Housing_Units check boxes, and make sure all of the list's other check boxes are cleared.

3. With the Replace Current Subtotals and the Summary Below Data check boxes still selected, click OK.

4. In the three outline buttons toward the top of the left margin (the area to the left of the row number indicators), click the button with the number 2 on it. The average housing units and population per state are displayed.

5. To remove the subtotals, in Excel 2007, click Data ➤ (Outline) ➤ Subtotal, and then click the Remove All button. In Excel 2003, click Data ➤ Subtotals, and then click the Remove All button.

6.6 Create a Data Table

Data tables, along with scenarios (see section "6.10: Create a Scenario" for more information), goal seeking (see section "6.11: Perform What-If Data Analysis with Goal Seek" for more information), and Solver (see section "6.12: Perform What-If Data Analysis with Solver" for more information) are part of Excel's what-if data analysis toolset. These tools allow you to change cell values to see how those changes are reflected in worksheet formula results. In the case of data tables, you can calculate and display the results of one or more input values. A multiplication table is an example of a simple data table. A mortgage payment schedule is an example of a more complicated data table.

There are two types of data tables. A *one-variable data table* is based on a formula that contains one replaceable input value, while a *two-variable data table* is based on a formula that contains two replaceable input values.

Data tables contain *input values*. Input values can consist of one *input cell* (in the case of one-variable data tables) or two input cells (in the case of two-variable data tables). These input cells contain the replaceable values in the formula that are substituted from the row or column input values (for one-variable data tables) or the row and column input values (for two-variable data tables).

Data tables also contain *result values*. Result values are, as the name suggests, the results of substituting the input values in the formula.

■Note A *data table* in Excel 2007 and Excel 2003 is different from a *table* (in Excel 2007). For more information on tables in Excel 2007, see section "6.9: Create a Table/List."

■Note For more information about data tables, see my book *Beginning Excel What-If Data Analysis Tools: Getting Started with Goal Seek, Data Tables, Scenarios, and Solver* (Apress, 2006).

Quick Start

To set up and create a one-variable data table, do the following:

1. Select the group of cells that contains the formula, the input values, and the cells for which you want to display the result values.

2. In Excel 2007, click Data ➤ (Data Tools) What-If Analysis ➤ Data Table. In Excel 2003, click Data ➤ Table.

3. Complete the Table dialog box, and then click OK.

To set up and create a two-variable data table, do the following:

1. Select the group of cells that contains the formula, the column and row of input values, and the cells for which you want to display the result values.

2. In Excel 2007, click Data ➤ (Data Tools) What-If Analysis ➤ Data Table. In Excel 2003, click Data ➤ Table.

3. Complete the Table dialog box, and then click OK.

How To

To set up and create a one-variable data table, do the following:

1. If the input values are listed down a column, type the formula in the row above the first column value and then one cell to the right of the column of values. If desired, type any additional formulas to the right of that first formula.

2. If the input values are listed across a row, type the formula in the column one cell below and to the left of the first row of values. If desired, type any additional formulas below the first formula.

3. Select the group of cells that contains the formula, the input values, and the cells for which you want to display the result values.

4. In Excel 2007, click Data ➤ (Data Tools) What-If Analysis ➤ Data Table. In Excel 2003, click Data ➤ Table.

5. If the input values are listed down a column, type or click the input cell reference in the Column Input box.

6. If the input values are listed across a row, type or click the input cell reference in the Row Input box.

7. Click OK.

To set up and create a two-variable data table, do the following:

1. Type the formula that will serve as the basis of the two-variable data table.

2. Type the list of column input values below the formula in the same column.

3. Type the list of row input values in the same row as the formula, just to the right of the formula.

4. Select the group of cells that contains the formula, the column and row of input values, and the cells for which you want to display the result values.

5. In Excel 2007, click Data ➤ (Data Tools) What-If Analysis ➤ Data Table. In Excel 2003, click Data ➤ Table.

6. In the Column Input box, type or click the column input cell reference.

7. In the Row Input box, type or click the row input cell reference.

8. Click OK.

Try It

In this exercise, you will practice creating a one-variable data table and a two-variable data table to calculate the total monthly charge for a single worker and multiple workers at various hourly pay rates.

First, open the practice Excel workbook as follows:

1. Start Excel.

2. Click Office Button ➤ Open (in Excel 2007) or File ➤ Open (in Excel 2003), browse to and select the ExcelDB_Ch06_06-12.xls file, and click Open.

On the DataTables tab, notice the formula in cell B4. It represents the number of workdays in January 2008 (with New Year's Day 2008 counted as a holiday) in cell B1, multiplied by the hourly rate in cell B2, which is then multiplied by the number of hours per workday in cell B3. Calculate result values for this one-variable data table:

1. Select cells A4 through B21.

2. In Excel 2007, click Data ➤ (Data Tools) What-If Analysis ➤ Data Table. In Excel 2003, click Data ➤ Table.

3. In the Column Input Cell box, type or click cell B2. This means that for cells B5 through B21, display the result of substituting cell B2 in the formula in cell B4 with the input values taken from cells A5 through A21.

4. Click OK, and note the results in cells B5 through B21.

Next on the DataTables tab, notice the formula in cell D5. It represents the number of workdays in January 2008 (with New Year's Day 2008 counted as a holiday) in cell E1, multiplied by the hourly rate in cell E2, multiplied by the number of hours per workday in cell E3, which is then multiplied by the number of workers in cell E4. Calculate result values for this two-variable data table:

1. Select cells D5 through I22.

2. In Excel 2007, click Data ➤ (Data Tools) What-If Analysis ➤ Data Table. In Excel 2003, click Data ➤ Table.

3. In the Row Input Cell box, type or click cell E4. This means that for cells E6 through I22, display the results of substituting cell E4 in the formula in cell D5 with the input values taken from cells E5 through I5.

4. In the Column Input Cell box, type or click cell E2. This means that for cells E6 through I22, display the result of substituting cell E2 in the formula in cell D5 with the input values taken from cells D6 through D22.

5. Click OK, and note the results in cells E6 through I22.

6.7 Consolidate Data

Excel can summarize similar data from multiple worksheets in the same workbook into a single worksheet. Excel can also summarize similar data from multiple workbooks into a single worksheet. For example, you may want to consolidate data taken from dozens of inventory clerks, each using their own Excel worksheet to enter their own inventory counts, into a single worksheet containing the total of all of the clerks' inventory counts.

Quick Start

To consolidate data across worksheets, do the following:

1. Select the worksheet cell where you want Excel to start putting the consolidated data.

2. In Excel 2007, click Data ➤ (Data Tools) ➤ Consolidate. In Excel 2003, click Data ➤ Consolidation.

3. Complete the Consolidate dialog box, and then click OK.

How To

To consolidate data across worksheets, do the following:

1. Select the worksheet cell where you want Excel to start putting the consolidated data.

2. In Excel 2007, click Data ➤ (Data Tools) ➤ Consolidate. In Excel 2003, click Data ➤ Consolidation.

While you are in the Consolidate dialog box, do the following:

1. In the Function list, select a function to apply to the consolidated data, such as Sum or Average.

2. In the Reference list, type or select a cell group to consolidate.

■**Tip** Data consolidation works best when each cell group to be consolidated has the same data field names, there are no blank rows or columns within the cell groups' data records, and each cell group has a defined name. To give each group of data records a name on each worksheet, select all of the cells containing the data records on the first worksheet, click Formulas ➤ (Defined Names) Define Name (in Excel 2007) or Insert ➤ Name ➤ Define (in Excel 2003), complete the New Name dialog box (in Excel 2007) or Define Name dialog box (in Excel 2003), and click OK. Then repeat this process for each worksheet that contains data records to be consolidated.

---

   3. Click the Browse button to define a cell group in a separate workbook.

■**Tip** Selecting a separate workbook simply adds the workbook's path to the Reference list. To complete the reference to the target cell group, add the cell group's worksheet tab name and cell group reference by using the following syntax: 'WorkbookPath[WorkbookFileName.xls]WorksheetName'!CellReference. For example, for a cell group named ApplianceCounts, on a worksheet tab named ItemCounts, in a workbook with the file name StoreInventory.xls, stored in the C:\My Documents path, the syntax would be 'C:\My Documents\ [StoreInventory.xls]ItemCounts'!ApplianceCounts.

---

   4. Click the Add button to add the contents of the Reference box to the All References list.

   5. Click the Delete button to delete the selected reference from the All References list.

   6. In the Use Labels In area, select the Top Row check box to use the data field names in each cell group's top row to assist Excel in consolidating data correctly, or select the Left Column check box to use any data record names in each cell group's far left column to assist Excel in consolidating data correctly.

   7. Select the Create Links to Source Data check box to update the consolidated data automatically whenever data in any of the target cell groups changes.

   8. Click OK to finish consolidating the data.

Try It

In this exercise, you will consolidate data on four separate worksheets of data into one worksheet. These worksheets contain data representing seasonal fish catches in three river tributaries.

   If the Excel workbook file is not open from the previous exercise, open it:

   1. Start Excel.

   2. Click Office Button ➤ Open (in Excel 2007) or click File ➤ Open (in Excel 2003), browse to and select the ExcelDB_Ch06_06-12.xls file, and click Open.

Notice on the SpringFish, SummerFish, FallFish, and WinterFish worksheet tabs that there are identical data record names in column A and identical data field names in row 1. Notice also that each set of data records on each of these worksheet tabs is defined as a named cell group. Preparing data records and using named cell groups in this manner helps ensure predictable data consolidation.

Consolidate the data:

1. On the ConsolidateData worksheet tab, click cell A1.

2. In Excel 2007, click Data ➤ (Data Tools) ➤ Consolidate. In Excel 2003, click Data ➤ Consolidation.

3. With the Function list showing Sum, click the Reference list, type **SpringFish**, and click Add.

4. In the Reference list, type **SummerFish**, and click Add.

5. In the Reference list, type **FallFish**, and click Add.

6. In the Reference list, type **WinterFish**, and click Add.

7. Select the Top Row and Left Column check boxes, and click OK. The data from all four worksheets are added together and placed on the ConsolidateData worksheet, starting with cell A1.

6.8 Group and Outline Data

Excel can group related data records together and then allow you to switch between the individual data records or summarized data with the click of a button. For example, you may have several sets of individual sales records sorted by sales transaction date. After each set of sales records, you could insert a row in the spreadsheet with the sales total. You can then group and outline the sales records so that you can easily switch between the individual sales records and the sales total with the click of a button.

■**Tip** Grouping and outlining data records is slightly different than subtotaling data records. Grouping and outlining data records works best when you have already summarized the data. If you did not have the sales total already created in the preceding example, you could use Excel's subtotaling feature to first create the subtotal and then outline the data.

Quick Start

To group and outline data records, click Data ➤ (Outline) (in Excel 2007) or Data ➤ Group and Outline (in Excel 2003), and then click one of the menu commands to do the following:

- Hide or display an already grouped set of data records.

- Group or ungroup selected data records.

- Have Excel automatically group and outline selected data records.

- Remove grouping and outlining for selected data records.

- Control grouping and outlining behavior for selected data records.

How To

To group and outline data records in Excel 2007, click Data, and in the Outline group, do the following:

1. Click Hide Detail or Show Detail to hide or display an already grouped set of data records related to the currently selected data record.

2. Click Group or Ungroup to manually group or ungroup the selected set of data records.

3. Click Group ➤ Auto Outline to have Excel automatically group and outline the selected set of data records, based on how the data records are already summarized.

4. Click Ungroup ➤ Clear Outline to remove grouping and outlining for the selected set of data records.

5. Click Outline to control grouping and outlining behavior through the Settings dialog box:

   a. In the Direction area, check the Summary Rows Below Detail check box and/or the Summary Columns to Right of Detail check box to specify whether the data record summaries are listed below and/or to the right of the individual data records.

   b. Select the Automatic Styles check box to have Excel apply cell formats, such as making the text of each summarized total bold, at the same time that the data records are grouped and outlined.

   c. Click the Apply Styles button to have Excel apply cell formats to data records that are already grouped and outlined.

In Excel 2003, click Data ➤ Group and Outline, and then do the following:

1. Click Hide Detail or Show Detail to hide or display an already grouped set of data records related to the currently selected data record.

2. Click Group or Ungroup to manually group or ungroup the selected set of data records, respectively.

3. Click Auto Outline to have Excel automatically group and outline the selected set of data records, based on how the data records are already summarized.

4. Click Clear Outline to remove grouping and outlining for the selected set of data records.

5. Click Settings to control grouping and outlining behavior through the Settings dialog box:

    a. In the Direction area, check the Summary Rows Below Detail check box and/or the Summary Columns to Right of Detail check box to specify whether the data record summaries are listed below and/or to the right of the individual data records.

    b. Select the Automatic Styles check box to have Excel apply cell formats, such as making the text of each summarized total bold, at the same time that the data records are grouped and outlined.

    c. Click the Apply Styles button to have Excel apply cell formats to data records that are already grouped and outlined.

Try It

In this exercise, you will practice grouping and outlining data records related to the number of shipping containers inspected in a country's regional seaports by month.

If the Excel workbook file is not open from the previous exercise, open it:

1. Start Excel.

2. Click Office Button ➤ Open (in Excel 2007) or click File ➤ Open (in Excel 2003), browse to and select the ExcelDB_Ch06_06-12.xls file, and click Open.

Group the data manually:

1. On the GroupOutline worksheet, select rows 2 through 13.

2. In Excel 2007, click Data ➤ (Outline) Group. In Excel 2003, click Data ➤ Group and Outline ➤ Group.

3. Repeat steps 1 and 2 for rows 15 through 26, rows 28 through 39, and rows 41 through 52.

4. In the outline area (the column to the left of the row numbers), click the 1 button. The details are hidden and only the totals are displayed. Click the 2 button to see the details again.

5. Clear the manual groupings by clicking cell A1 and in Excel 2007, click Data ➤ (Outline) Ungroup ➤ Clear Outline. In Excel 2003, click Data ➤ Group and Outline ➤ Clear Outline.

Now, group and outline more quickly by having Excel do it for you automatically. Click Data ➤ (Outline) Group ➤ Auto Outline (in Excel 2007) or Data ➤ Group and Outline ➤ Auto Outline (in Excel 2003). Excel detects that rows 14, 27, 40, and 53 contain SUM worksheet values and automatically groups the related detail cells.

6.9 Create a Table/List

Tables (in Excel 2007) and lists (in Excel 2003) allow you to add the following capabilities to a selected group of data records:

- Show or hide data records that meet your specified criteria using AutoFilter.

- Insert or delete data records and data fields and grow or shrink the table's/list's boundaries to accommodate these changes.

- Display a data form to help control data record management and minimize data entry errors.

- Publish the data records to a Microsoft Windows SharePoint web site, and then synchronize the version of the data in the worksheet with the version of the data on the SharePoint web site.

- Resize the table's/list's boundaries.

- Display or hide a row at the bottom of the table/list that summarizes the data records with a worksheet function, such as SUM.

- Create a chart based on the table's/list's data records.

- Print the table's/list's data records.

The unique thing about Excel tables/lists is that these capabilities will work against the selected table's/list's data records without affecting any other data records that may be on the same worksheet but not in the selected table/list.

■**Note** A *table* in Excel 2007 is different from a *data table*. For more information on data tables, see section "6.6: Create a Data Table."

Quick Start

To create a table/list, do the following:

1. In Excel 2007, click Insert ➤ (Tables) Table. In Excel 2003, click Data ➤ List ➤ Create List.

2. Complete the Create Table dialog box (in Excel 2007) or Create List dialog box (in Excel 2003), and then click OK. The table/list is created.

How To

To create a table/list, do the following:

1. In Excel 2007, click Insert ➤ (Tables) Table. In Excel 2003, click Data ➤ List ➤ Create List.

2. In the Create Table dialog box (in Excel 2007) or Create List dialog box (in Excel 2003), in the Where Is the Data for Your Table box (in Excel 2007) or the Where Is the Data for Your List box (in Excel 2003), select or type the cell reference for the data records.

3. If the data records have data field names in the first row of the selected cells, select the My Table Has Headers check box (in Excel 2007) or the My List Has Headers check box (in Excel 2003).

4. Click OK. The table/list is created.

To remove data records or data fields from a table/list, select the data records or data fields to delete, right-click the selected data records or data fields, and in Excel 2007, click Delete ➤ Table Columns or Delete ➤ Table Rows. In Excel 2003, click Delete ➤ Row or Delete ➤ Column.

To resize a table's/list's boundaries, select the table/list, and do the following:

1. In Excel 2007, click (Table Tools) Design ➤ (Properties) Resize Table. In Excel 2003, click Data ➤ List ➤ Resize List.

2. In the Resize Table dialog box (for Excel 2007) or Resize List dialog box (for Excel 2003), in the Select the New Data Range for Your Table box (for Excel 2007) or the Select the New Data Range for Your List box (for Excel 2003), select or type the cell reference for the data records that you want to be included in the resized table/list, and then click OK.

To insert into or delete a row or column from a table/list, do the following:

1. Select a cell in or adjacent to the row or column that you want to insert or delete.

2. Right-click the selected cell, and in Excel 2007, click Insert ➤ Table Columns to the Left, Insert ➤ Table Rows Above, Delete ➤ Table Columns, or Delete ➤ Table Rows. In Excel 2003, click Insert ➤ Row, Insert ➤ Column, Delete ➤ Row, or Delete ➤ Column.

To add a total row to a table/list, select the table/list, and in Excel 2007, click (Table Tools) Design ➤ (Table Style Options) Total Row. In Excel 2003, click Data ➤ List ➤ Total Row.

▓**Tip** To change the total row's worksheet function, click the cell containing the total row's worksheet function, click the arrow next to that cell, and select a different worksheet function from the list.

To show or hide specific data records in a table/list, select the table/list, click the arrow in the table's/list's data field header row, and do the following:

- To sort in ascending (A to Z, smallest to largest) order, click Sort A to Z or Sort Smallest to Largest (in Excel 2007) or Sort Ascending (in Excel 2003).

- To sort in descending (Z to A, largest to smallest) order, click Sort Z to A or Sort Largest to Smallest (in Excel 2007) or Sort Descending (in Excel 2003).

- To sort by color, click Sort by Color (Excel 2007 only).

- To display the top or bottom number or percentage of data records, click Number Filters ➤ Top 10 (for number-based data in Excel 2007) or (Top 10 . . .) (in Excel 2003).

- To display data records based on custom criteria that you specify, click Text Filters ➤ Custom Filter (in Excel 2007) or (Custom . . .) (in Excel 2003).

- To display data records by color, click Filter by Color (Excel 2007 only).

- To display data records that equal, do not equal, begin with, do not begin with, contain, or do not contain a particular data value, click Text Filters, and then click the respective command (Excel 2007 only).

- To display data records that match one of a selected list of specific data values, select the check box next to each specific data value (Excel 2007 only).

- To display data records that match a specific data value, click the specific data value in the list (Excel 2003 only).

To convert a table/list to a set of data records, select the table/list, and in Excel 2007, click (Table Tools) Design ➤ (Tools) Convert to Range. In Excel 2003, click Data ➤ List ➤ Convert to Range.

Try It

In this exercise, you will practice creating a table/list based on yearly newspaper circulation statistics for the United States, adding and removing data records and data fields from the table/list, adding a total row and changing the total row's worksheet function, and changing the table's/list's display format.

If the Excel workbook file is not open from the previous exercise, open it:

1. Start Excel.

2. Click Office Button Open (in Excel 2007) or click File ➤ Open (in Excel 2003), browse to and select the ExcelDB_Ch06_06-12.xls file, and click Open.

Create the table/list:

1. On the TableList worksheet tab, in Excel 2007, click Insert ➤ (Tables) Table. In Excel 2003, click Data ➤ List ➤ Create List.

2. In the Where Is the Data for Your Table box (in Excel 2007) or Where Is the Data for Your List box (in Excel 2003), type or select cells A1 through E21.

3. With the My Table Has Headers check box (in Excel 2007) or My List Has Headers check box (in Excel 2003) selected, click OK. The list is created.

Add and remove data records and data fields from the table/list:

1. Right-click cell A4 (which represents total newspaper circulation for 1970), and then click Insert ➤ Table Rows Above (in Excel 2007) or Insert ➤ Row (in Excel 2003).

2. In cell A4, type **1966**, and press Enter.

3. Right-click cell A4, and then click Delete ➤ Table Rows (in Excel 2007) or Delete ➤ Row (in Excel 2003).

4. Right-click cell E1 (which represents total Sunday circulation for all years), and then click Insert ➤ Table Columns to the Left (in Excel 2007) or Insert ➤ Column (in Excel 2003).

5. In cell E1, type **Evening and Sunday Run**, and press Enter.

6. Right-click cell E1, and then click Delete ➤ Table Columns (in Excel 2007) or Delete ➤ Column (in Excel 2003).

Add a total row to the table/list and change the total row's worksheet function:

1. Select the (Table Tools) Design ➤ (Table Style Options) Total Row check box (in Excel 2007), or click Data ➤ List ➤ Total Row (in Excel 2003).

2. Click cell E22 (in Excel 2007) or cell E23 (in Excel 2003) (the total row's worksheet function result), click the arrow in cell E22 (in Excel 2007) or cell E23 (in Excel 2003), and then click Average. The average yearly Sunday run for all years is displayed.

Change the table's/list's display format:

1. Click the arrow in cell E1, and then click Number Filters ➤ Custom Filter (in Excel 2007) or (Custom . . .) (in Excel 2003).

2. In the Custom AutoFilter dialog box, in the top left list, select Is Greater Than.

3. In the box to the right, type **55000000**.

4. With the And option selected, in the bottom left list, select Is Less Than.

5. In the box to the right, type **60000000**.

6. Click OK. Only data records with total yearly Sunday runs of between 55,000,000 and 60,000,000 are displayed.

6.10 Create a Scenario

Scenarios, along with data tables (see section "6.6: Create a Data Table" for more information), goal seeking (see section "6.11: Perform What-If Data Analysis with Goal Seek" for more information), and Solver (see section "6.12: Perform What-If Data Analysis with Solver" for more information) are part of Excel's what-if data analysis toolset. These tools allow you to change cell values to see how those changes are reflected in worksheet formula results. In the case of scenarios, you can display the outcome of a set of formulas. You can save these results, repeat the process of displaying another outcome of the same set of formulas multiple times, and then switch back and forth among these saved outcomes. For example, you could switch back and forth between different mortgage payment schedules to determine whether a mortgage for a three-bedroom house or a four-bedroom house meets your budget constraints.

■Tip For more information about scenarios, see my book *Beginning Excel What-If Data Analysis Tools: Getting Started with Goal Seek, Data Tables, Scenarios, and Solver* (Apress, 2006).

Quick Start

To create a scenario, do the following:

1. Select the worksheet containing the cell values and formulas that you want to serve as the basis of your scenario, and then in Excel 2007, click Data ➤ (Data Tools) What-If Analysis ➤ Scenario Manager. In Excel 2003, click Tools ➤ Scenarios.

2. Click Add.

3. Complete the Scenario Manager dialog box, and then click OK. The scenario is created.

How To

To create a scenario, do the following:

1. Select the worksheet containing the cell values and formulas that you want to serve as the basis of your scenario, and in Excel 2007, click Data ➤ (Data Tools) What-If Analysis ➤ Scenario Manager. In Excel 2003, click Tools ➤ Scenarios.

2. Click Add.

3. In the Scenario Name box, type a name for the scenario.

4. In the Changing Cells box, type or select the cell reference for the cells that will change.

5. Click OK.

6. For each changing cell, type a value.

7. Click Add to create the scenario and return to the Add Scenario dialog box, or click OK to create the scenario and return to the Scenario Manager dialog box.

To display an existing scenario's results on the current worksheet, do the following:

1. In Excel 2007, click Data ➤ (Data Tools) What-If Analysis ➤ Scenario Manager. In Excel 2003, click Tools ➤ Scenarios.

2. In the Scenarios list, click the scenario that you want to display.

3. Click Show.

To change an existing scenario on the current worksheet, do the following:

1. In Excel 2007, click Data ➤ (Data Tools) What-If Analysis ➤ Scenario Manager. In Excel 2003, click Tools ➤ Scenarios.

2. In the Scenarios list, click the scenario that you want to change.

Once you have selected the scenario, click Edit, and then do the following:

1. In the Scenario Name box, type a name for the scenario.

2. In the Changing Cells box, type or select the cell reference for the cells that will change.

3. In the Comment box, type a comment.

4. Click OK.

5. For each changing cell, type a value.

When you are done, click OK to return to save the changes and to return to the Scenario Manager dialog box.

To remove an existing scenario on the current worksheet, do the following:

1. In Excel 2007, click Data ➤ (Data Tools) What-If Analysis ➤ Scenario Manager. In Excel 2003, click Tools ➤ Scenarios.

2. In the Scenarios list, click the scenario that you want to remove.

3. Click Delete.

Try It

In this exercise, you will practice creating three scenarios with high and low temperatures and then switching back and forth between them.

If the Excel workbook file is not open from the previous exercise, open it:

1. Start Excel.

2. Click Office Button ➤ Open (in Excel 2007) or click File ➤ Open (in Excel 2003), browse to and select the ExcelDB_Ch06_06-12.xls file, and click Open.

Create the first scenario:

1. On the Scenarios worksheet tab, in Excel 2007, click Data ➤ (Data Tools) What-If Analysis ➤ Scenario Manager. In Excel 2003, click Tools ➤ Scenarios.

2. In the Scenario Manager dialog box, click Add.

3. In the Scenario Name box, type **Seattle Scenario**.

4. Clear the contents of the Changing Cells box, select cell B1, and, with the Ctrl key pressed, select cells B4 through D5. Then click OK.

In the Scenario Values dialog box, type a value for each of the boxes, and then click OK:

1. In the $B$1 box, type **Seattle**.

2. In the $B$4 box, type **74**.

3. In the $C$4 box, type **76**.

4. In the $D$4 box, type **77**.

5. In the $B$5 box, type **54**.

6. In the $C$5 box, type **55**.

7. In the $D$5 box, type **57**.

With the Scenario Manager dialog box open, create the second scenario:

1. In the Scenario Manager dialog box, click Add.

2. In the Scenario Name box, type **New York Scenario**, and with the Changing Cells box showing B1,B4:D5, click OK.

In the Scenario Values dialog box, type a value for each of the boxes, and then click OK:

1. In the $B$1 box, type **New York**.

2. In the $B$4 box, type **96**.

3. In the $C$4 box, type **100**.

4. In the $D$4 box, type **95**.

5. In the $B$5 box, type **84**.

6. In the $C$5 box, type **82**.

7. In the $D$5 box, type **77**.

With the Scenario Manager dialog box open, create the third scenario:

1. In the Scenario Manager dialog box, click Add.

2. In the Scenario Name box, type **Minneapolis Scenario**, and with the Changing Cells box showing B1,B4:D5, click OK.

In the Scenario Values dialog box, type a value for each of the boxes, and then click OK:

1. In the $B$1 box, type **Minneapolis**.

2. In the $B$4 box, type **72**.

3. In the $C$4 box, type **81**.

4. In the $D$4 box, type **88**.

5. In the $B$5 box, type **67**.

6. In the $C$5 box, type **66**.

7. In the $D$5 box, type **68**.

With the Scenario Manager dialog box open, switch between the three scenarios:

1. In the Scenario Manager dialog box, select Seattle Scenario, and click Show.

2. Repeat the previous step for the New York Scenario and the Minneapolis Scenario scenarios.

6.11 Perform What-If Data Analysis with Goal Seek

Goal seeking, along with data tables (see section "6.6: Create a Data Table" for more information), scenarios (see section "6.10: Create a Scenario" for more information), and Solver (see section "6.12: Perform What-If Data Analysis with Solver" for more information) are part of Excel's what-if data analysis toolset. In the case of goal seeking, you can calculate a formula's input value when you want to work backward from the formula's answer. For example, if you have a mortgage payment schedule and you know the mortgage amount, the monthly payment, and the number of months in the payment schedule, you can use goal seeking to calculate the mortgage's interest rate.

■Tip For more information about goal seeking, see my book *Beginning Excel What-If Data Analysis Tools: Getting Started with Goal Seek, Data Tables, Scenarios, and Solver* (Apress, 2006).

Quick Start

To perform goal seeking, do the following:

1. In Excel 2007, click Data ➤ (Data Tools) What-If Analysis ➤ Goal Seek. In Excel 2003, click Tools ➤ Goal Seek.

2. Complete the Goal Seek dialog box, and click OK.

How To

To perform goal seeking, do the following:

1. In Excel 2007, click Data ➤ (Data Tools) What-If Analysis ➤ Goal Seek. In Excel 2003, click Tools ➤ Goal Seek.

2. In the Set Cell box, type or click the reference for the single worksheet cell that contains the formula that you want to set to a desired value.

3. In the To Value box, type the value that you want the cell referred to in the Set Cell box to display.

4. In the By Changing Cell box, type or click the reference for the single worksheet cell that contains the value that you want to adjust. This cell must be referenced by the formula in the cell you specified earlier in the Set Cell box.

5. Click OK. The Goal Seek Status dialog box will appear, confirming whether Excel is able to find a solution. It will also display the target value sought in the To Value box and the current value of the cell in the By Changing Cell box, which may not necessarily match the target value. If Excel does find a solution, the target value and the current value will be equivalent.

Try It

In this exercise, you will use goal seek to determine how many widgets need to be produced per hour to come up with 1,000,000 widgets per month per manufacturing plant, given a fixed number of widget makers, fixed hours per day worked, and a fixed number of days per month worked.

If the Excel workbook file is not open from the previous exercise, open it:

1. Start Excel.

2. Click Office Button ➤ Open (in Excel 2007) or click File ➤ Open (in Excel 2003), browse to and select the ExcelDB_Ch06_06-12.xls file, and click Open.

Determine the number of widgets that need to be produced per hour:

1. On the GoalSeekSolver worksheet tab, in Excel 2007, click Data ➤ (Data Tools) What-If Analysis ➤ Goal Seek. In Excel 2003, click Tools ➤ Goal Seek.

2. In the Goal Seek dialog box, clear the contents of the Set Cell box, click the Set Cell box, and select cell B8.

3. In the To Value box, type **1000000**.

4. Click the By Changing Cell box, select cell B4, and click OK.

5. When the Goal Seek Status dialog box appears, click OK. Cell B4 should display the value 170.1. This means that 35 widget makers working eight hours per day and 21 days per month can produce 1,000,000 widgets if they produce 170.1 widgets per hour.

6. Repeat steps 1 through 5 for the Southworth, Downtown, and Westlake plants. Substitute in the Set Cell box the cell references C8, D8, and E8 respectively. Substitute in the By Changing Cell box the cell references C4, D4, and E4 respectively. Your results should be 198.4 for cell C4, 212.6 for cell D4, and 145.2 for cell E4.

6.12 Perform What-If Data Analysis with Solver

Solver, along with data tables (see section "6.6: Create a Data Table" for more information), scenarios (see section "6.10: Create a Scenario" for more information), and goal seeking (see section "6.11: Perform What-If Data Analysis with Goal Seek" for more information) are part of Excel's what-if data analysis toolset. In the case of Solver, Excel can find a single worksheet cell formula's target value or most favorable value. Solver does this by changing the worksheet cell values you specify to produce the selected cell formula's desired value. You can also apply restrictions to the cell values that Solver can use to find the desired value. For example, you can change a business's forecasted budget amount and see the effect on the projected business's profit.

To better work with Solver, you should understand a few Solver terms, specifically these:

- The *target cell* is the cell that you want Solver to set to a maximum, minimum, or specified value.

- The *objective* is the desired goal or outcome of the problem that you want Solver to reach. The target cell represents Solver's problem-solving goal.

- The *adjustable cells* (sometimes known as *changing cells*) are the cells that Solver will change or adjust the values of to achieve the desired objective.

- The *constraints* are the problem's restrictions that you place on the adjustable cells. Solver must adhere to these constraints as it tries to change the adjustable cells to meet the objective.

- A *model* is the set of target cells, all adjustable cells, and any constraints for the current problem that you want Solver to solve.

Tip For more information about Solver, see my book, *Beginning Excel What-If Data Analysis Tools: Getting Started with Goal Seek, Data Tables, Scenarios, and Solver* (Apress, 2006).

Quick Start

To run Solver, do the following:

1. In Excel 2007, click Data (Analysis) ➤ Solver. In Excel 2003, click Tools ➤ Solver.

2. Complete the Solver Parameters dialog box, and then click Solve.

Tip

Since Solver may not always be available when Excel is installed, you should confirm that Solver is available before you try to use it. If the Solver command doesn't appear in the Data (Analysis) group (in Excel 2007) or on the Tools menu (in Excel 2003), do this:

- In Excel 2007, click Office Button ➤ Excel Options. In the left pane, click Add-Ins. With the Manage list toward the bottom of the screen showing Excel Add-Ins, click Go. Select the Solver Add-In check box, click OK, and then click Data (Analysis) ➤ Solver.

- In Excel 2003, click Tools ➤ Add-Ins, select the Solver Add-In check box, click OK, and then click Tools ➤ Solver.

If, however, the Solver Add-In check box is not visible in the Add-Ins dialog box's Add-Ins available list, you must install Solver by running the Microsoft Office Setup program again and selecting Solver from the list of available Excel add-ins. Then you can start Excel and click Data (Analysis) ➤ Solver (in Excel 2007) or Tools ➤ Solver (in Excel 2003).

How To

To run Solver, do the following:

1. In Excel 2007, click Data (Analysis) ➤ Solver. In Excel 2003, click Tools ➤ Solver. The Solver Parameters dialog box appears.

2. In the Set Target Cell box, type or click a reference to a single worksheet cell that you want to set to a maximum, minimum, or specific value. This cell referenced in this box must contain a formula.

3. Use the Equal To options to specify whether you want the cell referenced in the Set Target Cell box to be maximized, minimized, or set to a certain value:

   - Click the Max option if you want Solver to try to reach the highest target cell value subject to any specified constraints.

   - Click the Min option if you want Solver to try to reach the lowest target cell value subject to any specified constraints.

   - Click the Value Of option if you want Solver to try to reach a specific value subject to any specified constraints. If you click the Value Of option, type the specific value in the Value Of box to the right of the Value Of option. The default value is 0 (zero).

4. In the By Changing Cells box, type or select a reference to the worksheet cells that you want Solver to try to adjust until the cell referenced in the Set Target Cell box reaches its specified maximum, minimum, or exact value, subject to any specified constraints. For Solver to work properly, the cells referenced in the By Changing Cells box must be somehow related to the cell referenced in the Set Target Cell box.

5. Click the Guess button if you want Solver to try to guess all nonformula cells related to the Set Target Cell box's referenced worksheet cell formula and place those nonformula cell references in the By Changing Cells box.

The Subject to the Constraints list displays the current restrictions for the problem. Click the Add button to display the Add Constraint dialog box and add a constraint to the problem as follows:

1. In the Cell Reference box, type or select the cell references for which you want to restrict their values.

2. In the Operator list between the Cell Reference and Constraint boxes, click the relationship that you want between the referenced cells and the constraint. The relationships are the following:

   - The <= item specifies that the referenced cell values must be less than or equal to the constraint.

   - The = item specifies that the referenced cell values must be equal to the constraint.

- The >= item specifies that the referenced cell values must be greater than or equal to the constraint.

- The int item specifies that the referenced cell values must be integers.

■**Caution** Adding integer constraints to a Solver problem can significantly increase a problem's complexity, resulting in lengthy delays and possibly even prematurely stopping Solver before it can find a solution.

- The bin item specifies that the referenced cell values must be only one of two values, such as yes or no, true or false, or 0 or 1.

■**Note** You can apply the int and bin relationships only to constraints on adjustable cells.

---

3. In the Constraint box, type a number, a cell reference, or a formula.

■**Note** If you click int in the operator list, integer appears in the Constraint box. If you click bin in the Operator list, binary appears in the Constraint box. Do not bother typing the words *int*, *integer*, *bin*, or *binary* in the Constraint box as Solver will do this for you.

---

4. Click the Cancel button to return to the Solver Parameters dialog box.

5. Click the Add button to accept the constraint and prepare to add another constraint without returning to the Solver Parameters dialog box first.

6. Click the Help button to display an Excel Help topic that describes how to use the Add/Change Constraint dialog box.

7. Click the OK button to accept the constraint and return to the Solver Parameters dialog box.

After you return to the Solver Parameters dialog box, you can change an existing constraint by selecting the constraint in the Subject to the Constraints list, and then click the Change button to display the Change Constraint dialog box. The Change Constraint dialog box's controls are identical to those in the Add Constraint dialog box.

In the Solver Parameters dialog box, to delete an existing constraint, select the constraint in the Subject to the Constraints list, and then click the Delete button.

In the Solver Parameters dialog box, you can click the Options button to display the Solver Options dialog box to specify Solver settings and advanced Solver options as follows:

- The Max Time box specifies the number of seconds that you want to allow Solver to try to reach your solution's objective. While you could enter a value as high as 32,767 seconds (that's more than nine hours!), the default value of 100 seconds (just more than one and a half minutes) is adequate for most small problems. If Solver does not find a solution by the time period in the Max Time box is reached, it pauses and displays the Show Trial Solution dialog box to give you the option of stopping without an optimal solution or allowing you to continue for another equal time period.

- The Iterations box specifies the maximum number of calculations that you want to allow Solver to try before it reaches your solution's objective or gives up. Like the Max Time box, while you could enter a value as high as 32,767 iterations, the default value of 100 iterations is adequate for most small problems. If Solver cannot reach the objective after the number of tries in the Iterations box, it stops and displays the Show Trial Solution dialog box to give you the option of stopping without an optimal solution or allowing you to continue for another equal set of iterations.

- The Precision box specifies to what level of exactness the value of a constraint cell meets a target value or satisfies a lower or upper bound. The Precision value must be a fractional number between 0 (zero) and 1. The smaller the number in the Precision box is (the higher the number of decimal places), the higher the degree of precision. For example, 0.000001 is a higher precision than 0.01. Solver continues trying to reach the problem's objective until the constraints are reached within this degree of precision. For example, if the value in this box is 0.000001, and some constraint states that a cell value must equal 19, Solver will stop when the cell's value is within 0.000001 of 19, that is, between 18.999999 and 19.000001.

- The Tolerance box specifies the percentage by which the target cell of a problem with integer constraints can differ from the true optimal value, and Solver still considers it an acceptable solution to the problem. A higher tolerance tends to speed up Solver's time to find a solution. Solver will stop when the target cell's value is within this percent of the constraint value. The default tolerance is 5%.

- The Convergence box specifies the amount of relative change you want to allow Solver in its last five calculations before Solver stops with a solution. Solver uses the value in the Convergence box to determine when a proposed solution is significantly better than the previous proposed solution. If the change in the two proposed solutions is less than or equal to the value in the Convergence box, Solver will stop and declare that it has found a solution. Convergence applies only to nonlinear problems and must be indicated by a fractional number between 0 (zero) and 1. The smaller the number in the Convergence box, the smaller the convergence is. For example, 0.0001 (the default value) is a smaller degree of relative change in two solutions that Solver may propose— and therefore a smaller convergence—than 0.01. However, the smaller the number in the Convergence box, the more time it takes for Solver to reach a solution.

After you've set Solver options, do the following:

1. Click the OK button to apply the selected Solver options and return to the Solver Parameters dialog box.

2. Click the Cancel button to disregard any changes to the current Solver options and return to the Solver Parameters dialog box.

3. Click the Load Model button to display the Load Model dialog box, where you can specify the cell references for the model that you want to load.

4. Click the Save Model button to display the Save Model dialog box, where you can specify where to save the current model. You only need to click this button when you want to save more than one model with a worksheet, as Solver automatically saves the first model in the current worksheet.

5. Click the Help button to display an Excel Help topic that describes how to use the Solver Options dialog box.

6. Select the Assume Linear Model check box to speed up Solver's solution process if you know that your problem can be solved with linear functions.

■**Note** A linear function is a function that can be written as the sum of a series of variables, where each variable is multiplied by some constant value. A nonlinear function involves using some mathematical operation other than summation.

■**Note** Solver sometimes struggles with arriving at a solution to nonlinear problems, because in a nonlinear problem, there may be many approaches that Solver could take to find solutions, and it is not always possible to determine which of these approaches is best. If a Solver problem is linear and you select the Assume Linear Model check box, Solver uses a very efficient algorithm (the simplex method) to find the model's solution. If a Solver model is linear and you do not select the Assume Linear Model check box, Solver uses a very inefficient algorithm (the GRG2 method) and might have difficulty finding the model's solution.

---

7. Select the Assume Non-Negative check box when you want Solver to assume a lower limit of 0 (zero) for all adjustable cells that you have not set lower limit constraints for.

8. Select the Use Automatic Scaling check box when problem input and output values have large differences in order of magnitude—for example, when maximizing the percentage of profit based on billion dollar cash flows.

■**Note** Poorly scaled models (models where the typical values of the problem's objective and its constraints differ by several orders of magnitude) are one of the most common reasons why Solver appears to stop early without reaching a true optimal solution. Therefore, it is a good idea to select the Use Automatic Scaling box if you think you're working with a poorly scaled model.

---

9. Select the Show Iteration Results check box when you want Solver to pause, display the Show Trial Solution dialog box, and show its interim results for each calculation of the current problem.

10. The Estimates area specifies the approach used to obtain initial estimates of the basic variables in each one-dimensional search. Click the Tangent option if you know you have a linear problem to solve. The Tangent option instructs Solver to use an algorithm that performs a linear extrapolation from a tangent vector, and therefore favors linear problems. Clicking the Tangent option is faster, but less accurate, than clicking the Quadratic option. Click the Quadratic option if you know you have a nonlinear problem to solve. The Quadratic option instructs Solver to use an algorithm that performs a quadratic extrapolation, which can greatly improve the results on highly nonlinear problems.

11. The Derivatives area specifies the algorithm that Solver uses to begin calculating possible solutions by estimating partial derivatives of the problem's objective and its constraints. Click the Forward option for most problems, especially those problems in which the constraint values change relatively slowly. Click the Central option for those problems in which you know that the constraints may change rapidly, especially near their limits.

■**Tip** Although clicking the Central option forces Solver to make more calculations, it might be useful to click the Central option if Solver ever displays a message stating that a solution could not be improved.

---

12. The Search area specifies the algorithm that Solver uses to determine the next direction it will search for a possible solution after each of its calculations. Click the Newton option to use a quasi-Newton algorithm that results in a highly accurate search for possible solutions. Click the Conjugate option to use a less accurate search when you have a large problem that consumes a lot of computing resources, or when using Solver to step through iterations reveals very slow progress.

After you click OK to close the Solver Options dialog box, you can click one of the following:

- Click the Reset All button to clear all of the settings in the Solver Parameters dialog box and reset all of the settings in the Solver Options dialog box to its default values.

- Click the Help button to display an Excel Help topic that describes how to use the Solver Parameters dialog box.

- Click the Close button to close the Solver Parameters dialog box without solving the specified problem.

■**Note** When you click the Close button, Solver retains any changes you make to the Solver Parameters dialog box on the current worksheet by using the Options, Add, Change, or Delete buttons. The next time you click Data (Analysis) ➤ Solver (in Excel 2007) or Tools ➤ Solver (in Excel 2003) on the current worksheet, those retained changes will reappear.

- Click the Solve button to have Solver start finding a solution for the specified problem.

Try It

In this exercise, you will use Solver to determine how many widgets need to be produced per hour to come up with 1,000,000 widgets per month per manufacturing plant, altering a number of factors such as the number of widget makers, the number of widgets produced per hour, the number of hours per day worked, and the number of days per month worked.

If the Excel workbook file is not open from the previous exercise, open it:

1. Start Excel.

2. Click Office Button ➤ Open (in Excel 2007) or click File ➤ Open (in Excel 2003), browse to and select the ExcelDB_Ch06_06-12.xls file, and click Open.

Use Solver to determine how to produce 1,000,000 widgets per month for the Plainsville manufacturing plant, making sure that there are no more than 30 widget makers, no more than 8 hours worked per day, and no more than 20 days worked per month.

On the GoalSeekSolver worksheet tab, in Excel 2007, click Data (Analysis) ➤ Solver. In Excel 2003, click Tools ➤ Solver.

In the Solver dialog box, do the following:

1. Clear the contents of the Set Target Cell box, click the Set Target Cell box, and select cell B8.

2. Click the Value Of option, and in the Value Of box, type **1000000**.

3. Click the By Changing Cells box, and select cells B3 through B6.

4. Click Add.

5. Click the Cell Reference box, and select cell B3.

6. With the Condition list showing <=, type **30** in the Constraint box.

7. Click Add.

8. Click the Cell Reference box, and select cell B5.

9. With the Condition list showing <=, type **8** in the Constraint box.

10. Click Add.

11. Click the Cell Reference box, and select cell B6.

12. With the Condition list showing <=, type **20** in the Constraint box.

13. Click OK.

14. Click Solve.

Solver finds a solution: 30 widget makers, producing 208.3 widgets per hour, working at eight hours a day for 20 days, can produce approximately 1,000,000 widgets.

6.13 Create a PivotTable and PivotChart

PivotTables and PivotCharts allow you to analyze data from a different perspective. Instead of looking at data in a data-record-by-data-record format, you can use a PivotTable to summarize the data in different ways, as shown in Figures 6-1 through 6-3.

Average of Score	
Subject ▼	Total
Computer Science	92
Cooking	94
Graphic Design	82
Handwriting	95
Language	83
Math	73
Metal Arts	68
Physical Education	64
Reading	89
Sociology	66
Grand Total	81

Figure 6-1. *PivotTable displaying scores summarized by average test score per subject*

Average of Score	
Student ▼	Total
A. Ahmed	79
B. Bailey	79
C. Cornell	88
D. Duncan	77
E. Ellington	77
F. Farrell	78
G. Goshua	81
H. Hanson	83
I. Ikesville	86
J. Jackson	78
Grand Total	81

Figure 6-2. *PivotTable displaying scores summarized by average test score per student*

Subject	Computer Science ▾
Average of Score	
Student ▾	Total
A. Ahmed	99
B. Bailey	83
C. Cornell	99
D. Duncan	89
E. Ellington	91
F. Farrell	99
G. Goshua	94
H. Hanson	80
I. Ikesville	97
J. Jackson	89
Grand Total	92

Figure 6-3. *PivotTable displaying scores summarized by average test score per student and subject*

In these figures, let's pretend there are more than 100 school records containing students' test scores. In Figure 6-1, these scores are summarized by average test score per subject. In Figure 6-2, these scores are summarized by average test score per student. In Figure 6-3, these scores are also summarized by average test score per student, but the PivotTable allows you also to show test scores per student and per subject at the same time.

Based on these three PivotTable views, the corresponding PivotCharts in Figures 6-4 through 6-6 provide another visual perspective on the data.

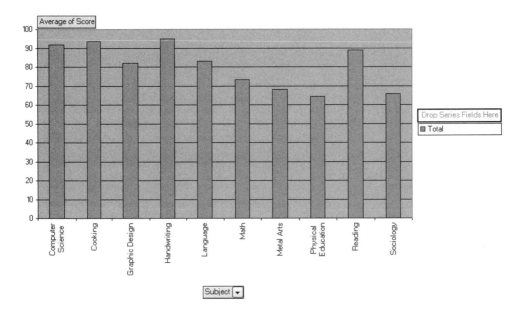

Figure 6-4. *PivotChart displaying scores summarized by average test score per subject*

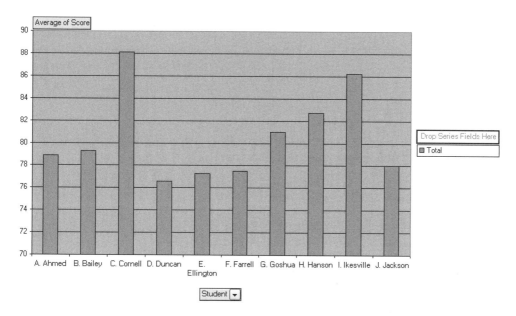

Figure 6-5. *PivotChart displaying scores summarized by average test score per student*

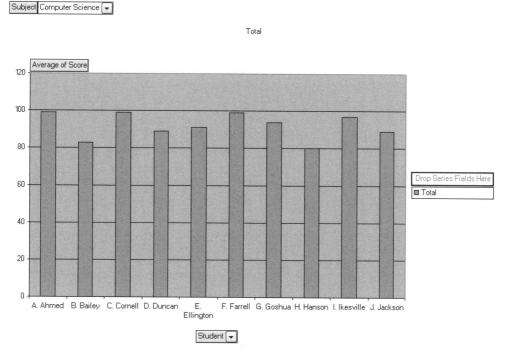

Figure 6-6. *PivotChart displaying scores summarized by average test score per student and subject*

In Figure 6-4, the PivotChart provides a visual representation of the average test score per subject. In Figure 6-5, the PivotChart provides a visual representation of the average test score per student. In Figure 6-6, the PivotChart also provides a visual representation of the average test score per student, but the PivotChart allows you also to show test scores per student and per subject at the same time.

There are a few terms you should familiarize yourself with to use PivotTables and PivotCharts more effectively:

The *row labels* (in Excel 2007) or the *row area* (in Excel 2003) in a PivotTable display the data field names that comprise the PivotTable's rows.

The *column labels* (in Excel 2007) or the *column area* (in Excel 2003) in a PivotTable display the data field names that comprise the PivotTable's columns.

The *values* (in Excel 2007) or the *data area* (in Excel 2003) in a PivotTable and a PivotChart display the individual or summarized data values.

The *report filter* (in Excel 2007) or *page area* (in Excel 2003) in a PivotTable and a PivotChart provide options for displaying individual or summarized data values that correspond to only a specific data field's matching data value.

The *axis fields* (in Excel 2007) or *category axis* (in Excel 2003) in a PivotChart display the data field values for each category of individual or summarized data value series.

The *legend fields* (in Excel 2007) or *series axis* (in Excel 2003) in a PivotChart display the series of individual or summarized data values for each category.

■**Tip** For more information about PivotTables and PivotCharts, see my book *A Complete Guide to PivotTables: A Visual Approach* (Apress, 2005).

Quick Start

To create a PivotTable and a PivotChart at the same time, in Excel 2007, do the following:

1. Click Insert ➤ (Tables) PivotTable ➤ PivotChart.

2. Complete the options in the Create PivotTable with PivotChart dialog box, and then click OK.

3. Use the PivotTable Field List, the (PivotTable Tools) Options ribbon, and the (PivotChart Tools) Design ribbon to define the PivotTable and PivotChart display format.

In Excel 2003, do the following:

1. Click Data ➤ PivotTable and PivotChart Report.

2. In the PivotTable and PivotChart Wizard – Step 1 of 3 page, in the What Kind of Report Do You Want to Create area, select the PivotChart Report (with PivotTable Report) option.

3. Complete the rest of the steps in the PivotTable and PivotChart Wizard.

4. Use the PivotTable Field List, the PivotTable, the PivotTable toolbar, the PivotChart, and the Chart toolbar to define the PivotTable and PivotChart display format.

How To

To create a PivotTable, or to create both a PivotTable and a PivotChart at the same time, in Excel 2007, do the following:

1. Click Insert ➤ (Tables) PivotTable ➤ PivotChart.

2. In the Create PivotTable with PivotChart dialog box, do the following:

   a. In the Choose the Data That You Want to Analyze area, select the Select a Table or Range option if the table or range is in an already open worksheet or workbook. In the Table/Range list, type or select the corresponding table or range reference. Or select the Use an External Data Source option if the data is in an external data source. Then click the Choose Connection button, complete the options in the Existing Connections dialog box, and click OK.

▓**Tip** For more information about how to complete the Existing Connections dialog box, see section "5.1: Create a Reusable Connection to External Data" in Chapter 5.

---

   b. In the Choose Where You Want the PivotTable and PivotChart to Be Placed area, select the New Worksheet option if you want to create a new worksheet in the current workbook and add the PivotTable and PivotChart to the new worksheet. Or select the Existing Worksheet option if you want to add the PivotTable and PivotChart to an existing worksheet. In the Location box, type or select the worksheet's location.

3. Click OK.

4. Use the PivotTable Field List, the PivotTable, the PivotTable toolbar, the PivotChart, and the Chart toolbar to define the PivotTable and PivotChart display format.

■**Tip** For information on how to change the PivotTable's and PivotChart's display format, see section "6.14: Change the View of a PivotTable and PivotChart."

In Excel 2003, do the following:

1. Click Data ➤ PivotTable and PivotChart Report.

2. In the PivotTable and PivotChart Wizard – Step 1 of 3 page, do the following:

   a. In the Where Is the Data That You Want to Analyze area, select the Microsoft Office Excel List or Database option to specify that the data source is a group of Excel cells; select the External Data Source option to specify that the data source is in a data file or a database other than Excel; select the Multiple Consolidation Ranges option to specify that the data source is in a set of multiple Excel cell groups; or select the Another PivotTable Report or PivotChart option to specify that the data source is in an existing PivotTable or PivotChart.

   b. In the What Kind of Report Do You Want to Create area, select the PivotChart Report (with PivotTable Report) option.

   c. Click Next.

3. Depending on the option you selected in step 2, the PivotTable and PivotChart Wizard – Step 2 of 3 page will differ. Do one of the following:

   • If you selected the Microsoft Office Excel List or Database option in step 2, the Step 2 of 3 page displays a Range box. Type or select the cell reference as your data source in the Range box, or click the Browse button to select a cell reference in another Excel workbook.

   • If you selected the External Data Source option in step 2, the Step 2 of 3 page displays a Get Data button. If you click this button, the Choose Data Source dialog box appears to allow you to specify details about the external data source.

■**Tip** For more information about how to complete the Choose Data Source dialog box, see section "5.2: Adjust External Data While Importing" in Chapter 5.

   • If you selected the Multiple Consolidation Ranges option in step 2, the Step 2 of 3 page is comprised of two subpages. The Step 2a of 3 page displays two options. Select the Create a Page Field for Me option to have Excel create a single page field for you, or select the I Will Create the Page Fields option to create your own page fields. The Step 2b of 3 page displays options for you to add each separate Excel cell group to the data source list. If you select the I Will Create the Page Fields option in the Step 2a of 3 page, there are additional options for you to specify the number and names of page fields.

4. Click Next.

5. The Step 3 of 3 page displays two options. Select the New Worksheet option to specify that Excel will create a new worksheet in the current workbook, and then it will place the PivotTable into the new worksheet that Excel created. Or select the Existing Worksheet option to specify that Excel will place the PivotTable beginning with the cell that you specify in the box below the Existing Worksheet option.

■**Note** When you select the PivotChart Report (with PivotTable Report) option in step 1, Excel will also create a new worksheet just for the PivotChart and place the PivotChart in this new worksheet.

---

6. Click Finish.

7. Use the PivotTable Field List, the PivotTable, the PivotTable toolbar, the PivotChart, and the Chart toolbar to define the PivotTable and PivotChart display format.

■**Tip** For information on how to change the PivotTable's and PivotChart's display format, see section "6.14: Change the View of a PivotTable and PivotChart."

Try It

In this exercise, you will practice creating a PivotTable and a PivotChart to display a summary of automotive sales statistics by sales year:

1. Start Excel.

2. Click Office Button ➤ Open (in Excel 2007) or click File ➤ Open (in Excel 2003), browse to and select the ExcelDB_Ch06_13-14.xls file, and click Open.

In Excel 2007, create the PivotTable and PivotChart:

1. On the AutoSales worksheet, click Insert ➤ (Tables) PivotTable ➤ PivotChart.

2. In the Create PivotTable with PivotChart dialog box, with the Select a Table or Range option selected, in the Table/Range box with the cell reference of the AutoSales worksheet and cells A1 through G33 showing (select cells A1 through G33 if this is not showing), and the New Worksheet option selected, click OK.

In Excel 2007, put data in the PivotTable and PivotChart:

1. Select the PivotTable and PivotChart worksheet (the worksheet with the Drop Here areas, the blank PivotChart area, and the PivotTable Field List showing).

2. With the PivotTable selected, in the PivotTable Field List, right-click the Compact check box, and click Add to Values.

3. Repeat step 2 for the following check boxes, respectively, clicking the Add to Values context menu command for each: Station Wagon, Sport Utility, Minivan, and Heavy Truck.

4. Right-click the Year check box and click Add to Row Labels.

5. Notice that the PivotTable and the PivotChart layouts are synchronized.

In Excel 2003, create the PivotTable and PivotChart:

1. On the AutoSales worksheet, click Data ➤ PivotTable and PivotChart Report.

2. In the PivotTable and PivotChart Wizard – Step 1 of 3 dialog box, with the Microsoft Office Excel list or Database option selected, select the PivotChart Report (with Pivot-Table Report) option, and then click Next.

3. In the PivotTable and PivotChart Wizard – Step 2 of 3 dialog box, in the Range box, with the cell reference of cells A1 through G33 showing (select cells A1 through G33 if this is not showing), click Next.

4. In the PivotTable and PivotChart Wizard – Step 3 of 3 dialog box, with the New Work-sheet option selected, click Finish. The PivotTable and PivotChart are created.

In Excel 2003, put data in the PivotTable and PivotChart:

1. Select the PivotTable worksheet (the worksheet with the Drop Here areas and the PivotTable Field List showing).

2. With the PivotTable selected, in the PivotTable Field List, click the Year field.

3. In the Add To list, select Row Area, and then click the Add To button.

4. In the PivotTable Field List, click the Compact field.

5. In the Add To list, select Data Area, and then click the Add To button.

6. Repeat steps 4 and 5 for the following fields, respectively, adding each to the Data area: Station Wagon, Sport Utility, Minivan, and Heavy Truck.

7. Notice that when you click the PivotChart worksheet (the worksheet with the word *Chart* in its name), the PivotChart reflects the data that is displayed in the PivotTable.

6.14 Change the View of a PivotTable and PivotChart

After you create a PivotTable or a PivotChart, you can use the PivotTable Field List as a tool to switch (or *pivot*) among different ways to view the summarized data. Figure 6-7 shows the PivotTable Field List in Excel 2007, and Figure 6-8 shows the PivotTable Field List in Excel 2003.

Figure 6-7. *PivotTable Field List in Excel 2007*

In Excel 2007, you can do the following in the PivotTable Field List:

- Click the Fields Section and Areas Section Stacked button to change how the Choose Fields to Add to Report area (the *fields*) and the Drag Fields Between Areas Below area (the *drop zones*) are displayed in the PivotTable Field List.

- Right-click any of the check boxes in the Choose Fields to Add to Report area and then click the drop zone into which the corresponding data field should be displayed.

- Click any data field in the Drag Fields Between Areas Below area to move the corresponding data field up, down, to the beginning, or to the end of the selected drop zone; move the data field to another drop zone; remove the data field from the PivotTable or PivotTable and PivotChart; or change the data field's display settings.

- Select the Defer Layout Update check box to not update the PivotTable and PivotChart display until the Update button is explicitly clicked. If the Defer Layout Update check box is cleared, the PivotTable and PivotChart display will update whenever you make a change to the data fields' layout or display options.

- Click the Update button to explicitly update the PivotTable and PivotChart display.

Figure 6-8. *PivotTable Field List in Excel 2003*

In Excel 2003, you can do the following in the PivotTable Field List:

- In the Drag Items to the PivotTable Report list, select the data field that you want to add to—or change the position of—the data field in the PivotTable or PivotChart.

- In the Add To list, select the area to which you want to add to—or change the position of—the data field in the PivotTable or PivotChart.

- Click the Add To button to add the selected data field to—or change the position of—the selected data field in the PivotTable or PivotChart.

■**Tip** For more information about creating PivotTable and PivotCharts, see section "6.13: Create a Pivot-Table and PivotChart." For more information on changing the views of PivotTables and PivotCharts, see my book *A Complete Guide to PivotTables: A Visual Approach* (Apress, 2005).

Quick Start

To change the view of an existing PivotTable or PivotChart, in Excel 2007, do the following:

1. In the PivotTable Field List, in the Choose Fields to Add to Report list, right-click the data field that you want to add to—or change position in—the PivotTable or PivotChart.

2. Select the area to which you want to add to—or change position in—the PivotTable or PivotChart (e.g., Add to Report Filter, Add to Row Labels, Add to Column Labels, or Add to Values).

In Excel 2003, do the following:

1. In the PivotTable Field List, in the Drag Items to the PivotTable Report list, select the data field that you want to add to—or change the position of the data field in—the PivotTable or PivotTable and PivotChart.

2. In the Add To list, select the area to which you want to add the selected data field to—or change the position of the selected data field in—the PivotTable or PivotTable and PivotChart (e.g., Row Area, Column Area, Page Area, Data Area, Category Axis, or Series Axis).

3. Click the Add To button.

How To

To add a data field to—or change the position of a data field in—a PivotTable or a PivotChart in Excel 2007, do the following:

1. In the PivotTable Field List, in the Choose Fields to Add to Report list, right-click the data field that you want to add to—or change position in—the PivotTable or PivotChart.

2. Select the area to which you want to add to—or change position in—the PivotTable or PivotChart (e.g., Add to Report Filter, Add to Row Labels, Add to Column Labels, or Add to Values).

In Excel 2003, do the following:

1. In the PivotTable Field List, in the Drag Items to the PivotTable Report list, select the data field that you want to add to—or change the position of the data field in—the PivotTable or PivotTable and PivotChart.

2. In the Add To list, select the area to which you want to add the selected data field to—or change the position of the selected data field in—the PivotTable or PivotTable and PivotChart (e.g., Row Area, Column Area, Page Area, Data Area, Category Axis, or Series Axis).

3. Click the Add To button.

To remove a data field from a PivotTable or a PivotChart, do the following:

1. In Excel 2007, clear the data field's check box in the PivotTable Field List's Choose Fields to Add to Report list.

2. In Excel 2003, drag the data field button (the button in the Row Area, Column Area, Page Area, Data Area, Category Axis, or Series Axis with the data field's name on it) outside of the PivotTable or PivotChart. When the mouse pointer changes to a red X, release the mouse button.

To change a data field's display format in a PivotTable, in Excel 2007, do the following:

1. Click the field in the PivotTable Field List's Drag Fields Between Areas Below area, and then click Field Settings.

2. Complete the options in the Field Settings dialog box, and then click OK.

In Excel 2003, do the following:

1. Right-click the data field button in the PivotTable, and click Format Cells or Field Settings.

2. Complete the options in the Format Cells or the PivotTable Field dialog boxes, respectively, depending on which display aspects of the data field you want to change, and then click OK.

To change a data field's display format in a PivotChart in Excel 2007, do the following:

1. Click the field in the PivotTable Field List's Drag Fields Between Areas Below area, and then click Field Settings.

2. Complete the options in the Field Settings dialog box, and then click OK.

In Excel 2003, do the following:

1. Right-click the data field button in the PivotChart, and click Format PivotChart Field.

2. Complete the options in the PivotTable Field dialog box, and then click OK.

Try It

This exercise assumes that you have first completed the exercise in the "Try It" section of section "6.13: Create a PivotTable and PivotChart," and that the corresponding PivotTable and PivotChart are set up per that section. In this exercise, you will change the view of the PivotTable and PivotChart so that you are looking at automotive sales statistics by sales region instead of by sales year. With the PivotTable from the "Try It" section of section "6.13" selected, in Excel 2007, do the following:

1. In the PivotTable Field List, clear the Year check box.

2. Right-click the Region check box and click Add to Row Labels.

3. Notice that the PivotTable and the PivotChart layouts are synchronized.

In Excel 2003, do the following:

1. Drag the Year field button outside of the PivotTable's boundaries. When the icon turns into a red X, release the mouse button.

2. In the PivotTable Field List, click the Region field.

3. In the Add To list, select Row Area, and then click the Add To button.

4. In the PivotTable, right-click the Region field button, point to Order, and click Move to Beginning.

5. Notice that when you click the PivotChart worksheet, the PivotChart reflects the data that is displayed in the PivotTable.

6.15 Perform Statistical Data Analysis

Excel includes a set of statistical data analysis tools that you can use to create a wide variety of statistical and engineering data analysis reports based on your selected data values. Some of these statistical data analysis tools include the following:

- The Descriptive Statistics tool provides a report displaying statistics such as the mean, median, mode, standard deviation, minimum, maximum, sum, count, and the largest and smallest data values.

- The Histogram tool provides a report displaying the frequency of specific data values.

- The Rank and Percentile tool provides a report displaying the ordinal and percentage ranking of specific data values.

Quick Start

To perform statistical data analysis, do one of the following and complete the steps in the Data Analysis dialog box:

- In Excel 2007, click Data (Analysis) ➤ Data Analysis.

- In Excel 2003, click Tools ➤ Data Analysis.

Tip

Since the Data Analysis tools may not always be available when Excel is installed, you should confirm that they are available before you try to use them. If the Data Analysis command doesn't appear in the Data (Analysis) group (in Excel 2007) or on the Tools menu (in Excel 2003), do one of the following:

- In Excel 2007, click Office Button ➤ Excel Options. In the left pane, click Add-Ins. With the Manage list toward the bottom of the screen showing Excel Add-Ins, click Go. Select the Analysis ToolPak check box, click OK, and then click Data (Analysis) ➤ Data Analysis.

- In Excel 2003, click Tools ➤ Add-Ins, select the Analysis ToolPak check box, click OK, and then click Tools ➤ Data Analysis.

  If, however, the Analysis ToolPak check box is not visible in the Add-Ins dialog box's Add-Ins available list, you must install the Analysis ToolPak by running the Microsoft Office Setup program again and selecting Analysis ToolPak from the list of available Excel add-ins. Then you can start Excel and click Data (Analysis) ➤ Data Analysis (in Excel 2007) or Tools ➤ Data Analysis (in Excel 2003).

How To

To perform statistical data analysis, do the following:

1. In Excel 2007, click Data (Analysis) ➤ Data Analysis. In Excel 2003, click Tools ➤ Data Analysis

2. In the Data Analysis dialog box, select an available analysis tool, and then click OK.

3. Follow the onscreen directions to run the selected analysis tool.

Try It

In this exercise, you will practice running the Descriptive Statistics tool on a set of data:

1. Start Excel.

2. Click Office Button ➤ Open (in Excel 2007) or click File ➤ Open (in Excel 2003), browse to and select the ExcelDB_Ch06_15.xls file, and click Open.

3. In Excel 2007, click Data (Analysis) ➤ Data Analysis. In Excel 2003, click Tools ➤ Data Analysis.

4. In the Data Analysis dialog box, select Descriptive Statistics, and then click OK.

5. Click the Input Range dialog box, and then type or select the cell reference for cells B2 through B41.

6. For the Grouped By options, click the Columns option.

7. Leave the Labels in First Row check box cleared.

8. In the Output options area, select the New Worksheet Ply option and the Summary Statistics check box. Leave the other check boxes in this area cleared.

9. Click OK. A new worksheet is created with the summary statistics displayed, including statistics such as the mean, median, mode, standard deviation, minimum, maximum, sum, and count of the selected data values.

■■■

CHAPTER 7

Automate Repetitive Database Tasks

The more you use Excel, the greater the chance that you will be performing the same sets of actions over and over again. For instance, you may frequently change the visual format of a selected set of worksheet cells to a similar font style, row height, and border style. Or perhaps you frequently sort data records that relate to sales transactions by transaction date. In this chapter, you will learn how to use Excel's macro recorder and the Excel programmatic object model with Visual Basic for Applications to automate these types of actions. By recording your Excel interactions and then customizing these recordings to automate Excel to get the desired results, you can save time and reduce errors when you want to do similar actions in the future.

7.1 Use the Macro Recorder

Excel's macro recorder works very similar to a digital music recorder. Just as a digital music recorder records music that you can play back, in Excel you can name a *macro* (a set of instructions to perform an action); the recorder starts, you perform a set of actions in Excel, and then you stop recording. Later, you can play the recorded macro as needed to perform the desired action. For example, you could record a set of actions to apply conditional formatting to a group of worksheet cells. You could then modify that set of actions and reuse them to quickly apply conditional formatting to another group of worksheet cells.

Quick Start

To use the macro recorder, do the following:

1. In Excel 2007, click Developer ➤ (Code) Record Macro. In Excel 2003, click Tools ➤ Macro ➤ Record New Macro.

2. Complete the options in the Record Macro dialog box.

3. In Excel, perform the actions that you want to automate.

4. When finished, in Excel 2007, click Developer ➤ (Code) Stop Recording. In Excel 2003, on the Stop Recording toolbar, click the Stop Recording button.

IF YOU DO NOT SEE THE DEVELOPER TAB IN EXCEL 2007

To display the Developer tab in Excel 2007, do the following:

1. Click Office Button ➤ Excel Options.

2. On the Popular tab, in the Top Options for Working with Excel area, select the Show Developer Tab In the Ribbon check box, and then click OK.

To run the macro, in Excel 2007, click Developer ➤ (Code) Macros, select the desired macro, and then click Run. In Excel 2003, click Tools ➤ Macros ➤ Macros, select the desired macro, and then click Run.

How To

To use the macro recorder, do the following:

1. In Excel 2007, click Developer ➤ (Code) Record Macro. In Excel 2003, click Tools ➤ Macro ➤ Record New Macro.

2. Complete the options in the Record Macro dialog box:

   - In the Macro Name box, you can type a name that you can easily remember later for reference.

   - In the Shortcut Key box, you can type a keyboard character that you want to use to associate with running this macro. For example, if you type the letter **J**, you can use the Ctrl+J shortcut key combination to run this macro later.

   - In the Store Macro In list, you can select the location in which you want to store this macro.

   - In the Description box, you can type a description for the macro for future reference.

3. In Excel, perform the actions that you want to automate.

4. When finished, in Excel 2007, click Developer ➤ (Code) Stop Recording. In Excel 2003, on the Stop Recording toolbar, click the Stop Recording button.

To run the macro, in Excel 2007, click Developer ➤ (Code) Macros, select the desired macro, and then click Run. In Excel 2003, click Tools ➤ Macros ➤ Macros, select the desired macro, and then click Run.

RECORDING AND RUNNING MACROS WITH EXCEL SECURITY SETTINGS

Depending on Excel's macro security level setting, you may not be able to record or run macros. To change your macro security level, do one of the following:

- In Excel 2007, click Developer ➤ (Code) Macro Security, select the desired macro security level on the Macro Settings tab, click OK, and then quit and restart Excel.

- In Excel 2003, click Tools ➤ Macro ➤ Security, select the desired macro security level on the Security Level tab, click OK, and then quit and restart Excel.

In Excel 2007, the macro security levels for documents that are opened from untrusted locations are the following:

- *Disable All Macros Without Notification*: Excel will not allow you to run macros in the workbook. Excel will not inform you that macros cannot be run, and Excel will not allow you to run macros in the workbook until you reopen the workbook and choose the Disable All Macros with Notification option or the Enable All Macros option.

- *Disable All Macros with Notification*: Excel will not allow you to run macros in the workbook. Excel will inform you that macros have been disabled in the workbook, and Excel will present you with an Options button to enable you to run macros in the workbook.

- *Disable All Macros Except Digitally Signed Macros*: If the workbook is opened from an untrusted location, and the macros are not digitally signed, Excel will not allow you to run macros in the workbook until the macros are digitally signed or you reopen the workbook and choose the Disable All Macros with Notification option or the Enable All Macros option.

- *Enable All Macros (Not Recommended; Potentially Dangerous Code Can Run)*: Excel will enable all macros in any workbook to be run, regardless of where the workbook originates or is stored. Because this setting can leave your computer very vulnerable to dangerous code, you should consider setting your macro security level to one of the other macro security levels.

In Excel 2003, the macro security levels are the following:

- *Very High*: Macros will run only if they are in a workbook stored in a trusted location.

- *High*: Macros will run only if they are in a workbook originating from a trusted source.

- *Medium*: If the workbook does not originate from a trusted source, Excel will ask if you want to enable the macros in the workbook to be run.

- *Low*: Excel will enable all macros in any workbook to be run, regardless of where the workbook originates or is stored. Because this setting can leave your computer very vulnerable to dangerous code, you should consider setting your macro security level to Medium or higher.

Be aware that changing Excel's macro security level can cause potentially unexpected and unwanted results in some cases. For example, in Excel 2003, setting your macro security level to Very High will prevent all of your macros from running unless they are in a workbook stored in a trusted location. Similarly, setting your macro security level to Low in Excel 2003 can unwittingly expose your computer to unwanted viruses hiding in macros created by others with malicious intent. In some organizations, your IT department may restrict or prevent your ability to change macro security levels such as Disable All Macros Without Notification or Very High.

Try It

In this exercise, you will practice using Excel's macro recorder to change the visual formatting of selected worksheet cells.

Open the workbook:

1. Click Office Button ➤ Open (in Excel 2007) or File ➤ Open (in Excel 2003).

2. Browse to and select the ExcelDB_Ch07_01-12.xls file, and then click Open.

Record the macro:

1. On the RecordMacros worksheet, select cells A2 through A9.

2. Do one of these:

   - In Excel 2007, click Developer ➤ (Code) Record Macro.

   - In Excel 2003, click Tools ➤ Macro ➤ Record New Macro.

3. In the Macro Name box, type **FormatSelectedCells**.

4. With the Store Macro in List showing This Workbook, click OK.

5. In Excel 2007, click Home ➤ (Cells) Format ➤ Format Cells. In Excel 2003, click Format ➤ Cells.

6. On the Font tab, in the Font Style list, select Bold Italic.

7. In the Color list, select the red box.

8. On the Fill tab (in Excel 2007) or the Patterns tab (in Excel 2003), in the Background Color area (in Excel 2007) or the Cell Shading area (in Excel 2003), click the yellow box, then click OK.

9. In Excel 2007, click Developer ➤ (Code) Stop Recording. In Excel 2003, on the Stop Recording toolbar, click Stop Recording.

Play back the macro:

1. Select cells C2 through C9.

2. In Excel 2007, click Developer ➤ (Code) Macros. In Excel 2003, click Tools ➤ Macro ➤ Macros.

3. In the list, select FormatSelectedCells, and click Run. The selected cells match the formatting in cells A2 through A9.

7.2 Understand Excel Visual Basic for Applications

If you're familiar with Microsoft Visual Basic, then Excel's Visual Basic for Applications (VBA) programming environment will also be very familiar. Even if you're not a Visual Basic programmer, using Excel's built-in programming environment is very straightforward.

When you want to write code to automate repetitive database tasks, you attach Excel VBA code to the desired workbook by using the Excel Visual Basic Editor (VBE). In the VBE, the

Project Explorer window displays the code attached to each open Excel workbook. To facilitate code reuse among Excel workbooks, you can also create modules that can be shared with other workbooks. For example, you could create a module that applies specific visual formatting to a group of worksheet cells. Then you could copy that module to other worksheets or share that module with your coworkers.

Quick Start

- To access the VBE, in Excel 2007, click Developer ➤ (Code) Visual Basic. In Excel 2003, click Tools ➤ Macro ➤ Visual Basic Editor.

■Note If you do not see the Developer tab in Excel 2007, see the sidebar in section 7.1 to learn how to display it.

- To create a module, right-click any node associated with the target workbook, click Insert, and then click the desired module type.

- To share a module, right-click the module, click Export File, and complete the Export File dialog box.

- To attach a module to a workbook, right-click any node associated with the target workbook, click Import File, and complete the Import File dialog box.

How To

To access the Visual Basic Editor (VBE) in Excel 2007, click Developer ➤ (Code) Visual Basic. In Excel 2003, click Tools ➤ Macro ➤ Visual Basic Editor.

To access the VBE's Project Explorer window, click View ➤ Project Explorer. Each Excel workbook has a corresponding node in the Project Explorer window, representing code attached to the workbook itself. To access the workbook's code, expand the workbook's node, and then double-click the ThisWorkbook icon. Each worksheet in a workbook has its own associated code as well, typically accessible only to that worksheet. To access a worksheet's code, double-click the corresponding worksheet icon.

To facilitate code reuse among Excel workbooks, you can also create three types of modules (*code modules*, *class modules*, and *UserForms*) that can be shared with other workbooks:

- *Code modules* are typically used to create reusable subroutines and functions.

- *Class modules* are used to create custom programmatic objects and classes that are best leveraged in object-oriented code solutions.

- *UserForms* are used to create interactive dialog boxes.

To create a code module, right-click in the Project Explorer any node associated with a workbook or worksheet, and then click Insert ➤ Module, Insert ➤ Class Module, or Insert ➤ UserForm. You can then attach code to the newly created code module by double-clicking that module in the Project Explorer window.

To share a code module, right-click in the Project Explorer the code module, click Export File, and complete the Export File dialog box to save a copy of the code. (Note that this copied code is a snapshot of the code module; future changes that you make to the original code module are not reflected in this saved copy of the code.) To attach an exported module to a workbook, right-click in the Project Explorer any node associated with the target workbook or worksheet, click Import File, and complete the Import File dialog box.

■**Tip** To learn more about how to use VBE in Excel 2007, in the VBE, click Help ➤ Microsoft Visual Basic Help, type phrases such as **Visual Basic Editor**, **Project Explorer**, **Code Window**, or **Toolbars** in the Type Words to Search For box, and click the Search Developer Reference button.

To learn more about how to use the VBE in Excel 2003, in the VBE, click Help ➤ Microsoft Visual Basic Help, and in the Table of Contents list, expand the Microsoft Visual Basic Documentation book, and expand the Visual Basic User Interface Help book. Read Help topics such as Project Explorer Window and Code Window (in the Windows book) and Standard Toolbar (in the Toolbars book), and the various Help topics in the Menus book.

If you've worked with other programming languages, you should be able to program in VBA with little difficulty. Here is a brief summary of the most common VBA language keywords:

- You begin a procedure or method with either the Sub keyword (for procedures and methods that don't return a value) or the Function keyword (for procedures and methods that can return a value), and you end the procedure or method declaration with End Sub or End Function—for example, Sub ChangeCellColor() and then End Sub.

- VBA defines data types such as Array, Boolean, Byte, Currency, Date, Decimal, Double, Integer, Long, Object, Single, String, and Variant, in addition to Excel-specific data types such as Workbook, Worksheet, and PivotTable. You declare a variable with the Dim keyword and specify the variable's data type. If the variable is an object data type, you then initialize the variable with the Set keyword—for example, Dim intNumberOfCells As Integer and then intNumberOfCells = 10 or Dim wbk As Workbook and then Set wbk = ThisWorkbook.

- VBA defines control flow constructs such as Do...Loop, For...Next, If...Then...Else, and Select Case—for example, For i = 1 to 10, then MsgBox i, and then Next to display the numbers 1 to 10.

■**Note** To learn more about how to use the VBA programming language in Excel 2007, in the VBE included with Excel 2007, click Help ➤ Microsoft Visual Basic Help, type phrases such as **writing declaration statements**, **data types keyword summary**, **control flow keyword summary**, or **keywords by task** in the Type Words to Search For box, and click the Search Developer Reference button.

To learn how to use the VBA programming language in Excel 2003, in the VBE included with Excel 2003, click Help ➤ Microsoft Visual Basic Help, and in the Table of Contents list, expand the Microsoft Visual Basic Documentation book, and expand the Visual Basic Conceptual Topics book. Read Help topics such as Writing a Sub Procedure; Declaring Variables; Creating Object Variables; Understanding Objects, Properties, Methods, and Events; and Looping Through Code.

Try It

In this exercise, you will practice attaching a module to an existing workbook. You will then export the module, attach the exported module to a new workbook, and run the module's code from the new workbook.

1. Start Excel.

2. Create two new Excel workbook files. Save the first Excel workbook with the file name Before.xlsm (in Excel 2007) or Before.xls (in Excel 2003) and the second Excel workbook with the file name After.xlsm (in Excel 2007) or After.xls (in Excel 2003). Both workbooks should be open in Excel at this point.

■Note In Excel 2007, click Office Button ➤ Save As ➤ Excel Macro-Enabled Workbook to save the workbook with the extension .xlsm.

---

3. Open the VBE:

   - In Excel 2007, click Developer ➤ (Code) Visual Basic.

■Note If you do not see the Developer tab, see the sidebar in section 7.1 to learn how to display it.

   - In Excel 2003, click Tools ➤ Macro ➤ Visual Basic Editor.

4. In the Project Explorer window, right-click the VBAProject (Before.xlsm in Excel 2007) or the VBAProject (Before.xls in Excel 2003) node, and then click Insert ➤ Module.

5. In the Code window, type this code:

```
Public Sub HelloWorld()

    MsgBox "Hello from the " & ThisWorkbook.Name & " workbook!"

End Sub
```

6. Click anywhere between the first and last lines of code, and then click Run ➤ Run Sub/User Form. The message "Hello from the Before.xlsm workbook!" (in Excel 2007) or "Hello from the Before.xls workbook!" (in Excel 2003) appears. Click OK.

7. Right-click the Module1 subnode in the VBAProject (Before.xlsm in Excel 2007) or the VBAProject (Before.xls in Excel 2003) node, and click Export File. Save the Module1.bas file to a convenient location.

8. In the Project Explorer window, right-click the VBAProject (After.xlsm in Excel 2007) or the VBAProject (After.xls in Excel 2003) node, and then click Import File.

9. Browse to and select the Module1.bas file, and then click Open.

10. In the Project Explorer window, expand the Modules subnode in the VBAProject (After.xlsm in Excel 2007) or the VBAProject (After.xls in Excel 2003) node, and double-click the Module1 node.

11. Click anywhere between the first and last lines of code, and then click Run ➤ Run Sub/User Form. The message "Hello from the After.xlsm workbook!" (in Excel 2007) or "Hello from the After.xls workbook!" (in Excel 2003) appears. Click OK.

12. Add one line of code (as shown in bold) to the body of the Module1 code module in the VBAProject (After.xlsm in Excel 2007) or the VBAProject (After.xls in Excel 2003) node:

```
Public Sub HelloWorld()

    MsgBox "Hello from the " & ThisWorkbook.Name & " workbook!"
    MsgBox "This code will not appear in the Before.xls(m) workbook."

End Sub
```

13. Click File ➤ Save After.xlsm (in Excel 2007) or File ➤ Save After.xls (in Excel 2003).

14. In the Project Explorer window, double-click the Module1 node in the VBAProject (Before.xlsm in Excel 2007) or the VBAProject (Before.xls in Excel 2003) node. Notice that the code you added to the Module1 subnode in the VBAProject (After.xlsm in Excel 2007) or the VBAProject (After.xls in Excel 2003) node does not appear in this code. The code in the Before.xlsm (in Excel 2007) or Before.xls (in Excel 2003) Module1 code module is now separate from the code in the After.xlsm (in Excel 2007) or After.xls (for Excel 2003) Module1 code module.

7.3 Understand the Excel Programming Model

Understanding Excel's collection of programmatic objects is key to being able to successfully automate Excel using VBA code. There are about 200 programmatic objects and collections of objects in Excel 2003 VBA, and close to 250 programmatic objects and collections of objects in Excel 2007 VBA. Fortunately you don't have to know them all to begin with. If you learn how to automate the five most important Excel objects—Application, Workbooks, Workbook, Worksheet, and Range—you can leverage them to automate the rest of the objects. For example, once you have access to a Workbook object, you can automate the workbook's individual worksheets, and in turn you can automate each worksheet's individual cells.

Quick Start

- To access the Excel application, use Excel VBA's Application object.

- To access a set of Excel workbooks, use Excel VBA's Workbooks collection.

- To access an Excel workbook, use Excel VBA's Workbook object.

- To access an Excel worksheet, use Excel VBA's Worksheet object.

- To access one or more Excel cells, use Excel VBA's Range object.

How To

To access the Excel application, call the Application object, as in this example:

```
Excel.Application.Speech.Speak Text:="Hello, World!"
```

To access a set of Excel workbooks, use the Workbooks collection, as in this example:

```
Dim wkbs As Excel.Workbooks

Set wkbs = Excel.Application.Workbooks

MsgBox Prompt:=wkbs.Count
```

To access an Excel workbook, use the Workbook object (or the ThisWorkbook object to access the current workbook), as in this example:

```
Dim wkb As Excel.Workbook

' And one of the following sets of code:

Set wkb = Excel.Application.Workbooks.Item _
    (Index:="ExcelDB_Ch07_01-12.xls")
MsgBox Prompt:=wkb.FullName

Set wkb = Excel.Application.ThisWorkbook
MsgBox Prompt:=wkb.FullName
```

To access an Excel worksheet, use the Worksheet object (or the ActiveSheet property to access the current worksheet), as in this example:

```
' One of the following lines of code:

MsgBox Prompt:=Excel.Application.Workbooks.Item _
    (Index:="ExcelDB_Ch07_01-12.xls"). _
    Worksheets.Item(Index:="Sample Data").Name

MsgBox Prompt:=Excel.Application.ThisWorkbook.ActiveSheet.Name

' Or:

Dim wks As Excel.Worksheet

' And one of the following sets of code:

Set wks = Excel.Application.Workbooks.Item _
    (Index:="ExcelDB_Ch07_01-12.xls"). _
    Worksheets.Item(Index:="Sample Data")
MsgBox Prompt:=wks.Name

Set wks = Excel.Application.ThisWorkbook.ActiveSheet
MsgBox Prompt:=wks.Name
```

EXCEL PROGRAMMING MODEL CODE SHORTCUTS

Excel VBA lets you omit the Excel library qualifier and the Application property to return the Application object, as long as you are not referring to any other Application objects defined in other libraries at the same time. For example, the following lines of code are equivalent to referring to an Excel workbook:

```
MsgBox Prompt:=Excel.Application.Workbooks.Item _
    (Index:="ExcelDB_Ch07_01-12.xls"). _
    Worksheets.Item(Index:="Sample Data").Name

MsgBox Prompt:=Excel.Workbooks.Item _
    (Index:="ExcelDB_Ch07_01-12.xls"). _
    Worksheets.Item(Index:="Sample Data").Name

MsgBox Prompt:=Application.Workbooks.Item _
    (Index:="ExcelDB_Ch07_01-12.xls"). _
    Worksheets.Item(Index:="Sample Data").Name

MsgBox Prompt:=Workbooks.Item _
    (Index:="ExcelDB_Ch07_01-12.xls"). _
    Worksheets.Item(Index:="Sample Data").Name
```

Similarly, the following lines of code are equivalent to accessing the current workbook by using the ThisWorkbook property to return the ThisWorkbook object:

```
MsgBox Prompt:=Excel.Application.ThisWorkbook.Worksheets.Item _
    (Index:="Sample Data").Name

MsgBox Prompt:=Excel.ThisWorkbook.Worksheets.Item _
    (Index:="Sample Data").Name

MsgBox Prompt:=Application.ThisWorkbook.Worksheets.Item _
    (Index:="Sample Data").Name

MsgBox Prompt:=ThisWorkbook.Worksheets.Item _
    (Index:="Sample Data").Name
```

To access one or more Excel cells, use the Range object, as in this example:

```
Dim rng As Excel.Range

Set rng = Excel.Application.Workbooks.Item(Index:="ExcelDB_Ch07_01-12.xls"). _
    Worksheets.Item(Index:="Sample Data").Range(Cell1:="A1")

MsgBox prompt:=rng.Value2
```

USING THE RANGE PROPERTY'S CELL1 AND CELL2 ARGUMENTS

You can access Excel cells with the Range property. To access a single cell, use code similar to
.Range(Cell1:="B5"). To access a group of cells, do one of the following:

- Use a cell reference for the Cell1 argument with code similar to .Range(Cell1:="B4:D11").

- Use a starting cell reference for the Cell1 argument and an ending cell reference for the Cell2
  argument with code similar to .Range(Cell1:="B4", Cell2:="D11").

- Use a named cell group for the Cell1 argument with code similar to .Range(Cell1:="StoreData").

Try It

To experiment with writing code to work with the Excel programming model, you can start with
the sample code that is provided in the ExcelDB_Ch07_01-12.xls file. See the following subroutines in the SampleCode code module to help you get started writing your own code: Access-
ExcelApplicationExample, AccessWorkbooksExample, AccessWorkbookExample, AccessWork-
bookByNameExample, AccessWorksheetsExample, AccessWorksheetExample, AccessWorksheet-
ByNameExample, and AccessCellRangeExample. For more information on how to work with
Excel VBA code in the VBE, see section "7.2: Understand Excel Visual Basic for Applications."

7.4 Automate Sorting Data

Just as you can use Excel's menu commands to manually sort data values, you can use Excel's
Sort method to automate sorting data values with Excel VBA code. For example, you may want
to automatically change how data values are sorted based on how the user types in or imports
certain data values.

Quick Start

To automate sorting data with code, use the Range object's Sort method.

How To

To automate sorting data values with Excel VBA code, do this:

1. Get an instance of a Range object that contains the data to be sorted. For example, consider this code:

```
Dim wks As Excel.Worksheet
Dim rng As Excel.Range

Set wks = ThisWorkbook.Worksheets.Item(Index:="Sample Data")
Set rng = wks.Range(Cell1:="StoreData")
```

This code accesses the cell group named StoreData on the Sample Data worksheet in
the active Excel workbook.

2. Call the `Range` object's `Sort` method. For example, consider this code:

```
rng.Sort Key1:="Employees", Order1:=xlAscending, Header:=xlYes
```

This code instructs Excel to sort the cell group named StoreData in ascending order, based on the values in the Employees column. The code `Header:=xlYes` instructs Excel to find the Employees column by searching the field names in the StoreData cell group's first row.

Try It

To experiment with writing code to automate sorting data, you can start with the sample code that is provided in the ExcelDB_Ch07_01-12.xls file. See the SampleCode code module's Sorting-DataExample subroutine and the ExcelHelpers code module's SortData subroutine. For more information on how to work with Excel VBA code in the VBE, see section "7.2: Understand Excel Visual Basic for Applications," and section "7.3: Understand the Excel Programming Model."

7.5 Automate Filtering Data

Just as you can use worksheet cells' AutoFilter buttons to display only those rows and columns that meet certain criteria, you can use the `AutoFilter` method to automate filtering data with Excel VBA code. For example, you may want to automatically change how data values are filtered depending on how certain data values are typed in or imported by the user.

Quick Start

To automate filtering data with code, use the `Range` object's `AutoFilter` method.

How To

To automate sorting data with Excel VBA code, do this:

1. Get an instance of a `Range` object that contains the data to be filtered. For example, consider this code:

```
Dim wks As Excel.Worksheet
Dim rng As Excel.Range

Set wks = ThisWorkbook.Worksheets.Item(Index:="Sample Data")
Set rng = wks.Range(Cell1:="StoreData")
```

This code accesses the cell group named StoreData on the Sample Data worksheet in the active Excel workbook.

2. Call the `Range` object's `Filter` method. For example, consider this code:

```
rng.AutoFilter Field:=4, Criteria1:=">500", VisibleDropDown:=True
```

This code instructs Excel to filter the cell group named StoreData based on the values in the fourth field from the left edge of the StoreData cell group. Only rows with a value of more than 500 in the fourth column are displayed. The code `VisibleDropDown:=True` instructs Excel to also display drop-down arrows in the cell group's first row.

Try It

To experiment with writing code to automate filtering data, you can start with the sample code that is provided in the ExcelDB_Ch07_01-12.xls file. See the SampleCode code module's Filtering-DataExample subroutine and the ExcelHelpers code module's FilterData subroutine. For more information on how to work with Excel VBA code in the VBE, see section "7.2: Understand Excel Visual Basic for Applications," and section "7.3: Understand the Excel Programming Model."

7.6 Automate Subtotaling Data

Just as you can use Excel's menu commands to manually subtotal data values, you can use Excel's Subtotal method to automate subtotaling data values with Excel VBA code. For example, you may want to automatically change how data values are subtotaled based on how the data values are typed in or imported by the user.

Quick Start

To automate filtering data with code, use the Range object's Subtotal method.

How To

To automate subtotaling data with Excel VBA code, do this:

1. Get an instance of a Range object that contains the data to be sorted. For example, consider this code:

```
Dim wks As Excel.Worksheet
Dim rng As Excel.Range

Set wks = ThisWorkbook.Worksheets.Item(Index:="Sample Data")
Set rng = wks.Range(Cell1:="StoreData")
```

This code accesses the cell group named StoreData on the Sample Data worksheet in the active Excel workbook.

2. Create an array of Variant objects to hold the column numbers by which to subtotal, and then add the field numbers to the array. For example, consider this code:

```
Dim fieldNumbers() As Variant
fieldNumbers = Array(4)
```

This code stores the number 4, which will be used in the Subtotal method to refer to the fourth column number. If you want to add more field numbers, you could substitute code such as fieldNumbers = Array(3, 4) to specify the third and fourth column numbers.

3. Call the Range object's Subtotal method. For example, consider this code:

```
rng.Subtotal GroupBy:=2, Function:=xlSum, TotalList:=fieldNumbers
```

This code instructs Excel to subtotal the cell group named StoreData. It groups the subtotals based on the values in the second column from the left edge of the StoreData cell group. Excel then adds up the values in the fourth column from the left edge of the StoreData cell group and displays the sum for each subtotal.

Try It

To experiment with writing code to automate subtotaling data, you can start with the sample code that is provided in the ExcelDB_Ch07_01-12.xls file. See the SampleCode code module's SubtotalingDataExample subroutine and the ExcelHelpers code module's SubtotalData subroutine. For more information on how to work with Excel VBA code in the VBE, see section "7.2: Understand Excel Visual Basic for Applications" and section "7.3: Understand the Excel Programming Model."

7.7 Automate Calculating a Worksheet Function

Just as you can manually type a worksheet function in a cell or use the Insert Function dialog box to assist you in inserting a worksheet function into a cell, you can use the Formula property to automate inserting a worksheet function in a cell. For example, you may want to insert a specific worksheet function based on how the data values in a certain column are typed in or imported by a user.

Quick Start

To automate calculating a worksheet function, use the Range object's Formula property.

How To

To automate calculating a worksheet function with Excel VBA code, do this:

1. Get an instance of a Range object that contains the cell into which the worksheet function will be inserted and then calculated. For example, consider this code:

```
Dim wks As Excel.Worksheet
Dim rng As Excel.Range

Set wks = ThisWorkbook.Worksheets.Item(Index:="Sample Data")
Set rng = wks.Range(Cell1:="D18")
```

This code accesses cell D18 on the Sample Data worksheet in the active Excel workbook.

2. Call the Range object's Formula property. For example, consider this code:

```
rng.Formula = "=SUM(D2:D17)"
```

This code instructs Excel to insert the SUM worksheet function into cell D18. This function displays the sum of the values in cells D2 through D17.

Try It

To experiment with writing code to insert worksheet functions, you can start with the sample code that is provided in the ExcelDB_Ch07_01-12.xls file. See the SampleCode code module's CalculatingWorksheetFunctionExample subroutine and the ExcelHelpers code module's CalculateWorksheetFunction subroutine. For more information on how to work with Excel VBA code in the VBE, see section "7.2: Understand Excel Visual Basic for Applications" and section "7.3: Understand the Excel Programming Model."

7.8 Automate Offsets

Just as you can use the OFFSET worksheet function to locate a cell that is a given distance from another cell, you can automate locating a cell with the `Offset` method using Excel VBA code. For example, you could automatically find the location of a given cell as rows or columns are inserted or deleted around that cell.

Quick Start

To automate calculating a cell offset, use the `Range` object's `Offset` method.

How To

To automate calculating a cell offset with Excel VBA code, do this:

1. Get an instance of a `Range` object from which to calculate the offset. For example, consider this code:

```
Dim wks As Excel.Worksheet
Dim rng As Excel.Range

Set wks = ThisWorkbook.Worksheets.Item(Index:="Sample Data")
Set rng = wks.Range(Cell1:="A16")
```

This code accesses cell A16 on the Sample Data worksheet in the active Excel workbook.

2. Get an instance of a `Range` object that will reference the offset cell. For example

```
Dim rngOffset As Excel.Range
```

3. Calculate the offset using the `Offset` method. For example, consider this code:

```
Set rngOffset = rng.Offset(rowOffset:=0, columnOffset:=3)

MsgBox Prompt:="After calculating the offset from cell " & _
    rng.Address & ", the value of cell " & rngOffset.Address & _
    " is " & rngOffset.Value2 & "."
```

This code returns the cell offset that is three columns to the right of cell A16 (which is cell D16), and displays the offset cell's value in a message box.

■Tip You could also insert the result of an offset calculation by using the `Range` object's `Formula` property with code similar to this:

```
Dim rngValue As Excel.Range

Set rng = wks.Range(Cell1:="A16")

rngValue.Formula = "=OFFSET(A16, 0, 3)"
```

Try It

To experiment with writing code to calculate cell offsets, you can start with the sample code that is provided in the ExcelDB_Ch07_01-12.xls file. See the SampleCode code module's Calculating-OffsetExample subroutine and the ExcelHelpers code module's CalculateOffset function. For more information on how to work with Excel VBA code in the VBE, see section "7.2: Understand Excel Visual Basic for Applications" and section "7.3: Understand the Excel Programming Model."

7.9 Automate HLOOKUP and VLOOKUP

Just as you can use the HLOOKUP and VLOOKUP worksheet functions to locate a given cell in a group of cells, you can automate locating cells with the `HLookup` and `VLookup` methods using Excel VBA code. For example, you could automatically find the location of given cells as rows or columns are inserted or deleted around those cells.

Quick Start

To calculate the result of an HLOOKUP worksheet function, call the `Worksheet` object's `HLookup` method.

To calculate the result of a VLOOKUP worksheet function, call the `Worksheet` object's `VLookup` method.

How To

To calculate the result of an HLOOKUP worksheet function with Excel VBA code, do this:

1. Get an instance of a `Range` object from which to calculate the horizontal lookup. For example, consider this code:

   ```
   Dim wks As Excel.Worksheet
   Dim rng As Excel.Range

   Set wks = ThisWorkbook.Worksheets.Item(Index:="Sample Data")
   Set rng = wks.Range(Cell1:="D19")
   ```

   This code accesses cell D19 on the Sample Data worksheet in the active Excel workbook.

2. Calculate the lookup using the HLookup method. For example consider this code:

```
rng.Value2 = Excel.Application.WorksheetFunction.HLookup(Arg1:="Store Number", _
    Arg2:=Range(Cell1:="StoreData"), Arg3:=7, Arg4:=False)
```

In this code, the HLookup method takes the following arguments:

- Arg1 is the field in the cells' first row to look up—in this case, the Store Number field.

- Arg2 is the cells to reference—in this case, the group of cells named StoreData.

- Arg3 is the row to reference—in this case, the seventh row.

- Arg4 is an approximate match (True) or an exact match (False, as in this case).

To calculate the result of a VLOOKUP worksheet function with Excel VBA code, do this:

1. Get an instance of a Range object from which to calculate the vertical lookup. For example, consider this code:

```
Dim wks As Excel.Worksheet
Dim rng As Excel.Range

Set wks = ThisWorkbook.Worksheets.Item(Index:="Sample Data")
Set rng = wks.Range(Cell1:="D20")
```

This code accesses cell D20 on the Sample Data worksheet in the active Excel workbook.

2. Calculate the lookup using the VLookup method. For example consider this code:

```
rng.Value2 = Excel.Application.WorksheetFunction.VLookup(Arg1:="South", _
    Arg2:=Range(Cell1:="StoreData"), Arg3:=4, Arg4:=False)
```

In this code, the VLookup method takes the following arguments:

- Arg1 is the value in the first column to look up—in this case, the value South.

- Arg2 is the cells to reference—in this case, the group of cells named StoreData.

- Arg3 is the column to reference—in this case, the fourth column.

- Arg4 is an approximate match (True) or an exact match (False, as in this case).

■**Tip** You could also insert the results of the HLOOKUP and VLOOKUP worksheet functions by using the Range object's Formula property with code similar to this:

```
rng.Formula = "=HLOOKUP(""Store Number"", StoreData, 7, False)"
rng.Formula = "=VLOOKUP(""South"", StoreData, 4, False)"
```

Try It

To experiment with writing code to calculate HLOOKUP and VLOOKUP worksheet functions, you can start with the sample code that is provided in the ExcelDB_Ch07_01-12.xls file. See the SampleCode code module's CalculatingHLOOKUPExample and CalculatingVLOOKUPExample subroutines and the ExcelHelpers code module's CalculateHLOOKUP and CalculateVLOOKUP subroutines. For more information on how to work with Excel VBA code in the VBE, see section "7.2: Understand Excel Visual Basic for Applications" and section "7.3: Understand the Excel Programming Model."

7.10 Automate Creating a PivotTable and PivotChart

Just as you can use the PivotTable and PivotChart Wizard to manually create a PivotTable and a PivotChart, you can automate creating a PivotTable and a PivotChart with Excel VBA code. For example, you may want to automatically create a PivotTable and a PivotChart based on data values that a user types in or references or imports from an external data source.

Quick Start

To create a PivotTable and a PivotChart, do this:

1. Create a `PivotCache` object, a `PivotTable` object, and a `Chart` object.

2. Call the `Add` method of the desired workbook's `PivotCaches` collection to set the `PivotCache` object to the desired workbook's `PivotCaches` collection.

3. Call the `PivotCache` object's `CreatePivotTable` method to create a PivotTable and set the PivotTable object to the result of the `CreatePivotTable` method call.

4. Add a `Chart` object to the desired workbook.

5. Call the `Chart` object's `SetSourceData` method, passing to the method the value of the `PivotTable` object's `TableRange2` property.

How To

To create a PivotTable and a PivotChart using Excel VBA code, do this:

1. Create a `Workbook` object, a `PivotCache` object, a `PivotTable` object, a `Worksheet` object, and a `Chart` object. For example, consider this code:

```
Dim wkb As Excel.Workbook
Dim pvc As Excel.PivotCache
Dim pvt As Excel.PivotTable
Dim wks As Excel.Worksheet
Dim cht As Excel.Chart
```

```
Set wkb = Excel.Application.ThisWorkbook
    Set wks = wkb.Worksheets.Add

wks.Name = "PivotTable Example"
```

This code references the active workbook, adds a new blank worksheet to the workbook, and names the new worksheet PivotTable Example.

2. Call the `Add` method of the desired workbook's `PivotCaches` collection to set the `PivotCache` object to the desired workbook's `PivotCaches` collection. For example, consider this code:

```
Set pvc = wkb.PivotCaches.Add(SourceType:=xlDatabase, _
    SourceData:=Range(Cell1:="StoreData"))
```

This code initializes a `PivotCache` object and sets its data source to the cell group with the name StoreData in the workbook.

3. Call the `PivotCache` object's `CreatePivotTable` method to create a PivotTable and set the `PivotTable` object to the result of the `CreatePivotTable` method call. For example, consider this code:

```
Set pvt = pvc.CreatePivotTable(TableDestination:=wks.Range(Cell1:="A3"), _
    TableName:="StoreDataPivotTable")
```

This code creates a PivotTable, inserts it at cell A3 in the PivotTable Example worksheet, and gives the PivotTable the name StoreDataPivotTable.

4. Add a `Chart` object to the desired workbook, with code similar to this:

```
Set cht = wkb.Charts.Add
```

5. Set the chart's display format; give the chart a name; and then call the `Chart` object's `SetSourceData` method, passing to the method the value of the `PivotTable` object's `TableRange2` property. For example, consider this code:

```
With cht

    .ChartType = xl3DColumn
    .Name = "PivotChart Example"
    .SetSourceData pvt.TableRange2

End With
```

This code sets the chart's display format to 3-D Column, names the chart PivotChart Example, and sets the chart's data source to the data source of the PivotTable named StoreDataPivotTable.

■**Tip** You can also create a PivotTable by calling the `Worksheet` object's `PivotTableWizard` method. Although this is a quicker approach, it provides less flexibility and can't be used with OLE DB-based data sources. For example, using this approach, you could write code similar to this:

```
Dim wkb As Excel.Workbook
Dim wks As Excel.Worksheet

Set wkb = Excel.Application.ThisWorkbook
Set wks = wkb.Worksheets.Add

wks.Name = "PivotTable Example"
wks.PivotTableWizard SourceType:=xlDatabase, _
    SourceData:=Range(Cell1:="StoreData"), _
    TableDestination:=wks.Range(Cell1:="A3"), _
    TableName:="StoreDataPivotTable"
```

Try It

To experiment with writing code to create PivotTables and PivotCharts, you can start with the sample code that is provided in the ExcelDB_Ch07_01-12.xls file. See the SampleCode code module's CreatingPivotTableAndPivotChartExample subroutine and the ExcelHelpers code module's CreatePivotTableAndPivotChart subroutine. For more information on how to work with Excel VBA code in the VBE, see section "7.2: Understand Excel Visual Basic for Applications" and section "7.3: Understand the Excel Programming Model."

7.11 Automate Changing the View of a PivotTable and PivotChart

Just as you can use the PivotTable Field List to manually change the view of a PivotTable and its associated PivotChart, you can automate these view changes using Excel VBA code. For example, you could automatically change the view of a PivotTable and its associated PivotChart based on how a user adds data to or deletes data from the underlying data source.

Quick Start

To change the view of a PivotTable and PivotChart, call the `PivotTable` object's `AddFields` and `AddDataField` methods. The linked PivotChart's view will change to synchronize with the PivotTable's view.

How To

To change the view of a PivotTable and PivotChart using Excel VBA code, do this:

1. Create a Workbook object, a Worksheet object, and a PivotTable object, and then initialize the Workbook, Worksheet, and PivotTable objects. For example, consider this code:

```
Dim wkb As Excel.Workbook
Dim wks As Excel.Worksheet
Dim pvt As Excel.PivotTable

Set wkb = Excel.Application.ThisWorkbook
Set wks = wkb.Worksheets(Index:="PivotTable Example")
Set pvt = wks.PivotTables(Index:="StoreDataPivotTable")
```

This code references a PivotTable with the name StoreDataPivotTable on a worksheet named PivotTable Example in the current workbook.

2. Call the PivotTable object's AddFields method to add fields to the row area or page area, and call the PivotTable object's AddDataField method to add a field to the data area. For example, consider this code:

```
With pvt

    .AddFields RowFields:=Array("Region", "State"), _
        PageFields:="Store Number"
    .AddDataField Field:=pvt.PivotFields(Index:="Employees"), _
        Function:=xlSum

End With
```

The AddFields method call adds the two fields, a Region field and a State field, to the row area. The AddDataField method call adds an Employees field to the data area, and the field displays the sum of the employees by region and by state.

Try It

To experiment with writing code to change PivotTable and PivotChart views, you can start with the sample code that is provided in the ExcelDB_Ch07_01-12.xls file. See the SampleCode code module's ChangingPivotTableAndPivotChartViewsExample subroutine. For more information on how to work with Excel VBA code in the VBE, see section "7.2: Understand Excel Visual Basic for Applications" and section "7.3: Understand the Excel Programming Model."

7.12 Automate Connecting to External Data

Just as you can manually connect to external data using Excel's menu commands and their associated tools and wizards, you can automate connecting to external data using Excel VBA code. For example, you may want to automatically change an external data source connection or its associated connection behavior based on how the user adds data to or removes data from the external data source.

Quick Start

To automate connecting to external data, use the QueryTable object, which represents a cell group that displays the external data in a worksheet.

How To

To automate connecting to external data with Excel VBA code, such as connecting to data in an external text file, do this:

1. Create a Workbook object and a Worksheet object, and then initialize the Workbook and Worksheet objects. For example, consider this code:

```
Dim wkb As Excel.Workbook
Dim wks As Excel.Worksheet

Set wkb = xlApp.ThisWorkbook
Set wks = wkb.Worksheets(Index:="Sample Data Connection")
```

This code references a worksheet named Sample Data Connection in the current workbook. This worksheet will be used to display the data from the external text file.

2. Create and initialize a String object representing a connection string that Excel will use to locate the external text file. For example, consider this code:

```
Dim strConn As String

strConn = "TEXT;C:\My Sample Excel Files\ExcelDB_Ch01_02.txt"
```

The connection string instructs Excel to find a text file named ExcelDB_Ch01_02.txt in the C:\My Sample Excel Files folder.

3. Create a QueryTable object, and then use the QueryTables collection's Add method to add a QueryTable object to the QueryTables collection. Then, for the QueryTable object, specify the connection string, where to begin displaying the data from the external text file, how to import the data, and what to name the cell group that displays the external data. For example, consider this code:

```
Dim qyt As Excel.QueryTable

Set qyt = wks.QueryTables.Add(Connection:=strConn, _
    Destination:=Range(Cell1:="A1"))

With qyt

    .TextFileCommaDelimiter = True
    .Refresh
    .Name = "ExcelDB_Ch01_02 Query Table"

End With
```

This code uses the `QueryTables` collection's `Add` method to set the `QueryTable` object's connection string and where to begin displaying the data from the external text file (beginning at cell A1 in the Sample Data Connection worksheet). The code then uses the `QueryTable` object's `TextFileCommaDelimiter` property to instruct Excel to use the comma characters in the external text file to determine how to display the data in the worksheet. The `QueryTable` object's `Refresh` method displays the external text file's data in the worksheet, and the `QueryTable` object's `Name` property instructs Excel to give the name ExcelDB_Ch01_02 Query Table to the cell group displaying the external text file's data.

Tip

The format of the `Connection` argument in the `QueryTables` collection's `Add` method depends on the external data source type. Here are some examples:

- For an OLE DB or ODBC external data source, specify a string containing an OLE DB or ODBC connection string. The ODBC connection string has the form `"ODBC;<connection string>"`.

- For an ADO or DAO recordset, create and initialize an ADO or DAO `Recordset` object, and then provide the name of the ADO or DAO `Recordset` object.

- For a Web-based external data source, specify a string in the form `"URL;<url>"`.

For additional examples, see the `Add` method documentation in Excel VBA Help.

Try It

To experiment with writing code to connect to external data, you can start with the sample code that is provided in the ExcelDB_Ch07_01-12.xls file. See the SampleCode code module's ConnectingToExternalTextFileExample subroutine. For more information on how to work with Excel VBA code in the VBE, see section "7.2: Understand Excel Visual Basic for Applications" and section "7.3: Understand the Excel Programming Model."

Index

Find it faster at http://superindex.apress.com/

You Need the Companion eBook

Your purchase of this book entitles you to buy the companion PDF-version eBook for only $10. Take the weightless companion with you anywhere.

We believe this Apress title will prove so indispensable that you'll want to carry it with you everywhere, which is why we are offering the companion eBook (in PDF format) for $10 to customers who purchase this book now. Convenient and fully searchable, the PDF version of any content-rich, page-heavy Apress book makes a valuable addition to your programming library. You can easily find and copy code—or perform examples by quickly toggling between instructions and the application. Even simultaneously tackling a donut, diet soda, and complex code becomes simplified with hands-free eBooks!

Once you purchase your book, getting the $10 companion eBook is simple:

❶ Visit **www.apress.com/promo/tendollars/**.

❷ Complete a basic registration form to receive a randomly generated question about this title.

❸ Answer the question correctly in 60 seconds, and you will receive a promotional code to redeem for the $10.00 eBook.

2560 Ninth Street • Suite 219 • Berkeley, CA 94710

eBookshop

THE EXPERT'S VOICE™

Offer valid through 7/07.